Prais… r Quests

It's been a constant battl… at will not only keep them interested in turning pages but will also compl…ment their preparation for grammar/ independent school entrance exams. This book ticked all the boxes. It's a fantastic story with a very clever and unique way of explaining the antonyms and synonyms within the text. This helped so much with my dyslexic son who reads very well but often misinterprets the meaning of the vocabulary. I would 100% recommend this book regardless of age and educational journey.

– *Mum of three boys*

☆☆☆☆☆

S L Ager combines the use of effective and useful vocabulary with an in-built dictionary all in one book. Definitely a winner!!!

We introduced this book to our Year 5 students at our tuition centre last year when we read it as a group… The children loved it and wanted the story to continue… This book is now on our recommended list of books to prepare children for the 11+ exams.

– *Mrs Win*

☆☆☆☆☆

My son loved reading this book, he couldn't put it down!! Excellent vocabulary list and perfect for those studying for 11plus exams. I highly recommend it. He's been asking for the second book *(Race for Gold)* EVERYDAY since he finished this one which we just purchased too! You won't regret purchasing this book.

– *Nomi_smiles*

THE CADWALADR CHRONICLES

11+ VOCABULARY

BOOK 3: SIEGE

S. L. AGER

This is a work of fiction.

Names, characters, places and incidents either are the product of the author's imagination or are used fictitiously.

Any resemblance to actual persons, living or dead, events or locales is entirely coincidental.

The Cadwaladr Chronicles books have no affiliation with CEM, Cambridge Assessment and Cambridge University Press, GL Assessment, any school or examination boards.

This book does not purport to be a dictionary, nor does it aim to replace one.

Reading this book does not guarantee your child will pass any exam, but I hope it will help to make learning vocabulary more enjoyable.

Developmental editor: Anna Bowles
Copyeditor and proofreader: Louis Greenberg
Cover design and interior formatting: Mark Thomas / Coverness.com

ISBN 978-1-913753-10-8 (paperback)
ISBN 978-1-913753-11-5 (ebook)

www.slager.co.uk

FOR ALL CHILDREN,
REGARDLESS OF DIFFICULT EXAMS

SPECIAL THANKS

I want to say a big thank you to some exceptional readers who helped me to develop *The Cadwaladr Chronicles.*

Thank you,

Janya Agarwal,

Arjun Pasumarti

and

Aaron Smith.

Table of Contents

PREFACE

I wrote *Siege*, the third of *The Cadwaladr Chronicles*, prequels to *The Cadwaladr Quests*, after receiving so many requests from parents asking for books more suited to years two, three and four.

Some readers of the original *The Cadwaladr Quests* are in year three, but I don't recommend that for most children as the narrative is more suited to readers from late year four and above, including, of course, year six.

Although the prequels are aimed at younger readers, the narrative and vocabulary are as challenging as in *The Cadwaladr Quests* but they are age-appropriate.

Many of the words included and defined in this book come from the practice materials I covered and amassed with my two children when working towards the 11+ exams and SATs in primary school. We worked with both GL and CEM materials.

Of course, no published aids can guarantee that their material will appear on any exam paper, and neither can I. However, considering *The Cadwaladr Chronicles: Siege* contains almost 2,000 word definitions and hundreds of corresponding synonyms and antonyms (in a fun story for girls and boys), what does any parent or young reader have to lose?

I hope you enjoy Callwen's gripping adventure in the third book of *The Cadwaladr Chronicles*, but moreover, I hope it helps you and your children with any challenging vocabulary exams they are facing.

HOW TO USE THIS BOOK

This story has been specially written to help young readers prepare for their 11+, SATs and independent schools' entrance exams. It includes difficult vocabulary embedded in a fun narrative that provides context for the new words and makes them easier to learn and understand.

On every page, key words are in bold, and each has a correlated footnote with a concise definition. The words are defined using the context in which they appear in the text, and definitions are as child-friendly as possible. Chosen key words are defined only once, usually when they first appear in the story, unless they appear again in a different context.

Synonyms and antonyms, where applicable, are also provided.

This book does not aim to replace a dictionary or purport to be one, but dictionaries have been used to check the accuracy of each definition.

PS: There are a few Welsh words in the story. To learn how to pronounce them, please visit: slager.co.uk/welsh-words.

TOP READING TIPS

- Children, you may find it beneficial to read this book for the first time with an adult, but you and your parents can decide.
- The definitions are included for convenience and to guide the learning, not as a definitive 'must learn' list.
- Chosen key words are defined only once, usually when they first appear in the story, unless they appear again in a different context.
- To make learning difficult words easier, try to associate the words with the relevant scene in the book and to picture their meanings.
- Chapter lengths vary, so do not necessarily aim to finish a chapter in each sitting.
- Some pages have more definitions than others to fit in with the storytelling.
- Read the book as often as is needed, and continue to use its vast resource of definitions, synonyms and antonyms to reinforce learning.
- The best way to learn new words is to read as widely and with as much variety as possible. Every book is a world of adventure waiting for you to turn to the first page. I hope my book helps in this journey of discovery and learning.

KEY TO ABBREVIATIONS OF WORD TYPE

(v) verb

(n) noun

(adj) adjective

(adv) adverb

(prep) preposition

(con) conjunction

(int) interjection

(s) synonym

(ant) antonym

PARENTS, GET FIVE FREE COMPREHENSION EXERCISES

Parents, to receive your free comprehensions (with answers) based on *The Cadwaladr Chronicles: Book 3 – Siege,* please leave a review for *Siege* on Amazon and email a screenshot to:

freebies@slager.co.uk.

I will add you to my mailing list[1] and send you the comprehensions by email.

1 You can unsubscribe from the mailing list at any time. Further details will be emailed to you as soon as you are added.

INTRODUCTION TO THE KEY CHARACTERS, ITEMS AND LOCATIONS

Callwen (Cad) Cadwaladr. Adopted daughter of Prince Llywelyn and his wife, Siân.

The Knights Hawk. A magical order of hand-picked knights.

The Gwalch Gem bracelet. A magical combination of Welsh gold and emerald cut into the shape of a hawk.

Instinct. Powers bestowed by the bracelet which must be earned in order to become a Knight Hawk.

Cadwaladr Castle. Prince Llywelyn's residence.

Catrin Castle. Prince Dewi's residence. Cad's current home.

Prince Llywelyn. Knight Hawk. Ruler of Wales. Adoptive father to Cad and father of her baby brother, Prince John.

Princess Siân Cadwaladr. Wife of Prince Llywelyn. Mother to baby Prince John. Cad's adoptive mother.

Prince Dewi. Prince Llywelyn's younger brother.

Prince John. Baby son of Llywelyn and Siân. Cad's brother.

Gelert. Prince Llywelyn's faithful hound.

Dylan Rogers. Cad's friend and fellow page.

Rhys Price. Cad's friend and fellow page.

May. A hawk.

Bryn Davis. An older squire.

Jack Jones. Bryn's trainee.

Sir Robert Evans. Llywelyn's associate. A Knight Hawk.

Sir Owain Glyn. Llywelyn's second-in-command. A Knight Hawk.

Peggy (Hari). Prince Dewi's former henchman.

Goodwife Hughes. A servant.

Hugh Hughes. Goodwife Hughes's son.

Ellis Williams. A groom and a page.

Fishy. A dog.

Midnight. Dewi's destrier.

Slippy. A snake.

Skip. A dog.

Sooty. A cat.

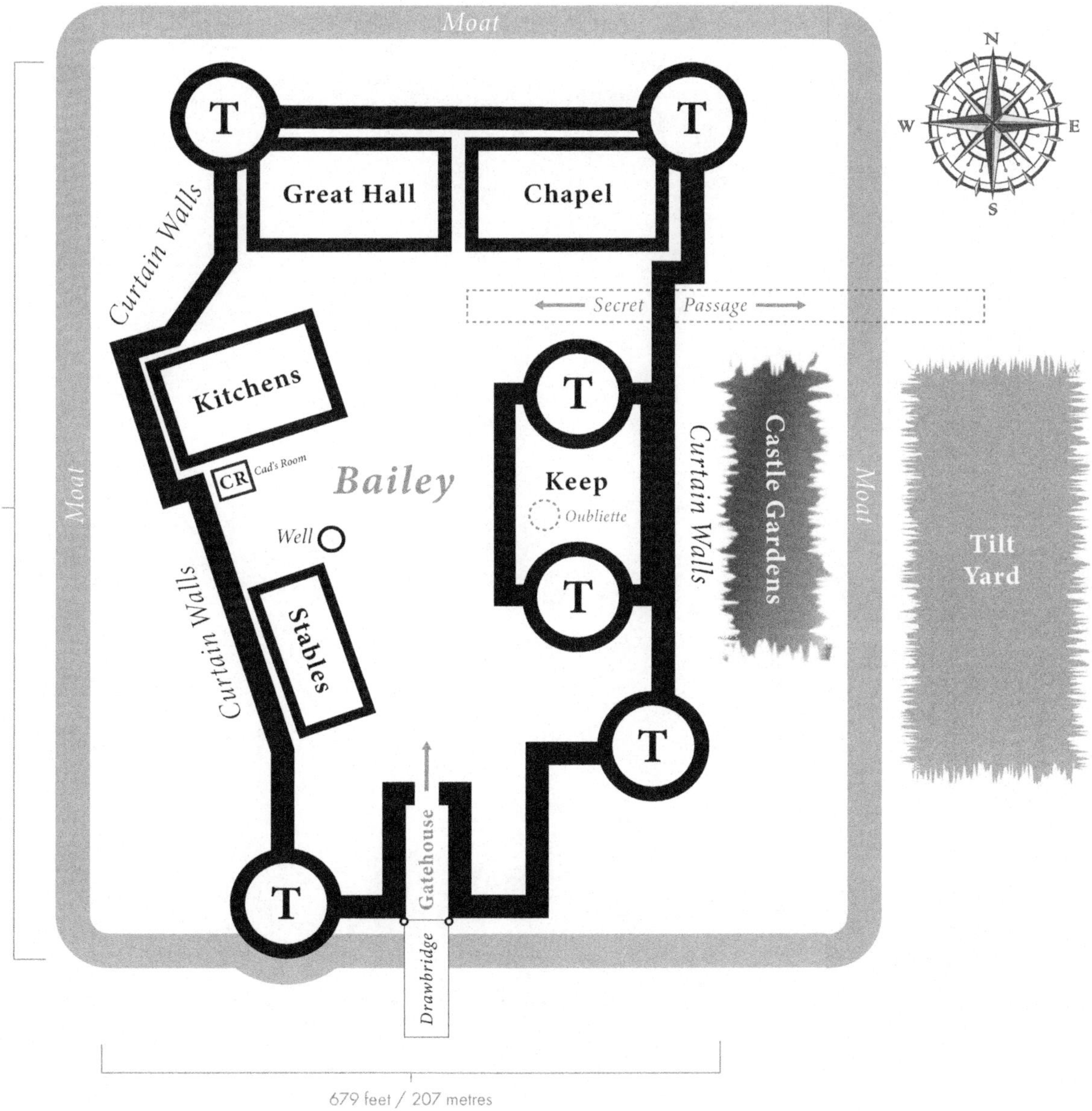

Map of Catrin Castle

TWELFTH-CENTURY WALES

CHAPTER ONE

A Knighthood

Cad knelt before Prince Llywelyn, one knee on the floor, the other perched on a red **velvet**[1] cushion, her **crested**[2] **helm**[3] placed beside her. The prince **shifted**[4] his attention from the **assembled**[5] **audience**[6] down to his daughter before him. Cad, so proud to be here, **relished**[7] her knight's **attire**[8]. Her body, **clad**[9] **entirely**[10] in **chain mail**[11], **bore**[12] the metal's weight with ease. The heavy **coif**[13], worn beneath the helm to protect the head, now **draped**[14] back between her

---

1 **velvet** *(n)* a fabric woven from silk, cotton or nylon with a dense, short pile on one side.

2 **crested** *(adj)* decorated with a coat of arms, badge or other emblem. *(s)* emblazoned. *(ant)* plain.

3 **helm** *(n)* a helmet, often made from metal and worn in medieval battle and jousting.

4 **shift** *(v)* move a short distance. *(s)* reposition. *(ant)* remain.

5 **assemble** *(v)* gather with others for a common purpose. *(s)* collect, convene. *(ant)* disperse.

6 **audience** *(n)* a group of people who listen or watch something. *(s)* spectators, onlookers.

7 **relish** *(v)* enjoy or like greatly. *(s)* love, delight in. *(ant)* detest, loathe.

8 **attire** *(n)* clothes. *(s)* clothing, dress, outfit, garments.

9 **clad** *(adj)* clothed or dressed. *(s)* attired, wearing, cloaked. *(ant)* unclothed, undressed.

10 **entirely** *(adv)* fully. *(s)* completely, totally, wholly. *(ant)* partially.

11 **chain mail** *(n)* flexible armour made of small metal rings that link together.

12 **bear** *(v)* carry the weight of (past tense: bore). *(s)* support. *(ant)* yield, collapse.

13 **coif** *(n)* a close fitting cap or head covering.

14 **drape** *(v)* arrange (cloth or material) around something. *(s)* cover. *(ant)* uncover.

shoulders. Over the mail which protected her **torso**[1], she wore a **scarlet**[2]-red **tunic**[3], **intricately**[4] worked in golden thread.

From the **broad**[5] leather belt at her waist hung a **sturdy**[6] **sheath**[7] for her newly **forged**[8] sword.

Siân, Cad's stunning mother, stood alongside her husband, Prince Llywelyn. Her red velvet **gown**[9], which matched Cad's tunic and its gold working, fell in **exquisite**[10] folds. Her long, waved **blonde** hair dazzled, **garlanded**[11] with **miniature**[12] white lilies, and topped with an emerald-studded crown. Both loving parents **gazed**[13] adoringly at Callwen, their **adopted**[14] daughter.

Cad had **yearned**[15] for this day since becoming a **novice**[16] **pageboy**[17] at Catrin Castle. The day for which Cad had **sacrificed**[18] her family and **assumed**[19] a false **gender,**[20] had arrived. She, Callwen Cadwaladr, was to be **sworn in**[21] to the magical order of the Knights Hawk.

Her younger brother, John, now a page himself, stood alongside his parents and beamed with

---

1 **torso** *(n)* the trunk (body without head or limbs) of a human. *(s)* upper body.

2 **scarlet** *(adj)* of a bright red colour. *(s)* crimson, vermillion.

3 **tunic** *(n)* a loose garment, often sleeveless and worn with a belt. *(s)* surcoat, robe.

4 **intricately** *(adv)* done in an intricate (detailed) manner. *(s)* artfully, exquisitely. *(ant)* simply.

5 **broad** *(adj)* physically wide. *(s)* big, large. *(ant)* narrow.

6 **sturdy** *(adj)* strong and solidly built. *(s)* robust, durable, substantial. *(ant)* weak.

7 **sheath** *(n)* a cover for a blade. *(s)* case, sleeve.

8 **forge** *(v)* make a metal object by heating in a fire and hammering it into shape. *(s)* cast, model.

9 **gown** *(n)* a long, formal dress. *(s)* robe, frock.

10 **exquisite** *(adj)* extremely beautiful. *(s)* elegant, graceful. *(ant)* ugly, crude.

11 **garland** *(v)* decorate with a garland (a ring of flowers and leaves). *(s)* festoon, loop.

12 **miniature** *(adj)* small compared to others. *(s)* tiny, diminutive. *(ant)* giant.

13 **gaze** *(v)* look steadily. *(s)* stare, gape, peer. *(ant)* glimpse glance.

14 **adopt** *(v)* legally take another person's child to raise as one's own.

15 **yearn** *(v)* really want something. *(s)* long, ache, crave, desire. *(ant)* reject.

16 **novice** *(adj)* someone new to and inexperienced in a situation or job. *(s)* beginner. *(ant)* expert.

17 **pageboy** *(n)* a boy in training for a knighthood, ranking one below a squire in a knight's personal service.

18 **sacrifice** *(v)* give up something for the sake of others. *(s)* forgo, forfeit. *(ant)* keep.

19 **assume** *(v)* adopt or take on (an identity or manner), sometimes falsely. *(s)* affect, fake, feign.

20 **gender** *(n)* characteristics pertaining to the two sexes; social and cultural identities beyond these established categories.

21 **swear in** *(v)* induct into a position or office by means of an oath (past participle: sworn). *(s)* inaugurate.

pride[1] for his elder sister. Cad's cheeks ached in fellow feeling for him as if they'd smiled for hours.

Cad's dearest friends, Dylan, Rhys and Ellis, sat in **awed**[2] silence, **spectating**[3] from the front row of Llywelyn's princely court. Llywelyn had **summoned**[4] all to Catrin Castle's great hall to **witness**[5] the **dubbing**[6] **ceremony**[7].

May, Cad's blind hawk, perched on Rhys's shoulder, and no doubt Slippy, the toothless snake, slept in a pouch at his waist. Fishy, Cad's **faithful**[8] dog, sat at Dylan's feet, and Cad was sure that if Ellis could have sneaked Flash, her pony, into the back of the hall to view the ceremony, he would have done so.

Everyone Cad cared for was here to see Llywelyn dub her a Knight Hawk. She, Callwen Cadwaladr, the girl **masquerading**[9] as a boy to become a knight, was about to make her father proud. Proud he had saved her from the depths of a well as a baby to raise her as his own.

As she fought back tears of joy, Cad stared into her father's eyes, his enormous sword now raised. Cad dared not peep at her mother, for those eager tears would win the fight if she did. With a **gulp**[10], she swallowed as Llywelyn's sword **descended**[11], her young life's work **culminating**[12] in this moment.

A ripple of delight thrilled Cad as she waited for the touch of Llywelyn's sword on her shoulder. Her green eyes fixed on its silvery tip. But the sword didn't reach Cad's shoulder. In mid-air, it stopped. She **glimpsed**[13] up, regarding her father's face in puzzlement, her eyes

---

1 **pride** *(n)* a feeling of satisfaction. *(s)* pleasure, delight, joy. *(ant)* shame.

2 **awed** *(adj)* filled with wonder. *(s)* amazed, wonderstruck. *(ant)* indifferent.

3 **spectate** *(v)* watch rather than take part in. *(s)* view, observe, witness. *(ant)* participate.

4 **summon** *(v)* order or ask someone to be present. *(s)* call, invite, request. *(ant)* dismiss.

5 **witness** *(v)* see something happen. *(s)* observe. *(ant)* ignore, overlook.

6 **dub** *(v)* make someone a knight by the custom of touching their shoulder with a sword. *(s)* knight. *(ant)* strip.

7 **ceremony** *(n)* a formal occasion to celebrate an event or achievement. *(s)* formality.

8 **faithful** *(adj)* remaining loyal, steadfast, constant and true. *(s)* dedicated, dependable, reliable. *(ant)* disloyal.

9 **masquerade** *(v)* make a false and deceptive show of pretence. *(s)* act, pose, behave. *(ant)* unmask.

10 **gulp** *(n)* a (sometimes audible) swallowing movement of the throat. *(s)* gasp.

11 **descend** *(v)* move or fall downwards. *(s)* dip. *(ant)* ascend, rise.

12 **culminate** *(v)* to reach the highest point or development. *(s)* conclude. *(ant)* begin, commence.

13 **glimpse** *(v)* to see briefly. *(s)* peek, peep. *(ant)* stare.

searching for **clues**[1]. The look in his eyes seemed changed.

Then, as though a spear of ice had passed through it, Cad's heart **lurched**[2] at the sight of Siân **ushering**[3] her brother from the dubbing **dais**[4]. Cad **observed**[5] in horror, seeing that Llywelyn's **expression**[6] had **dramatically**[7] **altered**[8].

The words Cad **longed**[9] to speak refused to form. Beneath Llywelyn's stony stare, her throat turned sandy. For a stunned moment, **bewildered**[10], her thoughts jammed. She looked to her friends for help, but only **blank**[11] faces stared back. Her stomach swirled as she knelt in the centre of a chilly silence, **gooseflesh**[12] running up her arms.

'Father, father,' she mouthed, as Llywelyn placed his **sleek**[13] sword back into its sheath. 'What are you doing?' Her voice was a **mere**[14] whisper.

Yet Llywelyn did not answer. He **uttered**[15] not a word, but turned away and followed her mother and brother from the dais, **accompanying**[16] both from the hall.

Cad watched, confusion **crippling**[17] her, **hopelessness**[18] **paralysing**[19] her **limbs**[20].

---

1 **clue** *(n)* a piece of information about something, especially a crime. *(s)* sign, indication. *(ant)* evidence.

2 **lurch** *(v)* move abruptly without control. *(s)* falter, pitch. *(ant)* steady.

3 **usher** *(v)* show, escort or guide someone somewhere. *(s)* accompany, shepherd, lead. *(ant)* follow.

4 **dais** *(n)* a low platform for a throne or lectern. *(s)* stage, rostrum, stand, podium.

5 **observe** *(v)* watch carefully. *(s)* see, study, regard. *(ant)* miss, ignore.

6 **expression** *(n)* a look that conveys (shows) a certain emotion. *(s)* face, appearance.

7 **dramatically** *(adv)* in a dramatic (powerful) way. *(s)* radically, noticeably. *(ant)* modestly.

8 **alter** *(v)* change in some way. *(s)* adjust. *(ant)* preserve.

9 **long** *(v)* to have great want. *(s)* yearn, desire. *(ant)* dislike, despise.

10 **bewildered** *(adj)* perplexed or confused. *(s)* baffled, mystified, confounded. *(ant)* enlightened.

11 **blank** *(adj)* figuratively showing a lack of understanding or reaction. *(s)* vacant, deadpan. *(ant)* expressive.

12 **gooseflesh** *(n)* small bumps on the skin caused by cold or emotion. *(s)* goosebumps, goose pimples.

13 **sleek** *(adj)* smooth and shining. *(s)* glistening, polished. *(ant)* dull, rough, coarse.

14 **mere** *(adj)* no more than. *(s)* just, only.

15 **utter** *(v)* speak *(s)* say, voice.

16 **accompany** *(v)* go with someone. *(s)* chaperone, escort. *(ant)* abandon, desert.

17 **cripple** *(v)* cause to become unable to move properly. *(s)* immobilise, paralyse. *(ant)* mobilise.

18 **hopelessness** *(n)* a state or feeling of extreme unhappiness or lack of hope. *(s)* distress, anguish. *(ant)* hope.

19 **paralyse** *(v)* cause to become unable to act or function properly. *(s)* disable, incapacitate. *(ant)* mobilise.

20 **limb** *(n)* an arm, leg or wing. *(s)* appendage, offshoot.

A **chorus**[1] of confused noises rose from the audience, **assailing**[2] her thoughts. Unable to move, her heart breaking, her body crumpling and her mind **reeling**[3], Cad **clutched**[4] her head with her hands and sobbed like never before.

---

1 **chorus** *(n)* a group of voices or singers performing at the same time. *(s)* ensemble. *(ant)* soloist.

2 **assail** *(v)* (of something unpleasant) come upon a person suddenly. *(s)* trouble, plague. *(ant)* soothe.

3 **reel** *(v)* feel bewildered and shocked. *(s)* spin, whirl. *(ant)* steady, stabilise.

4 **clutch** *(v)* grab or grasp something tightly. *(s)* hold, grip. *(ant)* release, let go.

CHAPTER TWO

Awakenings

Those darned **fleas**[1] were biting her again, or was it **pesky**[2] bed bugs? Cad neither knew nor cared. She wanted the pricking pain to stop as she **swiped**[3] at her arm. And the **cockroaches**[4], so many, **scuttling**[5] over her face, too **numerous**[6] to **bat**[7] away. Where were the pests coming from? Cad **detested**[8] cockroaches. Their shells cracking underfoot like dried acorns made her skin crawl and **bristle**[9] as she stumbled towards the **chamber pot**[10] in the corner of her room. Where were her shoes? If only she could find her blasted shoes, she wouldn't suffer the carpet of cockroaches beneath her feet.

'Please stop,' she whispered, but when she struggled to focus, nothing but a grey mist **lingered**[11] before her eyes.

---

1 **flea** *(n)* a tiny insect that feeds on the blood of mammals and birds.

2 **pesky** *(adj)* annoying. *(s)* irritating, irksome, vexing. *(ant)* welcome.

3 **swipe** *(v)* hit or try to hit. *(s)* swing, slap, lash out.

4 **cockroach** *(n)* a beetle-like insect with long antennae and legs. *(s)* roach, bug, creepy-crawly.

5 **scuttle** *(v)* run or scamper hurriedly or furtively (secretly). *(s)* dart, scurry. *(ant)* saunter.

6 **numerous** *(adj)* many. *(s)* plentiful, abundant, copious. *(ant)* few.

7 **bat** *(v)* hit something or someone with one's hand. *(s)* swipe, knock.

8 **detest** *(v)* dislike intensely. *(s)* abhor, despise, loathe, hate. *(ant)* love, adore.

9 **bristle** *(v)* recoil or react defensively. *(s)* prickle, shiver, flinch. *(ant)* accept.

10 **chamber pot** *(n)* a bowl in a bedroom used as a toilet during the night.

11 **linger** *(v)* be slow to disappear. *(s)* persist, remain, endure. *(ant)* vanish.

She tried to raise her arm, but it was **leaden**[1] – so heavy.

'Callwen. Callwen.'

Who was calling her Callwen? Who in Catrin Castle was foolishly using her real name? Her friends knew better than that, but she heard it from someone; from somewhere, somebody repeatedly called her Callwen.

'*Stop!*' she wanted to shriek, **vexed**[2] by their **persistence**[3]. 'My name is Cad.'

She knew she must protect her secret **identity**[4] with her life. Her voice wouldn't rise, staying trapped within her throat. When Cad opened her mouth to speak, silence **ensued**[5], and the calling continued.

Then from nowhere, but with agonising **clarity**[6], like knives through butter, she remembered the **crushing**[7] disappointment that pained her heart. Her anger at the voices calling 'Callwen' **faded**[8] along with her **resolve**[9]. The **betrayal**[10]. Her father's **treachery**[11]: he'd **humiliated**[12] her before his entire court, and even worse, her friends.

Why?

Why had her family turned their backs on her? Now she might never be a Knight Hawk. Nor could she quite grasp what had led to her failure. **Despair**[13] **devastated**[14] her.

Am I in bed? Cad asked herself, so **weary**[15], her eyes closed in search of peace, but her mind

---

1 **leaden** *(adj)* heavy. *(s)* weighted, lifeless. *(ant)* light.

2 **vexed** *(adj)* annoyed. *(s)* irked, riled, irritated. *(ant)* pacified, calm.

3 **persistence** *(n)* the act of continuing despite difficulty. *(s)* tenacity, resolve. *(ant)* apathy.

4 **identity** *(n)* the characteristics determining what someone or something is. *(s)* identification, existence.

5 **ensue** *(v)* happen afterwards or as a consequence. *(s)* arise, develop, follow. *(ant)* precede.

6 **clarity** *(n)* the quality of being clearly understood. *(s)* lucidity. *(ant)* ambiguity.

7 **crush** *(v)* make someone feel incredibly disappointed or embarrassed. *(s)* humiliate, devastate. *(ant)* please.

8 **fade** *(v)* slowly become faint. *(s)* wane, decrease, subside. *(ant)* increase.

9 **resolve** *(n)* firm determination. *(s)* steadfastness, willpower. *(ant)* doubt.

10 **betrayal** *(n)* the action of being gravely disloyal (untrue) to someone. *(s)* deception, treachery. *(ant)* loyalty.

11 **treachery** *(n)* a breach of trust. *(s)* betrayal, deceit, disloyalty. *(ant)* loyalty, honesty.

12 **humiliate** *(v)* make someone feel foolish or ashamed. *(s)* embarrass, mortify. *(ant)* praise.

13 **despair** *(n)* the loss of all hope. *(s)* hopelessness, desperation. *(ant)* hope, joy.

14 **devastate** *(v)* cause overwhelming shock or grief. *(s)* traumatise, crush, distress. *(ant)* comfort.

15 **weary** *(adj)* showing or feeling great tiredness. *(s)* exhausted, fatigued, shattered. *(ant)* fresh, refreshed.

battled with **conflicting**[1] thoughts, unable to find any **respite**[2]. Even when the **torment**[3] **subsided**[4], she slid into **fitful**[5] sleep only to be **roused**[6] again by insects, and those voices calling, 'Callwen. Callwen.'

Dazed[7], Cad's eyes **fluttered**[8] open, and through the mad spinning of her thoughts, she realised her surroundings and **swatted**[9] hard at the insect that bit her arm. 'Got you!' she **muttered**[10] before flopping back down. *So tired*, she thought as her eyes closed again, something odd yet familiar brushing at the edges of her memory.

Then through a swirling sea of mist, like a **cork**[11] atop water, it surfaced again.

'Callwen. Callwen.'

Those **wretched**[12] voices, louder now, more **urgent**[13] and **pleading**[14] than before. *Don't call me Callwen*, she tried to say, but managed only thoughts, when the insect she'd swatted **nipped**[15] her again as she finally **capitulated**[16] to sleep.

I'm dreaming. I must be. Why would Dylan and Rhys be here? They weren't here before. And Fishy?

'Cad! Cad!'

At least they're using my name.

The voice was louder now, persistent. 'Cad, it's us. It's Dylan and Rhys, and we have Fishy and

---

1 **conflicting** *(adj)* not being in harmony or agreement. *(s)* contradictory, clashing. *(ant)* harmonious.

2 **respite** *(n)* a period of rest or relief from something difficult. *(s)* break, interval. *(ant)* continuation.

3 **torment** *(n)* extreme mental or physical suffering. *(s)* pain, anguish, distress, trauma. *(ant)* pleasure.

4 **subside** *(v)* become less severe or intense. *(s)* diminish, ease, abate. *(ant)* increase.

5 **fitful** *(adj)* not regular or steady. *(s)* broken, disturbed, sporadic. *(ant)* constant, sound.

6 **rouse** *(v)* bring out of inactivity. *(s)* stimulate, provoke, arouse. *(ant)* calm, appease.

7 **dazed** *(adj)* not able to react or think well. *(s)* bewildered, stunned. *(ant)* clearheaded.

8 **flutter** *(v)* move with a light, irregular or trembling motion. *(s)* flicker, twitch. *(ant)* still.

9 **swat** *(v)* hit with a blow from a flat object or the hand. *(s)* swipe, slap. knock.

10 **mutter** *(v)* say something that is difficult to hear. *(s)* murmur, mumble, whisper. *(ant)* shout.

11 **cork** *(n)* a light substance that floats often used to seal liquid, such as wine, into bottles.

12 **wretched** *(adj)* extremely annoying. *(s)* despicable, loathsome. *(ant)* admirable.

13 **urgent** *(adj)* needing immediate attention or action. *(s)* pressing, acute. *(ant)* trivial, unimportant.

14 **pleading** *(adj)* making an emotional appeal. *(s)* beseeching, imploring. *(ant)* offering.

15 **nip** *(v)* pinch or bite sharply. *(s)* peck, nibble.

16 **capitulate** *(v)* stop resisting a demand or an opponent. *(s)* surrender, yield, relent. *(ant)* resist.

May here with us. We can bring Flash if you want us to.'

Who's speaking? Wondered Cad, not recognising this person who spoke of her friends.

As a nasty memory rattled around her head, one she fought to forget, something bit her so hard she **yelped**[1], and her eyes snapped wide open.

While coming to, she stared about her, the room drifting into focus. Was that Fishy sitting on her bed? Cad lifted her hand and touched her dog, feeling her soft fur between her fingers; she was real.

I'm not dreaming.

As her friends **materialised**[2] from behind a thick **fog**[3], Cad's mind struggled to make sense of the scene before her.

What in heaven? she thought, as she **massaged**[4] the insect bite on her arm.

As **realisation**[5] slowly **dawned**[6], **grappling**[7] its way through the **stupor**[8], confusion, fear and anger fought for first place in Cad's mind. Anger won. **Furious**[9], Cad **registered**[10] that Rhys Price had just pricked her arm with the emerald hairpin, but even worse, why, and how, had the little sneak-thief **nabbed**[11] it from her tunic again?

---

1 **yelp** *(v)* make a short, sharp cry, especially of pain or alarm. *(s)* squeal, yowl, yell.

2 **materialise** *(v)* appear or become present. *(s)* emerge, surface. *(ant)* disappear.

3 **fog** *(n)* a thick cloud of water droplets forming in the air that restricts or obscures visibility.

4 **massage** *(v)* rub with the hands. *(s)* knead, work, palpate.

5 **realisation** *(n)* the act of becoming aware that something is a fact. *(s)* understanding, awareness. *(ant)* ignorance.

6 **dawn** *(v)* become evident, be perceived or understood by the mind. *(s)* occur. *(ant)* obscure.

7 **grapple** *(v)* engage in a struggle. *(s)* wrestle, fight, battle. *(ant)* surrender.

8 **stupor** *(n)* a state of near unconsciousness or unawareness. *(s)* daze, torpor, blankness. *(ant)* consciousness.

9 **furious** *(adj)* extremely angry. *(s)* enraged, infuriated, fuming, seething. *(ant)* calm, mild.

10 **register** *(v)* become aware of. *(s)* notice, realise, understand. *(ant)* miss.

11 **nab** *(v)* (informal) steal, grab or take something. *(s)* pinch, nick, pilfer. *(ant)* give.

CHAPTER THREE

Stupor

'Rhys Price, how dare you **pilfer**[1] my pin *again*?' yelled Cad, her eyes **ablaze**[2] with **fury**[3].

Well, she tried to yell, swallowing against the dryness in her throat as a spear of fear sliced through her. She made to shout again, but what left her mouth was a string of **unintelligible**[4] baby-like sounds; **gibberish**[5] making no sense at all.

Suddenly, an explosion of arms surrounded her, patting her, stroking her, licking her. 'Cad! Oh, Cad! You're awake! You're alive!' chorused the **intrusive**[6] voices, drowned by the deafening sound of Fishy's barks.

But to Cad's **utter**[7] horror, no matter how she tried, she couldn't form words.

Thoughts tumbled into her head. *Why am I in bed? Why are they hugging me? Why are they saying 'You're alive'?*

When her friends released her, stepping away from her bed, their smiles shone and Fishy licked Cad's face in delight.

---

1 **pilfer** *(v)* steal. *(s)* rob, thieve, snatch, purloin. *(ant)* give.

2 **ablaze** *(adj)* (often used figuratively) on fire. *(s)* aflame, burning, blazing. *(ant)* extinguished.

3 **fury** *(n)* wild anger. *(s)* rage, wrath, outrage, temper. *(ant)* calmness.

4 **unintelligible** *(adj)* impossible to understand. *(s)* incomprehensible, unfathomable. *(ant)* intelligible, clear.

5 **gibberish** *(n)* nonsense speech. *(s)* blather, drivel, balderdash. *(ant)* sense.

6 **intrusive** *(adj)* disturbing and impossible to ignore. *(s)* inescapable, invasive, obtrusive. *(ant)* inconspicuous.

7 **utter** *(adj)* absolute. *(s)* total, complete, downright. *(ant)* partial.

As weak as a newborn kitten, blank-faced but wide-eyed, Cad took in the room while trying to nudge her dog away.

'Fishy, come,' said Dylan, relieving Cad of the dog's **slobbery**[1] tongue.

Is this my bedchamber? she wondered.

The room looked familiar. She blinked, **dredging**[2] her mind for memories. One thing seemed certain: Rhys Price stood before her, and he held her emerald hairpin in his hand.

Again, she tried to speak, but **gobbledygook**[3] formed on her tongue. She couldn't **pronounce**[4] words. *Where's my voice?* Hot **panic**[5] rose in her chest as a sharp pain stabbed her ribs, and not one caused by Rhys.

'Cad! Cad, relax,' Dylan **urged**[6], gently easing her shoulder into the pillow as Rhys shooed Fishy off her bed and onto his. 'Don't **jerk**[7] like that; you'll **aggravate**[8] your ribs.'

Cad frowned, and shaking her head, tried to point to her mouth.

What does he mean? she wondered, **mystified**[9] by his comments as she battled for clues from her **blurry**[10] mind. Her ribs pained her, yet she knew not why. Her last memory was of her father returning to Catrin early and planning a **feast**[11]. After that, things were hazy.

'Are you struggling to speak?' asked Dylan, his voice soft.

Cad nodded and lifted her hands in a 'why?' **gesture**[12], this simple movement **sapping**[13] her strength at once.

---

1 **slobbery** *(adj)* unpleasantly wet. *(s)* dribbly, sopping, salivating. *(ant)* dry.

2 **dredge** *(v)* search deeply. *(s)* explore, delve, probe. *(ant)* overlook.

3 **gobbledygook** *(n)* meaningless language. *(s)* claptrap, gibberish, hogwash. *(ant)* sense.

4 **pronounce** *(v)* sound out in a particular way. *(s)* say, speak, articulate. *(ant)* mispronounce.

5 **panic** *(n)* uncontrollable anxiety or fear. *(s)* fright, dread, alarm. *(ant)* calm, self-control.

6 **urge** *(v)* try to persuade someone. *(s)* encourage, press. *(ant)* deter, discourage.

7 **jerk** *(v)* move with a sudden, sharp movement. *(s)* jolt, lurch. *(ant)* glide, ease.

8 **aggravate** *(v)* make worse. *(s)* irritate. *(ant)* calm, soothe.

9 **mystified** *(adj)* completely perplexed or bewildered. *(s)* bamboozled, stumped. *(ant)* enlightened.

10 **blurry** *(adj)* not clear. *(s)* fuzzy, bleary. *(ant)* clear.

11 **feast** *(n)* a large celebratory meal. *(s)* banquet, feed, binge. *(ant)* snack.

12 **gesture** *(n)* an action to convey a feeling or intention of something. *(s)* act, indication, sign.

13 **sap** *(v)* weaken, erode, destroy or deplete power. *(s)* drain, debilitate. *(ant)* boost, bolster.

His expression **wrought**[1] with **concern**[2], Dylan poured water into a cup and, **coaxing**[3] Cad's head forward, offered her a drink. Something scratching the back of Cad's mind alarmed her, and momentarily she hesitated to drink it, but so **parched**[4], her throat demanded she take a sip. But as the liquid hit her **gullet**[5], it stuck, seeming to lose its way, and she almost **choked**[6] as it eventually found its way down. It was as if she'd forgotten how to swallow.

'Cad, what **ails**[7] you so?' cried Dylan, **cradling**[8] her head and trying to wipe away the water with which she'd showered him.

She shrugged her shoulders, blinking, her eyes now wide, wet with tears, and frightened.

What is happening to me?

'Do you remember anything?'

Cad closed her eyes seeing the dubbing ceremony, then shook her head. She remembered – and yet, she didn't. Her father had **spurned**[9] her with no explanation. She would never be a Knight Hawk. Tears like pearls sat on her cheeks and she was too weak to wipe them away.

'What bothers you so?' asked Dylan with such a pained **countenance**[10] that Rhys joined him beside her, hairpin still in hand.

Cad shook her head again, pointed to her mouth, then at Dylan. Then opening and closing the tips of her fingers making the shape of a duck's beak, gestured for Dylan to talk.

'Cad, you've been asleep – well, unwakeable – for two full days, if that is such a word,' said Dylan. 'Even **Physician**[11] Jordan couldn't rouse you. At first, we thought you dead, but Rhys **insisted**[12] you were not and said he'd seen you in deep **slumber**[13] like this before. He said he once

---

1 **wrought** *(adj)* (archaic past and past participle of 'work') shaped or formed. *(s)* cast, sculpted.

2 **concern** *(n)* worry. *(s)* anxiety, disquiet, apprehension, unease. *(ant)* serenity, calm.

3 **coax** *(v)* persuade gently to do something. *(s)* cajole, urge. *(ant)* force, compel.

4 **parched** *(adj)* very thirsty or dry. *(s)* dehydrated, gasping. *(ant)* hydrated.

5 **gullet** *(n)* the food passage from the mouth to the stomach. *(s)* oesophagus, throat.

6 **choke** *(v)* have difficulty in breathing due to lack of air. *(s)* gasp. *(ant)* breathe.

7 **ail** *(v)* trouble or afflict. *(s)* pain, distress, bother, worry.

8 **cradle** *(v)* hold gently and protectively. *(s)* support, embrace. *(ant)* drop.

9 **spurn** *(v)* reject with disdain (dislike). *(s)* snub, rebuff, ignore. *(ant)* accept.

10 **countenance** *(n)* a person's expression or face. *(s)* features, look, appearance.

11 **physician** *(n)* a medical doctor. *(s)* medical practitioner, physic.

12 **insist** *(v)* demand forcefully without allowing refusal. *(s)* command, require. *(ant)* give up.

13 **slumber** *(n)* sleep. *(s)* a rest, a nap.

couldn't wake you after you **imbibed**[1] the **draught**[2] from Physician Jordan.'

Cad's **brow**[3] **creased**[4] in **consternation**[5], and Dylan clearly noticed, mirroring her look and **tilting**[6] his head in surprise.

'The **potion**[7] **prescribed**[8] by Physician Jordan is to ease the pain from your broken ribs. Don't you remember it?'

Clueless, Cad felt her eyes widen again, but she nodded at Dylan to speak. Then pointing at her middle and shaking her head, she signalled that she didn't understand the 'ribs' part.

'You don't remember falling from Flash in the practice **joust**[9]?'

Cad shook her head. She remembered nothing of a joust, only the **hideous**[10] knighting ceremony, which hurt her to **recall**[11] even for an instant.

'Three days ago, you were riding in the **tilt yard**[12] preparing for a **tournament**[13] arranged by your father—'

Dylan **abruptly**[14] stopped, seeming to search Cad's eyes for recognition of her father, and on seeing it, continued.

'Your father arrived home early from his quest and arranged celebrations for your brother's first birthday, here at Catrin Castle.'

Dylan, observing Cad closely, waited for a sign to carry on.

Cad thought for a moment. *A quest?* She remembered something about her uncle Dewi

---

1 **imbibe** *(v)* drink. *(s)* consume, swallow, swig, down.

2 **draught** *(n)* liquid with medicinal properties. *(s)* medicine, potion, elixir.

3 **brow** *(n)* the forehead.

4 **crease** *(v)* make a line in something. *(s)* wrinkle, pucker. *(ant)* smooth, straighten.

5 **consternation** *(n)* a feeling of dismay or worry. *(s)* concern, trepidation. *(ant)* relaxation, comfort.

6 **tilt** *(v)* move into a sloping position. *(s)* incline, cock. *(ant)* level.

7 **potion** *(n)* a medicinal liquid. *(s)* drink, brew, concoction, mixture.

8 **prescribe** *(v)* (of medicine) advise and authorise the use and dose of.

9 **joust** *(n)* a medieval contest in which two opponents fought on horseback using lances. *(s)* tourney, tilt.

10 **hideous** *(adj)* extremely unpleasant. *(s)* appalling, monstrous. *(ant)* pleasant.

11 **recall** *(v)* bring something back into one's mind. *(s)* remember, recollect. *(ant)* forget.

12 **tilt yard** *(n)* a place or courtyard where jousts took place, sometimes enclosed.

13 **tournament** *(n)* a series of contests with multiple contestants. *(s)* competition, series, event.

14 **abruptly** *(adv)* in an abrupt (unexpected and sudden) way. *(s)* hastily, quickly, immediately. *(ant)* gradually.

having stolen a magical bracelet, but it was hazy; then something deeper within her **stirred**[1]. Something she couldn't quite grasp, but she knew it was floating to the top of her memory, and she **fretted**[2] that when it finally broke the surface, she would not welcome its news at all.

Now struggling to swallow her own **saliva**[3], Cad dipped her chin at Dylan to continue. All her **prior**[4] anger at Rhys's use of her hairpin had vanished completely: she was certain Dylan would have an **apt**[5] explanation for everything. All Cad could do was listen, and hope that her voice, her strength and her memory would soon return, because something was **severely**[6] **impairing**[7] all three.

Dylan, making himself comfortable on Cad's bed, continued.

'Pages were to **demonstrate**[8] the skills we'd learned before the court, and you were practising on Flash, doing very well, I might add.' He beamed at her before **resuming**[9] his story. 'For an odd reason, thanks to Rhys here, we now understand, Bryn Davis challenged you to a **duel**[10], and *you took him on!*'

Dylan's voice had risen an **octave**[11], but **currently**[12] the story meant little to Cad, who nodded at him to carry on, her throat **clogged**[13] with questions.

'Bryn **duped**[14] you. You were expecting Jack Jones, but Bryn appeared, riding his **destrier**[15], Lightning, and you were mounted on little Flash. He challenged you to joust, one-on-one. We

---

1 **stir** *(v)* prompt or arouse a feeling or memory. *(s)* awaken, rouse. *(ant)* discourage, stop.

2 **fret** *(v)* be anxious. *(s)* worry, fuss, agonise, anguish.

3 **saliva** *(n)* the watery liquid found in the mouth. *(s)* spit, spittle, slaver.

4 **prior** *(adj)* coming or existing before. *(s)* earlier, previous. *(ant)* later, subsequent.

5 **apt** *(adj)* suitable in the circumstances. *(s)* appropriate, relevant. *(ant)* inappropriate.

6 **severely** *(adv)* to a great degree. *(s)* seriously, gravely, acutely. *(ant)* slightly, somewhat.

7 **impair** *(v)* damage or weaken. *(s)* compromise, hinder, disable. *(ant)* improve.

8 **demonstrate** *(v)* practically explain or show something. *(s)* display, illustrate, exhibit.

9 **resume** *(v)* continue or begin again (after pausing or an interruption). *(s)* restart, recommence. *(ant)* stop.

10 **duel** *(n)* a contest of honour fought between two people with deadly weapons. *(s)* head-to-head.

11 **octave** *(n)* eight musical notes or the interval between the top and bottom of these eight notes.

12 **currently** *(adv)* at the present time. *(s)* presently, right now. *(ant)* previously.

13 **clog** *(v)* become blocked. *(s)* obstruct, choke. *(ant)* unblock, clear.

14 **dupe** *(v)* deceive. *(s)* fool, trick, hoodwink, mislead, cheat.

15 **destrier** *(n)* a heavy-set, large medieval knight's war horse. Also known as the Great Horse due to its importance.

begged[1] you to stop, but you wouldn't listen. You took Davis on, who was riding a *destrier!*'

She hoped it was the stupor **addling**[2] her mind, because at this moment, Cad wasn't sure what a destrier was, but as she'd **apparently**[3] been riding Flash at the time, she **assumed**[4] it was a horse. She seemed to remember Flash was her pony.

'Madness really, but the **marvellous**[5] part is, you did *really* well,' continued Dylan, with Rhys nodding **furiously**[6] in agreement. 'But Bryn cheated – it's a long story – and he took you from your saddle with a massive **blow**[7] to your torso. You banged your head, and you broke some ribs.'

Dylan stopped again, as if studying her face for signs of **distress**[8], but she lifted her chin and showed none. She was listening **intently**[9], trying to piece back the puzzle that had become her life.

'You hit your head when you landed, but the main injury was to your ribs. Physician Jordan **diagnosed**[10] them as broken and prescribed a pain-killing draught and bed rest while they healed.'

Cad's hawk eyes fixed on Dylan, then on Rhys and back again. She knew from their faces that more story bubbled beneath the surface. Had the knock to her head **wiped**[11] her memory and silenced her speech? How long had she **languished**[12] here, stuck in this sweaty stupor?

Feeling like a mouse **at the mercy of**[13] a cat, just managing to lift her hand, Cad pinched

---

1 **beg** *(v)* ask honestly. *(s)* beseech, implore, plead, request. *(ant)* offer, give.

2 **addle** *(v)* make someone unable to think properly. *(s)* confuse, muddle, stupefy, daze.

3 **apparently** *(adv)* as far as one knows or can see. *(s)* seemingly, evidently. *(ant)* implausibly.

4 **assume** *(v)* presume to be the case without any proof. *(s)* suppose, conclude, believe. *(ant)* prove.

5 **marvellous** *(adj)* causing great wonder and amazement. *(s)* awesome, sensational. *(ant)* ordinary.

6 **furiously** *(adv)* in a furious (energetic) manner. *(s)* energetically, feverishly, frantically. *(ant)* slowly.

7 **blow** *(n)* a strike with a weapon, hand or hard object. *(s)* punch, thump, thwack.

8 **distress** *(n)* extreme sorrow, anxiety or pain. *(s)* upset, disquiet, torment. *(ant)* peace, calm.

9 **intently** *(adv)* in an intent (eager) way. *(s)* closely, attentively. *(ant)* casually.

10 **diagnose** *(v)* identify a medical condition or injury. *(s)* determine, confirm, pronounce.

11 **wipe** *(v)* remove completely. *(s)* eradicate, expunge, erase. *(ant)* add.

12 **languish** *(v)* be forced to remain in a situation. *(s)* suffer. *(ant)* thrive.

13 **at the mercy of** (phrase) to be completely in the power of someone or something else.

her thumb and **forefinger**[1] together and **scrawled**[2] in the air as though writing. It was time for answers.

'You want a **quill**[3] and **parchment**[4]?' asked Rhys, nodding and moving to the table at the back of their room.

Cad gestured the slightest of nods. But as she lowered her hand, the blood drained from her face, her body turned to rags, and she flopped back into her pillows, **exhaustion**[5] **consuming**[6] her once more.

---

1 **forefinger** *(n)* the first finger (the one next to the thumb). *(s)* pointer, index finger, indicator.

2 **scrawl** *(v)* write in a hurried way. *(s)* scribble.

3 **quill** *(n)* a pen made from the main wing or tail feathers of a large bird.

4 **parchment** *(n)* prepared animal skin with a papery appearance used in ancient writing. *(s)* vellum, scroll.

5 **exhaustion** *(n)* extreme mental or physical tiredness. *(s)* fatigue, weariness. *(ant)* vigour.

6 **consume** *(v)* strongly affect or overwhelm with a feeling. *(s)* dominate, overpower. *(ant)* abandon.

CHAPTER FOUR

Cad and Rhys

Despite[1] having slept for hours, Cad's eyes were still sore and heavy-lidded, and she struggled to sit up against her pillows to relieve the **congestion**[2] in her chest. **Groggy**[3], and with **mounting**[4] **trepidation**[5], she **pondered**[6] her situation and the shock of knowing, thanks to Rhys, that someone had **poisoned**[7] her.

Apparently, Rhys's idea to prick Cad with her hairpin had eventually roused her from the deep stupor. Perhaps its magic did work in that strange way: rescuing folks from death's door. They would never know, but she was **conscious**[8], and that's what mattered.

Cad realised that what she'd imagined being insect bites while she was **unconscious**[9] were probably pricks from the pin. Why in her **delirium**[10] she'd seen **myriad**[11] cockroaches, she

---

1 **despite** *(prep)* in spite of, regardless of. *(s)* even though. *(ant)* because of.

2 **congestion** *(n)* the state of being congested (blocked). *(s)* obstruction, blockage. *(ant)* flow.

3 **groggy** *(adj)* dazed or weak especially from illness. *(s)* muzzy, befuddled. *(ant)* alert.

4 **mount** *(v)* grow more intense. *(s)* escalate, increase, soar, spiral. *(ant)* decrease, diminish.

5 **trepidation** *(n)* anxiety or fear about what may happen. *(s)* dread, apprehension. *(ant)* assurance.

6 **ponder** *(v)* think carefully about. *(s)* consider, contemplate, deliberate. *(ant)* disregard.

7 **poison** *(v)* give something very dangerous or life threatening to someone or something.

8 **conscious** *(adj)* aware of and responding to one's surroundings. *(s)* alert, responsive, awake. *(ant)* unconscious.

9 **unconscious** *(adj)* not awake or aware of one's environment. *(s)* asleep, comatose. *(ant)* conscious.

10 **delirium** *(n)* a disturbed state of mind. *(s)* incoherence, irrationality. *(ant)* lucidity, coherence.

11 **myriad** *(adj)* many. *(s)* numerous, multiple. *(ant)* few.

couldn't **fathom**[1], but for sure: she now **despised**[2] them even more. The memories of their crackling shells underfoot sent shivers of **disgust**[3] through her.

In one corner of their room, Rhys lay quietly on his bed, Fishy by his side. The **sulking**[4] dog was forbidden from jumping onto Cad's bed **lest**[5] she harm Cad's broken ribs.

From the corner of her eye, Cad observed the **taciturn**[6] boy, and her heart **swelled**[7] at his **loyalty**[8]. Rhys was such a dear friend, having plucked Cad from **dire straits**[9] twice, and probably saving her life on both occasions.

Earlier, as she'd drifted in and out of sleep, he'd explained how he'd rescued her from Catrin Castle's well. How he'd **hauled**[10] as she'd clung to the well's **pail**[11] to find her **smeared**[12] in a green slime-like **substance**[13]: the poison which had caused Cad to be unconscious for days. It seemed the poison was **administered**[14] into the castle's water system by someone with the means to make a **contraption**[15] to do so. Cad had much to thank Rhys for. How could she ever show him such **gratitude**[16]?

Cad thought of her other dear friend, Dylan. He was somewhere in the castle, doing what, Cad wasn't sure. Before Dylan had finally left her side earlier, Physician Jordan had visited, **doling**[17] out lotions and potions, pretending he'd never believed her dead. Then he'd

---

1 **fathom** *(v)* comprehend after much thought. *(s)* understand, grasp, perceive. *(ant)* misunderstand.

2 **despise** *(v)* dislike greatly. *(s)* hate, detest, loathe. *(ant)* love, admire.

3 **disgust** *(n)* a feeling of great dislike or revulsion. *(s)* loathing, horror. *(s)* pleasure.

4 **sulk** *(v)* be silent because one is disgruntled. *(s)* brood, mope. *(ant)* be cheerful.

5 **lest** *(con)* because of the possibility of something bad happening. *(s)* just in case, for fear that.

6 **taciturn** *(adj)* (of a person) quiet. *(s)* untalkative, silent. *(ant)* talkative.

7 **swell** *(v)* become larger in size. *(s)* expand, bulge. *(ant)* shrink, contract.

8 **loyalty** *(n)* the quality of giving constant support. *(s)* faithfulness, reliability. *(ant)* disloyalty.

9 **dire straits** (idiom) in an extremely bad or difficult situation.

10 **haul** *(v)* drag or pull with force or effort. *(s)* heave, yank. *(ant)* push, shove.

11 **pail** *(n)* a bucket.

12 **smeared** *(adj)* spread or coated over something. *(s)* streaked, smudged.

13 **substance** *(n)* a particular type of matter which has uniform qualities. *(s)* material, stuff.

14 **administer** *(v)* dispense (give out) or apply. *(s)* deliver, distribute. *(ant)* withhold, deny.

15 **contraption** *(n)* a device. *(s)* gadget, mechanism, apparatus.

16 **gratitude** *(n)* the quality of being thankful and showing appreciation. *(s)* gratefulness. *(ant)* ingratitude.

17 **dole** *(v)* share something. *(s)* allocate, allot, assign.

left in a hurry, leaving the boys to **tend**[1] her.

Hitherto[2], Cad's biggest relief had been the realisation that the insects and the knighting ceremony had indeed been **fantastical**[3] **demons**[4] brought on by imbibing **excess**[5] potion. Either the one Jordan had prescribed, or the green slime that had smeared itself over her when she'd been stuck down the well. Goodness knows how much she'd **ingested**[6], but she **suspected**[7] an awful lot. It seemed that her body had then shut down due to the **overdose**[8]. Luckily, she had pulled through. Whether her magic hairpin had woken her, or the poison had run its course, was a mystery.

Earlier, Goodwife Hughes had called in to care for her. The goodwife had cried and fussed, helping Cad to drink, and feeding her tiny amounts of her best bone **broth**[9] from a baby's spoon. Soon, Cad's throat had remembered how to swallow again, and within minutes of eating, she'd improved. Oddly, she still couldn't form words, but had **communicated**[10] with Dylan by roughly scribbling down the code they'd **invented**[11] between themselves and, of course, she now knew Rhys understood it too.

Thinking of codes **triggered**[12] the memory of the **cipher**[13], which Sir Robert had taken from her. When her father had returned early from his quest, she'd told him of it, and he'd been shocked and concerned and had wanted to see it immediately. She wondered whether her father had seen it yet, and if so, what he'd made of it.

Stuck in bed, where she'd spent two days locked behind the doors of sleep, Cad **brooded**[14] over

---

1 **tend** *(v)* look after, care for. *(s)* attend to, minister to. *(ant)* neglect.

2 **hitherto** *(adv)* until this point. *(s)* thus far. *(ant)* henceforth.

3 **fantastical** *(adj)* strange or weird in appearance. *(s)* bizarre, outlandish. *(ant)* normal, mundane.

4 **demon** *(n)* a bad spirit. *(s)* devil, fiend. *(ant)* angel.

5 **excess** *(adj)* more than a desirable amount; too much. *(s)* excessive. *(ant)* exact, too little.

6 **ingest** *(v)* swallow or absorb into the body. *(s)* consume, eat, drink. *(ant)* vomit.

7 **suspect** *(v)* believe in the existence or truth of something without proof. *(s)* assume, think, suppose. *(ant)* know.

8 **overdose** *(n)* too much of a dangerous substance or drug.

9 **broth** *(n)* a soup, usually made with meat, vegetables and stock from bones.

10 **communicate** *(v)* exchange or share information. *(s)* converse.

11 **invent** *(v)* design or create something never made before. *(s)* devise, develop.

12 **trigger** *(v)* (of a person) cause to think or do something. *(s)* activate. *(ant)* prevent, halt.

13 **cipher** *(n)* a disguised or secret way of writing something. *(s)* cryptograph, code, cryptogram.

14 **brood** *(v)* think deeply about something that makes one concerned, angry or unhappy. *(s)* ponder, contemplate.

her **absent**[1] father. Hurt and **perplexed**[2], she questioned why he'd not yet visited. Surely he should have come the moment she'd woken. Yet when she'd asked Dylan, he'd said she was too tired for visitors, insisting that the physician's **brew**[3] would soon **render**[4] her **incoherent**[5] and that she'd be best seeing the prince tomorrow. He **reassured**[6] Cad that her father would probably visit when she could hopefully speak more. Thank goodness her words were coming back, **albeit**[7] slowly.

That **conversation**[8] with Dylan was hours back; at least Cad thought it had been, but still **discombobulated**[9], she wasn't sure. She wriggled with a **wince**[10], trying to find a comfortable position. Without the **intoxicating**[11] draught, those blasted ribs hurt and breathing was **laboured**[12]. Sore and still **shattered**[13], she closed her eyes.

Finding little respite, Cad **meandered**[14] between fitful sleep and consciousness, reliving the **ordeal**[15] in the well. She saw nothing of the joust and falling from Flash, but her **plummet**[16] into the well materialised in **random**[17], **vivid**[18] pictures.

After **scant**[19] rest, Cad woke with a start, her body bathed in sweat. **Stubborn**[20] tears sprang to her eyes, her mind wrought with tangled thoughts. When Goodwife Hughes had visited earlier,

---

1 **absent** *(adj)* not present. *(s)* gone, unavailable. *(ant)* present.

2 **perplex** *(v)* completely confuse. *(s)* baffle, confound, flummox. *(ant)* enlighten.

3 **brew** *(n)* a blended drink. *(s)* beverage, mixture.

4 **render** *(v)* cause to become. *(s)* make, leave.

5 **incoherent** *(adj)* unintelligible or delirious. *(s)* unclear, incomprehensible. *(ant)* coherent.

6 **reassure** *(v)* do or say something to remove someone's fears or doubts. *(s)* comfort, hearten. *(ant)* unnerve.

7 **albeit** *(con)* although. *(s)* though, even though, while.

8 **conversation** *(n)* a talk between two or more people. *(s)* discussion, chat, dialogue, exchange.

9 **discombobulated** *(adj)* confused. *(s)* disconcerted, baffled, bemused. *(ant)* clear, informed.

10 **wince** *(n)* an instance of wincing (flinching) in reaction to pain or distress. *(s)* grimace. *(ant)* smile.

11 **intoxicating** *(adj)* (of a drug) likely to cause someone to lose control of their senses or behaviour. *(s)* potent.

12 **laboured** *(adj)* something done with great difficulty and effort. *(s)* strained, heavy. *(ant)* easy.

13 **shattered** *(adj)* extremely tired. *(s)* exhausted, weary, drained, fatigued. *(ant)* fresh, lively.

14 **meander** *(v)* wander. *(s)* drift, rove, roam.

15 **ordeal** *(n)* a prolonged and horrid experience. *(s)* trauma, nightmare. *(ant)* joy.

16 **plummet** *(n)* a rapid and steep fall or drop. *(s)* plunge. *(ant)* ascent.

17 **random** *(adj)* without method or organisation. *(s)* irregular, odd, arbitrary. *(ant)* regular.

18 **vivid** *(adj)* powerful or strong. *(s)* graphic, lifelike. *(ant)* vague, weak.

19 **scant** *(adj)* barely sufficient or adequate. *(s)* little, meagre, limited. *(ant)* extensive.

20 **stubborn** *(adj)* difficult to stop, move or cure. *(s)* persistent. *(ant)* yielding, weak.

it had disturbed Cad to recall that she had been the one to administer her dose that **fateful**[1] night. The dose's **composition**[2] had proved too strong, even though she'd taken little; its effects had been **overpowering**[3]. However, vomiting violently that night had probably saved her life. Now **burdened**[4] by a despairing **vulnerability**[5], she dashed away tears on her sleeve.

Rhys turned his head towards her.

Does that boy miss nothing? wondered Cad. Was he gifted with some sort of **sixth sense**[6]? It mattered not. Cad knew Rhys was special, **intelligent**[7] beyond his years, yet not in a **scholarly**[8] **fashion**[9]. Rhys had something else, something she struggled to **perceive**[10], but it was there.

Their eyes met and, without asking, Rhys read her look and joined her on the bed, Fishy hopping up beside them. Rhys **scowled**[11] at Fishy, who knew she shouldn't be there, but a nod from Cad wiped his cross look away.

'Cad, you look so **sorrowful**[12],' said Rhys, his voice **drenched**[13] with **genuine**[14] **sympathy**[15]. At least he'd finally stopped calling her 'Master Cad'.

With great effort, Cad managed a **feeble**[16] 'yes' along with an accompanying nod. She lifted a weak hand and rested it **atop**[17] Fishy's broad head. The **prospect**[18] of not fully recovering filled Cad

---

1 **fateful** *(adj)* involving far-reaching consequences. *(s)* significant, pivotal. *(ant)* insignificant.

2 **composition** *(n)* the way in which a mixture or whole is made up. *(s)* constitution, formation.

3 **overpowering** *(adj)* very strong or intense. *(s)* overwhelming. *(ant)* mild.

4 **burden** *(v)* cause worry, hardship or distress. *(s)* afflict, overload. *(ant)* relieve.

5 **vulnerability** *(n)* the state of being exposed to possible physical or emotional harm. *(s)* weakness. *(ant)* invulnerability.

6 **sixth sense** *(n)* a supposed ability to know things that are inexplicable in terms of normal perception. *(s)* instinct.

7 **intelligent** *(adj)* clever. *(s)* smart, bright, sharp, quick. *(ant)* unintelligent.

8 **scholarly** *(adj)* having or showing a love of academic learning. *(s)* learned. *(ant)* unenlightened.

9 **fashion** *(n)* a way of being or doing something. *(s)* manner, approach, style.

10 **perceive** *(v)* interpret or view in a particular way. *(s)* recognise, see, discern. *(ant)* misinterpret.

11 **scowl** *(v)* frown in an angry way. *(s)* glare, glower, grimace. *(ant)* smile.

12 **sorrowful** *(adj)* feeling or showing sadness. *(s)* miserable, desolate. *(ant)* cheerful.

13 **drench** *(v)* flood with. *(s)* satiate, soak.

14 **genuine** *(adj)* real, truthful or sincere. *(s)* honest, candid. *(ant)* insincere, false.

15 **sympathy** *(n)* feelings of sorrow and pity for the misfortunes of another. *(s)* empathy. *(ant)* callousness.

16 **feeble** *(adj)* lacking strength. *(s)* weak, frail, infirm. *(ant)* forceful, strong.

17 **atop** *(prep)* on the top of. *(s)* upon.

18 **prospect** *(n)* a future or anticipated event. *(s)* thought, idea, contemplation.

with such **dread**[1] she dared not **broach**[2] the **outcome**[3]. **Mortified**[4] at her reaction, she wiped away another **stray**[5] tear. Too **frail**[6] and **frustrated**[7] to try to speak, she sought **solace**[8] in her friends' **proximity**[9].

'Cad, we're here for you; Dylan, Ellis and I. We'll stay by your side as you recover from this **ailment**[10] and help find the **culprit**[11] who did this. Sir Robert has sealed off the well, all thanks to your **shrewdness**[12] and **courage**[13]. *You* checked the water supply. And because of that, many have gone **unscathed**[14], including me.'

Cad said nothing. Rhys gazed at her, his eyes searching her face, reading her emotions. He **absent-mindedly**[15] stroked Fishy, who clearly **adored**[16] having two in **attendance**[17].

'You may well have **prevented**[18] my **spewing**[19]!' Rhys cracked a half-smile, looking **embarrassed**[20] by his **debilitating**[21] **phobia**[22] of vomiting. It had **plagued**[23] him since childhood.

---

1 **dread** *(n)* fear. *(s)* apprehension, trepidation. *(ant)* confidence, cheer.

2 **broach** *(v)* raise a difficult subject for discussion. *(s)* propose, mention. *(ant)* close.

3 **outcome** *(n)* the way something turns out. *(s)* result, conclusion.

4 **mortified** *(adj)* embarrassed or ashamed. *(s)* appalled. *(ant)* pleased, gratified.

5 **stray** *(adj)* unexpected or not in the usual place. *(s)* random. *(ant)* expected.

6 **frail** *(adj)* weak. *(s)* infirm, feeble. *(ant)* strong.

7 **frustrated** *(adj)* feeling annoyed from being out of control. *(s)* exasperated, irritated. *(ant)* content.

8 **solace** *(n)* comfort in a bad situation. *(s)* support, relief. *(ant)* aggravation.

9 **proximity** *(n)* nearness. *(s)* closeness, adjacency. *(ant)* remoteness, distance.

10 **ailment** *(n)* an illness or condition. *(s)* affliction, disorder. *(ant)* wellness, health.

11 **culprit** *(n)* a person or thing responsible for a wrongdoing. *(s)* offender, criminal, baddie. *(ant)* victim.

12 **shrewdness** *(n)* the quality of showing or having good judgement. *(s)* cleverness, sharpness. *(s)* stupidity.

13 **courage** *(n)* the ability to do something frightening. *(s)* bravery, pluck. *(ant)* cowardice.

14 **unscathed** *(adj)* without suffering, harm or injury. *(s)* safe, unhurt. *(ant)* injured, harmed.

15 **absent-mindedly** *(adv)* done without proper thought or awareness. *(s)* dreamily. *(ant)* attentively.

16 **adore** *(v)* love. *(s)* treasure, prize. *(ant)* hate.

17 **attendance** *(n)* the state of being present. *(s)* attending. *(ant)* absence.

18 **prevent** *(v)* stop something from happening. *(s)* halt, avert. *(ant)* cause, permit.

19 **spew** *(v)* (informal) be sick. *(s)* vomit, retch, reach.

20 **embarrassed** *(adj)* showing or feeling embarrassment (shame or awkwardness). *(s)* sheepish, mortified. *(ant)* unabashed.

21 **debilitating** *(adj)* making weak and infirm. *(s)* wearing, crippling. *(ant)* fortifying.

22 **phobia** *(n)* an extreme or illogical fear of something. *(s)* loathing, aversion. *(ant)* liking, comfort.

23 **plague** *(v)* cause continual distress to. *(s)* afflict, torment, harass. *(ant)* soothe, support.

Rhys knew not why it **afflicted**[1] him, for he had no parents to explain it to him. He too was **orphaned**[2], like Cad, taken in by Llywelyn to serve as a page at Catrin Castle, and **funded**[3] **solely**[4] by the prince. He was most fortunate; many were not so.

Cad reached for her parchment and scribbled on it. Rhys read her note and smiled.

'You see the true me. I don't want to be a knight like you. I'm so sorry you suffered that awful nightmare of the dubbing ceremony. I am sure you will be a Knight Hawk one day.'

Cad scribbled some more. Rhys read it and grinned.

'I can't fight. I'm clumsy.'

Cad giggled, nodding at him as she stroked Fishy, happy to chat with Rhys in this way.

'I want to study the law, even if that means working with Sir Robert at some point. He thought me an **imbecile**[5] until I began to **fleece**[6] the court **gentry**[7] of their money.'

Cad let out such a hoot her throat **clenched**[8] in **protest**[9]. Dylan had recently **confessed**[10] to Cad, with just a hint of **envy**[11], how brilliant a chess player Rhys had become, having **trounced**[12] Dylan with **aplomb**[13] during their last few **bouts**[14].

You give me such cheer, she wrote in **Latin**[15].

'And Evans certainly doesn't know I taught myself to read.'

Neither did I until recently, thought Cad.

With a broad smile, Rhys patted Cad's hand, then rubbed Fishy's head.

---

1 **afflict** *(v)* cause pain or trouble to and affect adversely. *(s)* bother, ail, plague. *(ant)* aid.

2 **orphan** *(v)* make a child an orphan (without birth parents).

3 **fund** *(v)* provide with money. *(s)* pay for, finance. *(ant)* withdraw.

4 **solely** *(adv)* involving nothing or no one else. *(s)* only, exclusively, just. *(ant)* not only.

5 **imbecile** *(n)* a stupid person. *(s)* halfwit, clod, ninny, dunce. *(ant)* genius.

6 **fleece** *(v)* (informal) take money from someone (sometimes by cheating). *(s)* exploit.

7 **gentry** *(n)* people of nobility by birth (privileged). *(s)* the establishment. *(ant)* proletariat.

8 **clench** *(v)* contract or tighten. *(s)* constrict, tense. *(ant)* relax.

9 **protest** *(v)* express an objection to something. *(s)* object, complain. *(ant)* agree.

10 **confess** *(v)* admit or make known. *(s)* tell, reveal, divulge, disclose. *(ant)* deny, conceal.

11 **envy** *(n)* an unpleasant feeling of wanting what other people have. *(s)* jealousy, desire. *(ant)* generosity.

12 **trounce** *(v)* beat dramatically in a contest. *(s)* thrash, crush. *(ant)* lose.

13 **aplomb** *(n)* self-confidence. *(s)* assurance, surety, composure. *(ant)* fear, anxiety.

14 **bout** *(n)* a contest of strength. *(s)* match, encounter, fight, clash.

15 **Latin** *(n)* the classical language of ancient Rome.

Cad regarded her astute[1] friend with gratitude. Her father **disapproved**[2] of **gambling**[3] but turned a blind eye so long as it remained in hand. It was a difficult **scenario**[4] to police. In the castle, folks, and especially bored guards, would find many ways to **clandestinely**[5] play cards, dice or chess, and it seemed Rhys knew where they sought this sport. Cad remembered Dylan saying that Rhys regularly beat the castle's best players, noting his moves and naming them for future **reference**[6]. Cad now guessed that Rhys Price didn't lie awake at night counting sheep, but probably **revised**[7] chess moves in his head.

Still **racked**[8] with **indescribable**[9] exhaustion, Cad's quill slipped from her hand and onto the floor beside her bed. Rhys bent down to pick it up. 'Weary?' he asked, placing the quill on the table next to her. But Cad didn't answer.

Immediately concerned, Rhys **appraised**[10] her, then smiled and took the parchment from atop the bed covers, placing it next to the quill. Cad had drifted back off into the **remnants**[11] of her poisoned stupor and would remain that way for some time; he'd seen the pattern these last hours while tending his friend.

As she slept, Rhys gazed at Cad, who he saw as a sister. She dozed fitfully, her head turning, **strangled**[12] moans rising from her throat, her eyelids fluttering open and closed. He wished he could **cure**[13] her, **banish**[14] her **woes**[15]. This girl who'd befriended him as a small child. The girl who

---

1 **astute** *(adj)* able to quickly assess and turn something to one's advantage. *(s)* shrewd, clever. *(ant)* dim-witted.

2 **disapprove** *(v)* dislike. *(s)* criticise, denounce. *(ant)* approve, like.

3 **gambling** *(n)* the playing of games for money. *(s)* betting, wagering.

4 **scenario** *(n)* a possible sequence of events. *(s)* situation, state.

5 **clandestinely** *(adv)* in a clandestine (secretive) manner. *(s)* covertly, stealthily. *(ant)* overtly.

6 **reference** *(n)* the use of a source of information to work something out. *(s)* usage.

7 **revise** *(v)* revisit something to improve one's skills or knowledge. *(s)* study, go over, memorise.

8 **rack** *(v)* cause extreme discomfort. *(s)* beset, torment. *(ant)* comfort, relieve.

9 **indescribable** *(adj)* too extreme or unusual to describe. *(s)* intense, powerful. *(ant)* definable.

10 **appraise** *(v)* assess a situation or thing. *(s)* evaluate, gauge, review.

11 **remnant** *(n)* a part of something that is left over. *(s)* remainder, leftover.

12 **strangled** *(adj)* sounding as if coming from a constricted throat. *(s)* choked, squeezed.

13 **cure** *(v)* make better or relieve from illness. *(s)* heal, restore. *(ant)* sicken.

14 **banish** *(v)* get rid of. *(s)* eliminate, eradicate. *(ant)* accept, allow.

15 **woe** *(n)* great distress, misery or sorrow. *(s)* anguish, despair, gloom. *(ant)* happiness, joy.

never **judged**[1] his **peculiar**[2] ways. The girl who shared with him her deepest secret.

Rhys saw exactly what drove Cad, and he understood it too. She battled an **overwhelming**[3] need to prove herself worthy in the eyes of her father. Yet the one thing no one could **convince**[4] her of, was, that Llywelyn loved her regardless. **Nevertheless**[5], she would listen to no one, and Llywelyn knew that too. Cad was the most **stubborn**[6] and **strong-willed**[7] person Rhys had ever met, and nothing would stop her **personal**[8] quest to be a Knight Hawk. Only then would she feel she'd earned her place at the **noble**[9] prince's side.

Never a God-fearing boy, Rhys now placed his palms together and prayed Cad would recover, for if she didn't, he despaired for her future well-being. In that moment, he **vowed**[10] that no matter how far she fell, he would break her fall.

As he watched Cad sleep, knowing what he must soon tell her ripped his heart **asunder**[11]. He had **mulled**[12] over his decision for hours, torn between telling her today and waiting until tomorrow, as he'd agreed with Dylan. After much **deliberation**[13] and **reflection**[14], he'd decided to wait, with only her best interests at heart. He would let her recover for another day, before breaking the news that would no doubt devastate her.

---

1 **judge** *(v)* form an opinion (view) about something or someone, sometimes negatively.

2 **peculiar** *(adj)* different from normal or usual. *(s)* bizarre, uncanny, odd. *(ant)* normal.

3 **overwhelming** *(adj)* having a strong emotional effect. *(s)* profound, overpowering. *(ant)* underwhelming.

4 **convince** *(v)* persuade. *(s)* assure. *(ant)* dissuade.

5 **nevertheless** *(adv)* all the same. *(s)* however, even so, nonetheless.

6 **stubborn** *(adj)* being unwilling to change. *(s)* obstinate, headstrong, wilful. *(ant)* compliant.

7 **strong-willed** *(adj)* determined to do as one wishes. *(s)* stubborn, resolute. *(ant)* weak-willed.

8 **personal** *(adj)* affecting or belonging to a certain person (yours). *(s)* own, private. *(ant)* public.

9 **noble** *(adj)* belonging to the aristocracy or having fine moral and personal qualities. *(s)* aristocrat, honourable.

10 **vow** *(v)* make a solemn (serious) promise. *(s)* swear, guarantee, assure.

11 **asunder** *(adv)* apart. *(s)* in two, into pieces. *(ant)* together.

12 **mull** *(v)* think about. *(s)* ponder, muse, reflect. *(ant)* disregard.

13 **deliberation** *(n)* careful consideration or discussion. *(s)* thought, reflection, musing.

14 **reflection** *(n)* careful thought or consideration. *(s)* pondering, deliberation, contemplation.

CHAPTER FIVE

Dylan and Rhys

As dawn broke, Dylan and Rhys observed Cad as she lay in her drug-**induced**[1] sleep, their faces **drawn**[2] with worry. Neither boy had slept much. In turn, they'd **monitored**[3] Cad throughout the night. Then, tossing and turning, they'd waited for the time when they must break the distressing news to her. Even Fishy looked **downcast**[4], sensing something was deeply **amiss**[5].

'I dread telling her,' whispered Dylan as he crawled towards the end of his bed to be nearer to Rhys and out of Cad's **earshot**[6]. Although he doubted he'd wake her from the draught's effects until her body was ready, and they were not about to **resort**[7] to her hairpin again.

The next few days would be **torturous**[8] for Cad. Dylan knew she'd **crave**[9] to be involved, to help Catrin Castle and her father, but he also recognised that she was **incapable**[10] and must rest in the hope of making a full recovery. Since yesterday, Dylan had noticed improvements in her

---

1 **induce** *(v)* bring about. *(s)* cause, generate. *(ant)* prevent.

2 **drawn** *(adj)* (of a person) appearing strained due to a discomfort of some sort. *(s)* pinched, drained. *(ant)* relaxed.

3 **monitor** *(v)* observe and review, watch over. *(s)* check, supervise. *(ant)* mismanage.

4 **downcast** *(adj)* (of a person) feeling disheartened. *(s)* despondent, dispirited. *(ant)* upbeat.

5 **amiss** *(adj)* out of place or not right. *(s)* wrong, awry, untoward. *(ant)* right, in order.

6 **earshot** *(n)* the distance within which one can hear or be heard. *(s)* close range, hearing range.

7 **resort** *(v)* adopt a course of action to resolve a difficult situation. *(s)* employ, apply, use.

8 **torturous** *(adj)* involving or causing pain or suffering. *(s)* agonising, harrowing. *(ant)* pleasant, pleasing.

9 **crave** *(v)* feel great desire for. *(s)* want, yearn for, long for. *(ant)* dislike, spurn.

10 **incapable** *(adj)* unable to achieve or do something. *(s)* helpless, incapacitated. *(ant)* capable.

condition, and he now **willed**[1] her to make a full recovery. Her speech had progressed, but she'd been unable to rise from bed unaided, needing help to use the chamber pot. At first, Dylan had been mortified, but needs must, and they would assist Cad with anything, come what may. After all, Goodwife Hughes couldn't help her, for she wasn't **privy**[2] to Cad's secret.

Dylan and Rhys assumed that Physician Jordan, Llywelyn's man, was aware of Cad's gender, for he'd examined her after she'd fallen from Flash. Dylan and Rhys had to **ensure**[3] Bryn Davis get nowhere near Cad while she was **incapacitated**[4] in this way. Dylan wondered who in the castle knew of Cad's true identity and he **reflected**[5] for a while, **evaluating**[6] the mental list in his head.

Sir Robert was aware of Cad's pretence. He'd spent most of Cad's early childhood with her at Cadwaladr Castle. Owain Glyn, who Dylan trusted completely, had been with Llywelyn at Cad's rescue from the well. Obviously Dewi and Siân were on the list: Siân was her **adoptive**[7] mother and Dewi her uncle. Their **whereabouts**[8] with the stolen Gwalch Gem bracelet remained unknown, but Dylan fretted because perhaps they'd already shared secrets with the **traitors**[9] and spies at play in this castle. Indeed, Bryn Davis seemed to have discovered Cad's secret. Who'd told him? Dylan doubted he'd worked it out for himself; Bryn was no scholar, just a **thug**[10]. Who might he have shared Cad's secret with since?

Dylan gazed at Cad's sleeping **form,**[11] and wished more than anything that she could accept that her father loved her for who she was. Before John's birth, Llywelyn, perhaps foolishly, had **sanctioned**[12] her knight's training and there was no way she would stop now, unless this injury

---

1 **will** *(v)* use all mental powers and desires to make something happen or hope that it will.

2 **privy** *(adj)* having knowledge of something secret. *(s)* wise to, in on.

3 **ensure** *(v)* make certain. *(s)* guarantee. *(ant)* deny.

4 **incapacitate** *(v)* prevent from functioning normally. *(s)* debilitate, disable. *(ant)* enable.

5 **reflect** *(v)* think about carefully. *(s)* consider, contemplate. *(ant)* disregard.

6 **evaluate** *(v)* form an idea of. *(s)* assess, appraise, consider.

7 **adoptive** *(adj)* (of a person) related by adoption (legally raising someone else's child).

8 **whereabouts** *(n)* the place where something or someone is. *(s)* position, location.

9 **traitor** *(n)* someone who betrays (double-crosser). *(s)* conspirator, turncoat. *(ant)* loyalist.

10 **thug** *(n)* a violent person. *(s)* bully, hoodlum, ruffian, bandit.

11 **form** *(n)* the visible shape of something or someone. *(s)* outline, profile.

12 **sanction** *(v)* approve or permit. *(s)* allow, authorise, consent. *(ant)* veto, disapprove.

intervened[1]. Dylan wasn't sure which scenario was worse: her gender being revealed by Davis, or an ailment ending her **ambitions**[2]. Either way, Dylan felt wretched, not only for Cad, but for what currently occurred beyond Catrin Castle's walls. For if that wasn't **resolved**[3], Cad's problems were the least of their worries.

'Dylan, you look most troubled,' whispered Rhys, stroking Fishy's head.

'I'm **considering**[4] Cad, and her secrets.'

'We must be even more careful now,' said Rhys. 'We can't leave Cad alone, even with Goodwife Hughes. One of us must remain here at all times.'

'Yes, you're right. I'll approach Sir Robert and ask for **leave**[5] from castle **duties**[6] for us both. I'm sure he'll agree, even in these **dire**[7] times. However, I've heard **gossip**[8] that Sir Robert's command has been **quashed**[9] here at Catrin.'

'Really?' Rhys's voice rose along with his eyebrows.

Dylan put a finger to his lips and **cast**[10] his eyes towards Cad. 'Yes. **Rumours**[11] **abound**[12] that he's been replaced. I know not why or by whom. Not yet, but I *will* find out.'

Rhys muttered a low, 'Heaven above! That's a turn I didn't **foresee**[13]. Sir Robert won't take well to that. What on earth has he done?'

'I'm not sure,' said Dylan. 'But I suspect it relates to the cipher Cad found in his rooms, and the weapon plans it **evidently**[14] hid upon its parchment—'.

---

1 **intervene** *(v)* make happen or do to prevent or alter someone or something. *(s)* interfere, interrupt. *(ant)* avoid.

2 **ambition** *(n)* great desire to achieve or do something. *(s)* objective, aim, hope, goal. *(ant)* apathy.

3 **resolve** *(v)* find a solution. *(s)* settle, rectify. *(ant)* cause.

4 **consider** *(v)* think about before making a decision. *(s)* contemplate, examine, ponder.

5 **leave** *(n)* the permission to be absent from work. *(s)* break, sabbatical. *(ant)* work.

6 **duty** *(n)* an action or task one must do as part of one's job. *(s)* chore, responsibility, obligation.

7 **dire** *(adj)* serious or urgent. *(s)* dreadful, appalling, frightful. *(ant)* favourable.

8 **gossip** *(n)* casual talk or rumour that has not been confirmed as true. *(s)* tattle, tales, hearsay. *(ant)* facts.

9 **quash** *(v)* put an end to or reject as invalid. *(s)* cancel, reverse, revoke. *(ant)* allow.

10 **cast** *(v)* direct one's expression at someone or something. *(s)* aim, level.

11 **rumour** *(n)* a circulating story of little or doubtful truth. *(s)* gossip, hearsay, tittle-tattle. *(ant)* fact.

12 **abound** *(v)* exist in large amounts or numbers. *(s)* flourish, thrive. *(ant)* fail, decline.

13 **foresee** *(v)* be aware of something beforehand. *(s)* anticipate, predict.

14 **evidently** *(adv)* clearly. *(s)* obviously, plainly, manifestly. *(ant)* doubtfully.

Both boys stopped speaking, **astonishment**[1] colouring their faces as they turned towards Cad's bed.

Awake, pushing herself up with her hands and **reclining**[2] into her pillow, Cad muttered a **garbled**[3] but just understandable, 'What exactly was written on that parchment?'

---

1 **astonishment** *(n)* extreme surprise. *(s)* amazement, shock, surprise. *(ant)* indifference.

2 **recline** *(v)* lean or lie back with one's back supported. *(s)* repose, rest. *(ant)* stand.

3 **garbled** *(adj)* unclear or distorted. *(s)* confused, muddled. *(ant)* clear, understandable.

CHAPTER SIX

Bad News

'What do you mean by "evidently hid upon its parchment"?' Cad asked again, **emphasising**[1] her words as much as she could.

Neither Dylan nor Rhys answered, but Cad registered the **anxious**[2] looks passing between them. Her heart clenched, their words still marching around her ears.

'What is it?' Their faces panicked her. 'Fishy, off,' snapped Cad, with a hard edge to her voice as she shooed her dog away.

Both boys' eyes widened: Cad never spurned Fishy.

'What are you hiding from me?'

Terrified[3], Cad pictured her life ending. *Is the poison's damage* ***irreparable***[4]*?* she wondered. *Will I never fully* ***regain***[5] *my* ***faculties***[6]*?*

Another pained look passed between Rhys and Dylan. Rhys swallowed hard. Dylan cleared his throat.

---

1 **emphasise** *(v)* stress a word when speaking. *(s)* highlight, accentuate. *(ant)* understate.

2 **anxious** *(adj)* worried. *(s)* concerned, fearful, uneasy. *(ant)* carefree, unconcerned.

3 **terrify** *(v)* cause to feel great fear. *(s)* horrify, petrify. *(ant)* calm, soothe.

4 **irreparable** *(adj)* impossible to make better or repair. *(s)* irreversible. *(ant)* repairable.

5 **regain** *(v)* recover something, get back. *(s)* repossess. *(ant)* lose.

6 **faculty** *(n)* one's mental and physical power. *(s)* sense, ability, capability.

'Cad, when you were **overcome**[1] by the poison, the castle's feast, albeit late, was interrupted by a **herald**[2] bringing news.' Dylan paused, a dark look clouding his face.

'Go on. Go on,' she urged.

'The herald stated he'd witnessed an army marching towards Catrin Castle. One that would soon be upon us. He said the army's crest was unknown, but that its soldiers appeared strong. He called them "Giant-like men". The messenger **quaked**[3] in his boots as he spoke. I was there when he **relayed**[4] the news.'

Cad's mind, still unable to work at its normal **pace**[5], struggled to **fathom**[6] Dylan's words. A horrid shiver of **foreboding**[7] crept through her body as he continued.

'At once, your father sent out a **party**[8] of fast riders, but... but ...'

'But what?' asked Cad, her voice **shrill**[9].

'They didn't return.' Dylan gulped, **stifling**[10] a sob.

Engulfed[11] in panic, Cad's chest **constricted**[12], and her **temples**[13] **pounded**[14] with blood – bad news was **imminent**[15].

'Catrin Castle is under **siege**[16].' It wasn't Dylan who spoke now, but Rhys, and he held Cad's

---

1 **overcome** *(v)* overwhelm or overpower. *(s)* grip, seize, affect. *(ant)* underwhelm.

2 **herald** *(n)* an official employee who acts as a messenger, especially in medieval times. *(s)* crier, courier.

3 **quake** *(v)* tremble or shake. *(s)* shudder, wobble, vibrate, rock.

4 **relay** *(v)* receive and pass on messages or information. *(s)* deliver, communicate, convey. *(ant)* withhold.

5 **pace** *(n)* speed. *(s)* rapidity, swiftness, quickness.

6 **fathom** *(v)* comprehend after much thought. *(s)* understand, grasp, perceive. *(ant)* misunderstand.

7 **foreboding** *(n)* a feeling that something bad is about to happen. *(s)* apprehension. *(ant)* contentment.

8 **party** *(n)* a particular group of people. *(s)* company, contingent.

9 **shrill** *(adj)* high-pitched in sound. *(s)* sharp, piercing. *(ant)* low, soft.

10 **stifle** *(v)* restrain a reaction or stop oneself acting on an emotion. *(s)* suppress, repress, curb. *(ant)* encourage.

11 **engulf** *(v)* sweep over or surround completely. *(s)* envelop, overtake, overwhelm.

12 **constrict** *(v)* make narrower. *(s)* tighten, contract. *(ant)* expand, swell.

13 **temple** *(n)* the flat part of the head situated between the forehead and the ear.

14 **pound** *(v)* beat with a strong rhythm. *(s)* pulse, pulsate, throb.

15 **imminent** *(adj)* about to happen. *(s)* pending, forthcoming, likely. *(ant)* remote.

16 **siege** *(n)* a military operation that surrounds or blocks a castle or other place by force, cutting off essential supplies.

hand in his. 'We are **fending off**[1] an unknown **foe**[2]. From **intelligence**[3], it's thought the enemy is currently **constructing**[4] the cipher's plan: a weapon, the likes never seen before.'

Cad stared into Rhys's eyes: they mirrored hers, deep pools of confusion, pain and panic.

'My father,' Cad cried. 'Please bring Llywelyn to me, now.'

'Cad, no. Stay in bed.' Rhys placed a hand on her shoulder, firmly **restraining**[1] her movements.

'I must rise,' Cad **persisted**[6]. 'I must pee and wash before my father arrives. I stink like a pig.'

Rhys eyed Dylan, who gave the slightest of nods.

'Cad, you *stay* in bed!'

Her eyes widened at Rhys's new-found **assertiveness**[7]. However, overcome by **fatigue**[8] and distress, loose-limbed, she flopped back, her head hitting her pillow in relief. She would just have to **reek**[9] and use the **commode**[10] as before.

'Your father cannot visit you today.'

Dylan's voice brought immediate trepidation to Cad. Her face **contorted**[11] into a question. 'Why?' she asked, as something deep and **grim**[12] gripped her inside. What weren't they telling her?

A **yawning**[13] silence followed. Dylan and Rhys **exchanged**[14] fretful **glances**[15].

Rhys finally spoke.

'Because your father insisted on seeing the army for himself, he led the party of riders that

---

1 **fend off** *(v)* defend oneself from something. *(s)* stop, repel, parry. *(ant)* encourage.

2 **foe** *(n)* an enemy, nemesis or opponent. *(s)* antagonist, rival, opposition. *(ant)* friend, ally, comrade.

3 **intelligence** *(n)* the collection of information for military or political value or gain. *(s)* surveillance.

4 **construct** *(v)* make or build. *(s)* assemble. *(ant)* deconstruct, demolish.

1 **restrain** *(v)* prevent from doing something. *(s)* stop, hinder, impede, hamper. *(ant)* help.

6 **persist** *(v)* continue stubbornly or repeat insistently. *(s)* carry on, push, persevere. *(ant)* stop, yield.

7 **assertiveness** *(n)* forceful and confident behaviour. *(s)* boldness, confidence. *(ant)* timidity.

8 **fatigue** *(n)* extreme tiredness. *(s)* exhaustion, weariness, weakness. *(ant)* refreshment.

9 **reek** *(v)* smell strongly and often unpleasantly. *(s)* stink, pong.

10 **commode** *(n)* a chamber pot (a pot used as a toilet) that is concealed in a piece of furniture.

11 **contort** *(v)* bend or twist out of normal shape. *(s)* distort, deform. *(ant)* straighten.

12 **grim** *(adj)* serious or bleak. *(s)* horrid, miserable. *(ant)* pleasant, amiable.

13 **yawning** *(adj)* long. *(s)* large, big, great. *(ant)* short, brief.

14 **exchange** *(v)* swap. *(s)* transfer.

15 **glance** *(n)* a hurried look. *(s)* glimpse, peep, peek. *(ant)* stare.

night. And … and, they have yet to return …' Rhys's voice had dropped to a whisper, his eyes staring at the floor until eventually they rose to meet Cad's.

So weak and fighting to find her voice, Cad asked, 'Has there been any news since?'

Dylan and Rhys shook their heads in **unison**[1].

'Then I take that as good news.'

She forced **positivity**[2] into her **tone**[3], when inside her heart **shrivelled**[4] with sorrow. Even so, she shuffled out of bed, and this time, the boys stepped back to let her.

'I must speak with Sir Robert. Can you please ask him to visit me here? I must wash and dress.' She **shuffled**[5] about her bedside with the **gait**[6] of an **octogenarian**[7].

'That might be tricky.'

'Tricky? Why?'

'Rumours abound that he's no longer in charge.'

Cad sat, her head buzzing. 'What rumours? Please, Dylan, stop beating bushes and get to the point. I'm struggling as it is without your **waffle**[8].'

Seeing the hurt crush Dylan's face, Cad immediately regretted her **brusqueness**[9]. 'Forgive me,' she **blurted**[10]. 'I'm not myself. Tell me everything, but make it as brief as possible. I must act fast, yet my mind is slow.'

Dylan pinched his lips to **quell**[11] their **quivering**[12]. Cad felt wretched. No doubt he'd hardly slept, and she'd just bitten him like a **vicious**[13] dog.

---

1 **in unison** *(adj)* at the same time. *(s)* together, simultaneously. *(ant)* independently.

2 **positivity** *(n)* the practice of being upbeat in attitude. *(s)* optimism, confidence. *(ant)* negativity.

3 **tone** *(n)* the sound of one's voice. *(s)* pitch, timbre, intonation.

4 **shrivelled** *(adj)* contracted. *(s)* shrunken, withered. *(ant)* expanded.

5 **shuffle** *(v)* walk with one's feet dragging or catching on the ground. *(s)* shamble, lumber, dodder.

6 **gait** *(n)* the way a person walks or strides. *(s)* step, posture, carriage, movement.

7 **octogenarian** *(n)* someone who is aged between eighty and eighty-nine years old.

8 **waffle** *(n)* trivial (unimportant) talk or writing. *(s)* drivel, nonsense, tripe, wittering.

9 **brusqueness** *(n)* the state or quality of being brusque (impolite or unfriendly). *(s)* bluntness, curtness. *(ant)* politeness.

10 **blurt** *(v)* say something suddenly and without consideration. *(s)* announce, exclaim, cry.

11 **quell** *(v)* suppress, subdue or stop. *(s)* quash, control. *(ant)* intensify.

12 **quiver** *(v)* tremble or shake. *(s)* quaver, tremor. *(ant)* steady, still.

13 **vicious** *(adj)* deliberately violent or dangerous. *(s)* ferocious, savage. *(ant)* docile, gentle.

'I'm sorr—' she began, but Rhys **interjected**[1].

'Cad, we're all **drained**[2]. None of us knows what's really happening. It's **chaotic**[3] beyond that door.'

Cad's focus **flitted**[4] to where Rhys pointed. **Guilt**[5] consumed her. How could she be so **selfish**[6] to Dylan? Her shoulders slumped as she studied her feet.

'Now more than ever, we must **tolerate**[7] each other, or the **consequences**[8] may be dire,' said Rhys, **astounding**[9] Cad with his **maturity**[10] and **eloquence**[11] of speech. She looked up and met his kind gaze. She had so **underestimated**[12] this once **modest**[13] boy, who had now found his **footing**[14].

'Sir Owain didn't accompany your father on the intelligence gathering mission,' Dylan added. 'He remains here, and rumour has it, *he* now controls Catrin Castle.'

Cad considered this **revelation**[15], both its good and bad **connotations**[16]. Sir Robert would **deplore**[17] his loss of **rank**[18]; Cad knew him to be **petulant**[19] when he lost at anything. But having Owain Glyn commanding Catrin Castle would be a huge **boon**[20] while Catrin suffered a siege.

---

1 **interject** *(v)* interrupt someone who is speaking. *(s)* intervene, comment, cut in, butt in.

2 **drain** *(v)* take away or use up the energy of. *(s)* deplete, exhaust. *(ant)* fill, recuperate.

3 **chaotic** *(adj)* in a state of confusion and disorder. *(s)* frenzied, tumultuous. *(ant)* orderly.

4 **flit** *(v)* move swiftly. *(s)* dart, flick. *(ant)* remain, still.

5 **guilt** *(n)* a bad feeling about one's own wrongdoing. *(s)* regret, remorse, shame. *(ant)* innocence.

6 **selfish** *(adj)* lacking thought for other people. *(s)* self-centred, thoughtless. *(ant)* selfless.

7 **tolerate** *(v)* put up with. *(s)* accept, support. *(ant)* disapprove.

8 **consequence** *(n)* a result or effect. *(s)* outcome. *(ant)* cause.

9 **astound** *(v)* greatly surprise or shock. *(s)* astonish, stun, amaze. *(ant)* underwhelm, bore.

10 **maturity** *(n)* the state of being mature (adult-like). *(s)* wisdom. *(ant)* immaturity.

11 **eloquence** *(n)* clear and fluent speech or writing. *(s)* expressiveness. *(ant)* inarticulacy.

12 **underestimate** *(v)* regard someone as less capable than they really are. *(s)* misjudge. *(ant)* overestimate.

13 **modest** *(adj)* showing or having a low estimate of one's achievements and abilities. *(s)* humble. *(ant)* boastful.

14 **footing** *(n)* a social position or status. *(s)* standing, place.

15 **revelation** *(n)* a previously unknown fact that has been disclosed (revealed) to others. *(s)* divulgence. *(ant)* concealment.

16 **connotation** *(n)* a quality or idea suggested by a word or thing. *(s)* implication, meaning.

17 **deplore** *(v)* express or feel strong dislike. *(s)* hate, despise. *(ant)* admire.

18 **rank** *(n)* a position in an organisation. *(s)* standing, grade, level, status.

19 **petulant** *(adj)* sulky and ill-tempered. *(s)* crabby, fractious, irritable, peevish. *(ant)* affable, pleasant.

20 **boon** *(n)* a thing that is helpful or beneficial. *(s)* benefit, bonus. *(ant)* disadvantage, curse.

Although **fraught**[1] with concern for her father, she was relieved Owain was here. And she knew Llywelyn had **intended**[2] that, for that is why he'd left him behind, in case his mission failed. That outcome shot through Cad like an arrow. She would not accept her father's death until she saw his lifeless body laid out before her.

'Rhys, Dylan, thank you for your loyalty. It means more to me than any riches.'

Both boys nodded with **coy**[3] half-smiles.

'But no matter how pain ails my ribs, or poison **befuddles**[4] my mind, I cannot sit **idly**[5] by while Catrin Castle is under siege. I must rise to this challenge to help my father.'

'Cad!' Dylan cried, about to **admonish**[6] her.

But Cad **batted**[7] his words away like flies.

'Dylan, don't worry. I don't plan on charging into battle; that would be a death wish.' Cad's fingers crossed behind her back. 'But I must do *something*. Or, I should say, *we* must do something.'

Cad eyed both boys, not wanting to make them guilty but to urge them to be part of a team, her team.

The boys checked each other briefly, then nodded. Their **enthusiasm**[8] was **somewhat**[9] weak, but Cad chalked that up to fatigue.

'Good!' **chirped**[10] Cad, resetting her shoulders. 'Let's get down to business then. So who's going to bed first?'

Both boys frowned in puzzlement.

'Well, at the moment, I'm still stupid.' She **jabbed**[11] her temple with her forefinger. 'I can't make apt decisions; and without sleep, you two are equally daft as I. So who's going to sleep first?'

---

1 **fraught** *(adj)* stressed and extremely anxious. *(s)* apprehensive, troubled, upset. *(ant)* calm.

2 **intend** *(v)* to have in mind to do with something or someone. *(s)* plan, expect, propose.

3 **coy** *(adj)* modest or shy. *(s)* bashful, evasive, reserved. *(ant)* brazen.

4 **befuddle** *(v)* make someone unable to think clearly. *(s)* confuse, perplex, baffle. *(ant)* clear.

5 **idly** *(adv)* in a lazy or aimless fashion. *(s)* inertly, inactively. *(ant)* vigorously.

6 **admonish** *(v)* reprimand (tell off) firmly. *(s)* warn, chide, caution. *(ant)* praise.

7 **bat** *(v)* hit something or someone with one's hand. *(s)* swipe, knock.

8 **enthusiasm** *(n)* eager enjoyment, approval or interest. *(s)* fervour, zeal. *(ant)* apathy.

9 **somewhat** *(adv)* a little but not a lot. *(s)* a bit, rather, quite. *(ant)* extremely.

10 **chirp** *(v)* speak in a sing-song way. *(s)* sing, trill. *(ant)* groan.

11 **jab** *(v)* poke roughly or quickly. *(s)* prod, stab, push.

'Looks like the boss is better.'

Rhys nodded at his friend with a chuckle. 'Indeed, she is. Dylan, you rest. You've done far more than I. I'll watch Cad and update her on the castle's position the best I can.'

'Watch me?' cried Cad.

But Rhys ignored her and nodded towards Dylan's bed.

A look of relief softened Dylan's face, and without further **ado**[1], the boy pulled back his bedding, climbed in, placed his cap over his face, and within minutes was snoring like a **pug-nosed**[2] dog.

1 **ado** *(n)* fuss. *(s)* trouble, bother, upset, delay. *(ant)* order, haste.

2 **pug-nosed** *(adj)* (of the nose) having a concave bridge and flattened nostrils.

CHAPTER SEVEN

Eavesdropping Ellis

'What do you mean you're going to watch me!' snapped Cad.

It wasn't a question, more an **admonishment**[1], but Rhys didn't **flinch**[2] at Cad's tone.

'I'm not **festering**[3] here like a **craven**[4] fool while my father is **stranded**[5] beyond the castle walls. I must help him. Who's in charge? Let's hope it's Owain Glyn.' She hadn't yet stopped for breath.

Again, Rhys **barely**[6] moved; his eyes remained locked onto Cad's as she spoke. 'I will wash and dress. While I do so, find out who commands Catrin Castle. If it is Owain Glyn, arrange for him to visit me here.'

Cad **grimaced**[7], her hand gripping the **bindings**[8] beneath her tunic. Wincing, she checked the strapping that secured her ribs in place.

'Oh, and please, ask Physician Jordan to call by as soon as possible.' If she were to help her

---

1 **admonishment** *(n)* a firm telling off or warning. *(s)* scolding, reprimand. *(ant)* encouragement.

2 **flinch** *(v)* shy away from instinctively. *(s)* move, twitch, recoil, wince. *(ant)* stand firm.

3 **fester** *(v)* rot. *(s)* decay, moulder. *(ant)* flourish, thrive.

4 **craven** *(adj)* completely lacking in courage. *(s)* cowardly, gutless, spineless. *(ant)* brave, bold.

5 **stranded** *(adj)* left without the means (capability) to leave. *(s)* trapped, stuck, marooned. *(ant)* rescued.

6 **barely** *(adv)* almost not. *(s)* hardly.

7 **grimace** *(v)* make an ugly, twisted expression on one's face. *(s)* scowl, frown. *(ant)* smile.

8 **binding** *(n)* a bandage or bandages. *(s)* wrapping, swaddling.

father, she must seek a weaker version of the potion he'd **concocted**[1] for her to at least dull the pain plaguing her side.

Rhys regarded her in silence for what felt like **aeons**[2], then said, 'Cad, you dearly you wish to help Llywelyn, but stop to reflect a while. An unknown substance has poisoned you, you broke your ribs and you're weak due to lack of food and water. Do you not think it wiser to remain in bed a while longer? Until your ribs have healed at least a little?'

Without doubt, Cad knew he was right, but she simply could not lie in bed while the castle was under attack. She fiddled with her tunic, **weighing up**[3] her choices.

'Can you at least **compromise**[4]?' Rhys looked hopeful.

Cad thought on his words, unsure how to take her friend's new-found strength. Should she welcome it, fear it, fight it? Even Dylan had looked to Rhys for **guidance**[5]. Maybe that was due to his **sheer**[6] exhaustion, for he was still snoring like a **hog**[7] on his bed. Little roused that boy once he slept.

'I can't compromise. I must help my father to fight this foe.'

'But Cad, your current health is a **hindrance**[8], not a *help*.'

She was about to bite back, when an impatient rapping on the door cut the conversation short. Cad **started**[9], gripped by the pain clutching her ribs.

'Get back into bed,' hissed Rhys. 'You're not looking very boy-like just now.'

Cad **scrambled**[10] back to bed as a rush of heat spread through her chest then **flushed**[11] her

---

1 **concoct** *(v)* devise or create. *(s)* invent, make.

2 **aeons** *(n)* an indefinite and long time. *(s)* eternity, forever. *(ant)* moment, jiffy, flash.

3 **weigh up** *(v)* assess something or someone carefully. *(s)* evaluate, gauge. *(ant)* calculate.

4 **compromise** *(v)* accept something or a situation that is of a lower standard than desired. *(s)* strike a balance.

5 **guidance** *(n)* advice given to help someone. *(s)* instruction, direction.

6 **sheer** *(adj)* absolute. *(s)* pure, utter, total, downright, outright.

7 **hog** *(n)* another word for a pig. *(s)* swine, grunter, porker.

8 **hindrance** *(n)* a thing that causes a problem or a delay. *(s)* obstacle, barrier, handicap. *(ant)* help.

9 **start** *(v)* jump or jerk from surprise. *(s)* flinch, wince.

10 **scramble** *(v)* make one's way quickly. *(s)* clamber, scrabble, crawl.

11 **flush** *(v)* become red. *(s)* blush. *(ant)* pale.

face. Her heart skipped **several**[1] beats. Rhys was right. With **dishevelled**[2] hair, which **sorely**[3] needed cutting, and in her long nightclothes, she very much **resembled**[4] a girl.

Once in bed, covers up at her neck, Rhys opened the door. Ellis Williams, fellow page and Flash's groom, stood there, his face a mix of **anxiety**[1] and **anticipation**[6].

'Rumours are **rife**[7] that Cad has woken from his stupor. Is this true?' he blurted.

But before Rhys could speak, Ellis let out a yelp, flew through the door and crushed Cad with hugs.

'Master Cad, you're awake. You're awake. I was terrified you wouldn't live. I feared you dead. Flash has **pined**[8] in the stables, missing your nightly visits.'

'Ellis, please don't clutch me so; I have broken ribs.' But Cad was beaming, so pleased to see Ellis. Ellis, the friend in whom she trusted Flash's care, her **beloved**[9] pony.

'Sorry, Cad. I forgot your ribs.' Ellis blushed with a coy grin.

Suddenly, a huge snorting snore rose from Dylan's bed, accompanied by the loudest fart Cad had ever heard. All three friends exchanged astounded glances, then burst into a chorus of such **cacophonous**[10] laughter that tears filled Cad's eyes.

'It's so **heartening**[11] to see and hear you laugh again,' said Rhys with a gentle smile as their **chortles**[12] subsided.

'In my delight to see you, I forgot to tell you why I'm here,' said Ellis. 'I was **mucking out**[13] the stables when Owain Glyn passed with a **dour**[14]-looking Sir Robert. I heard Owain Glyn say he

---

1 **several** *(adj)* more than two but not a vast quantity of. *(s)* some, various. *(ant)* many.

2 **dishevelled** *(adj)* (hair or clothes) made untidy. *(s)* mussed, messy, tousled. *(ant)* tidy, groomed.

3 **sorely** *(adv)* to a large degree. *(s)* badly, really.

4 **resemble** *(v)* look or seem like something else. *(s)* favour. *(ant)* differ from.

1 **anxiety** *(n)* a worried and nervous feeling. *(s)* apprehension, unease, disquiet. *(ant)* calmness, reassurance.

6 **anticipation** *(n)* the action of expecting something to happen. *(s)* expectation, hope.

7 **rife** *(adj)* widespread. *(s)* ubiquitous, everywhere, extensive. *(ant)* scarce.

8 **pine** *(v)* miss someone or something greatly. *(s)* long, yearn, moon.

9 **beloved** *(adj)* much loved. *(s)* adored, favourite, treasured.

10 **cacophonous** *(adj)* noisy. *(s)* loud, raucous. *(ant)* harmonious.

11 **heartening** *(adj)* increasing happiness. *(s)* encouraging, comforting. *(ant)* saddening.

12 **chortle** *(n)* a noisy, happy laugh. *(s)* chuckle, guffaw. *(ant)* howl.

13 **muck out** *(v)* to clean the place where an animal, such as a horse, lives.

14 **dour** *(adj)* unfriendly, gloomy or miserable. *(s)* sour, stern, severe. *(ant)* kindly, cheerful.

was about to pay you a visit. I'm not sure why the great and the good were discussing a fellow page, so I came straight away.'

Cad quickly collected her **wayward**[1] thoughts, remembering that Ellis wasn't privy to her gender, or her being the daughter of Prince Llywelyn. Of course Ellis wouldn't understand why Llywelyn's **deputy**[2] wanted to visit her, unless to **chide**[3] her for a wrongdoing.

'It will concern my fall into the well,' she said, unsure how much he knew of her findings. Then, quickly changing the subject, she added, 'Ellis, you're a dear friend. Thank you for warning me. Now I must rise and wash. You may want to leave. Dylan snores like a pig, but I smell like one.' She laughed, nodding towards the door. 'I'll visit Flash later.'

'But your ribs, Master Cad.'

'**Piffle**[4] to my ribs. I've potions and lotions to help with those. I must see and smell my horse if I'm to **recuperate**[5], not fester away in this room like an old **scab**[6]. And don't call me master,' she added, wondering why fellow pages seemed to do this.

'Then I shall be off to dole the horses' **rations**[7]. We're **preserving**[8] food for the ...' A dark look **scudded**[9] across Ellis's face.'

'Rhys and Dylan told me of the siege. Don't worry.'

Cad rose as Ellis headed towards the door. With **tentative**[10] moves, she swung round her legs, putting her feet to the floor.

'Flash misses her master.'

Cad smiled at him, a warmth lifting her; she adored Flash.

---

1 **wayward** *(adj)* difficult to control or predict. *(s)* wilful, straying. *(ant)* compliant.

2 **deputy** *(n)* someone's second-in-command. *(s)* number two. *(ant)* chief.

3 **chide** *(v)* tell off, rebuke or scold. *(s)* reprimand, reproach, reprove. *(ant)* praise, applaud.

4 **piffle** *(n)* nonsense. *(s)* cobblers, tripe. *(ant)* sense.

5 **recuperate** *(v)* recover from an illness. *(s)* convalesce, improve. *(ant)* deteriorate.

6 **scab** *(n)* the crust that forms over a wound as it heals.

7 **ration** *(n)* a fixed amount of something. *(s)* allowance, portion. *(ant)* abundance.

8 **preserve** *(v)* keep something in its original state. *(s)* protect, conserve. *(ant)* spoil, neglect.

9 **scud** *(v)* move fast and in a straight line as if driven by the wind. *(s)* speed, streak, race.

10 **tentative** *(adj)* done without confidence. *(s)* cautious, faltering, reluctant. *(ant)* sure, certain.

'But Flashy was so much livelier once Hugh Hughes returned Midnight to his **stall**[1],' added Ellis, turning to leave.

'What did you just say?' asked Cad, her eyes narrowing at the comment.

Ellis paused and turned back, a look of consternation on his face. 'Just that Flash was happier once Hugh Hughes returned Midnight to his stable on the feast night.'

Cad seemed to remember that Midnight's stall had been empty when she'd seen that hooded figure **slope**[2] by. Her thoughts tumbled about her head.

'Why was Hugh returning Midnight at all?'

'He was the one to **herald**[3] the bad news of the approaching army,' said Ellis in all **innocence**[4], clearly wondering if he'd upset Cad.

Cad turned over this **statement**[5], her mind whirring. Why would Hugh be riding Midnight *again*? Hugh, Goodwife Hughes's son, was an **architect**[6] and law **apprentice**[7]. He worked for Sir Robert. He wasn't training to be a knight. Why was he riding Midnight at such a late hour? Why was he the one to deliver bad news to Catrin Castle? That wasn't his job, yet Evans had allowed this once before, when her father first began his quest.

Nothing **tallied**[8]. It seemed peculiar. Midnight was Dewi's destrier, and the only person who could have **permitted**[9] Hugh to ride him that night other than her father was Sir Robert. She doubted Llywelyn had sanctioned that ride. It would not cross his mind that Hugh could handle the **stallion**[10], yet it seemed Evans knew differently. Why would Sir Robert be allowing Hugh out on Dewi's **steed**[11], and **moreover**[12] why on a feast night **hosted**[13] by Llywelyn?

---

1 **stall** *(n)* a holding compartment for an animal, enclosed on three sides. *(s)* cubicle.

2 **slope** *(v)* (informal) sneak off or move aimlessly. *(s)* leave, go.

3 **herald** *(v)* indicate that something is about to happen. *(s)* announce, signal.

4 **innocence** *(n)* lacking corruption (dishonesty). *(s)* honesty. *(ant)* guilt.

5 **statement** *(n)* a clear or definite expression of something. *(s)* declaration, divulgence, utterance.

6 **architect** *(n)* someone who designs buildings and often supervises their construction. *(s)* designer, planner.

7 **apprentice** *(n)* someone who is learning from a skilled person. *(s)* trainee, novice, pupil. *(ant)* veteran, master.

8 **tally** *(v)* add up, agree or correspond to. *(s)* match, work.

9 **permit** *(v)* allow to do something. *(s)* enable. *(ant)* prohibit.

10 **stallion** *(n)* a male horse that has not been gelded (neutered).

11 **steed** *(n)* a horse that one can ride.

12 **moreover** *(adv)* as a further matter. *(s)* also, furthermore, additionally.

13 **host** *(v)* entertain or receive people as guests. *(s)* throw, give. *(ant)* guest.

'Master Cad, please don't overdo things,' pleaded Ellis as he left. 'I'll take great care of Flash, and Owain Glyn will never **surrender**[1] to the **rabble**[2] **preying**[3] beyond our gates.'

Cad smiled and nodded, but she was no longer listening. As Rhys closed the door behind Ellis, she was up, **hobbling**[4] to the washstand and trusting its water wasn't poisoned.

---

1 **surrender** *(v)* stop resisting an enemy or opponent. *(s)* submit, capitulate, yield. *(ant)* fight, beat.

2 **rabble** *(n)* a disorderly group of people. *(s)* mob, throng, gang, body.

3 **prey** *(v)* hunt or cause constant distress. *(s)* target, hound, harass.

4 **hobble** *(v)* walk in a difficult manner. *(s)* limp, dodder, totter. *(ant)* stride.

CHAPTER EIGHT

Without Water

Cad, not prepared to wait for Owain Glyn's visit, now faced him in her father's rooms from where he'd assumed command of Catrin Castle. The **minuscule**[1] amount of potion she'd licked from the empty **vial**[2] by her bed had hitherto proved **futile**[3]. Her ribs both ached and stabbed **simultaneously**[4].

'Callwen, I cannot **condone**[5] your involvement in this siege. You are in no fit state. Look at you. You could barely walk across the **bailey**[6] because you are supposed to be **abed**[7].'

'Sir Owain, please,' she **countered**[8], but he **wafted**[9] away her words, cutting her short before she could repeat herself for the tenth time. The stubborn knight refused to **budge**[10].

'Your father would not sanction my **yielding**[11] to your demands. If something happens to you

---

1 **minuscule** *(adj)* incredibly small. *(s)* tiny, minute. *(ant)* gigantic, vast.
2 **vial** *(n)* a small cylindrical glass container. *(s)* ampoule, phial.
3 **futile** *(adj)* useless and pointless. *(s)* ineffective, fruitless. *(ant)* useful.
4 **simultaneously** *(adv)* at the same time. *(s)* concurrently, instantaneously. *(ant)* separately.
5 **condone** *(v)* approve something. *(s)* allow. *(ant)* deny, disapprove.
6 **bailey** *(n)* a castle's inner courtyard, enclosed by an outer wall.
7 **abed** *(adv)* in bed.
8 **counter** *(v)* oppose. *(s)* counteract, retaliate, parry. *(ant)* assist.
9 **waft** *(v)* move with a waving motion. *(s)* fan.
10 **budge** *(v)* move a small amount or change one's mind. *(s)* shift, yield.
11 **yield** *(v)* give way to pressure. *(s)* move, bend. *(ant)* resist.

now, after your poisoned stupor, and on my watch, I could not, and would not, live with myself.'

Cad knew Owain was right, but she could not sit idly by. She must help Llywelyn.

'Do you agree to my rules or must I place a guard outside your room? One we can **scarcely**[1] spare?' he said with a deep frown.

Cad placed her hands behind her back, crossed her fingers and muttered a weak, 'Yes', hoping that might smooth over the moment.

'Good. Then you start right now with a visit from Physician Jordan. Goodwife Hughes will continue your care.'

'What about Rhys and Dylan? Why can't they be my carers?'

'Because we need them in the castle. We are under siege. We need all spare **manpower**[2].'

What about girl power? Cad **pouted**[3].

As if reading her thoughts, Owain added, 'Your time will come. Do not force **fate**[4]. It might not treat you kindly if you do so.'

The great knight observed Cad with such **intensity**[5], she looked away.

'Right now, improve your scholarly skills from the safety of your room, and eat whilst we still have **sufficient**[6] foods to **sustain**[7] us. Supplies will run low, and even *you* will be **rationed**[8] soon.'

Cad nodded, but her mind was already elsewhere, clicking and whirring, **hatching**[9] plans. Food was of no concern yet. They had plenty because of the cancelled tournament, but water was **vital**[10].

'May I sit with you and drink some water before I am **incarcerated**[11]?' she asked with a hint of **sarcasm**[12].

---

1 **scarcely** *(adv)* only just, almost not. *(s)* hardly, barely. *(ant)* generously, greatly.

2 **manpower** *(n)* the number of people available for work. *(s)* labour, workforce.

3 **pout** *(n)* the thrusting out or protrusion of the lips. *(s)* pursing, puckering. *(ant)* smile, grin.

4 **fate** *(n)* the developments of future outcomes that are out of one's control. *(s)* destiny, chance, luck.

5 **intensity** *(n)* the quality of being forceful. *(s)* vehemence, seriousness. *(ant)* indifference.

6 **sufficient** *(adj)* enough. *(s)* ample, adequate. *(ant)* insufficient.

7 **sustain** *(v)* provide nourishment or support. *(s)* maintain, nourish. *(ant)* sap.

8 **ration** *(v)* allow only a fixed amount of something. *(s)* limit, restrict. *(ant)* lavish.

9 **hatch** *(v)* make up. *(s)* devise, concoct, invent.

10 **vital** *(adj)* completely necessary. *(s)* essential, key, crucial. *(ant)* unimportant, secondary.

11 **incarcerate** *(v)* confine. *(s)* imprison, detain, lock up. *(ant)* free, release.

12 **sarcasm** *(n)* the use of irony (the opposite) to mock or convey dislike. *(s)* derision, scorn, disdain. *(ant)* flattery.

'Of course,' he replied, ignoring her **barbed**[1] comment and pouring a cup from his **ewer**[2].

'How long remains until the water runs out?' Cad knew this would decide the siege's outcome. She now realised that whoever had poisoned the well had known that an army approached. Without clean water, and unable to access the **spring**[3] beyond the castle's walls, they were **doomed**[4].

Owain hesitated before meeting Cad's **intense**[5] gaze. 'Not long,' he replied. 'We are rationing and **siphoning**[6] what we can from the stables' supplies, but that will dry up if we cannot access the spring. Currently, with their weaponry and positioning, that is impossible.'

Cad's heart sank. Only now did it hit her that the animals' water supply would dry up first. Of course it would. Flash, Fishy; they would be the first to die.

At least May will live. May could fly to water.

May! I wonder if May could find my father? Cad's heart **soared**[7]. Why hadn't that occurred to her sooner? But she knew the answer: the poison was still befuddling her thoughts. She must beware of her impaired **judgement**[8] when making decisions in the coming days.

Without water, Cad knew **disorder**[9] would arise. Folks within the castle would lose their animals and then turn on each other. Chaos would ensue, leading to **carnage**[10]. Over her crumbling bones was she about to sit in her bed and let that happen.

'Sir Owain.'

'No need for "sir".' He shook his head.

'Did my father **retrieve**[11] the cipher I found in Sir Robert's rooms? The one Sir Robert took back from me?'

---

1 **barbed** *(adj)* (of a comment) deliberately rude or hurtful. *(s)* cutting, spiteful, unkind. *(ant)* kind.

2 **ewer** *(n)* a big jug with a wide opening, formerly used for carrying water. *(s)* urn, vessel.

3 **spring** *(n)* a natural source of water which wells up from beneath the ground.

4 **doomed** *(adj)* likely to have a bad outcome. *(s)* finished, condemned, done. *(ant)* blessed.

5 **intense** *(adj)* very serious or earnest. *(s)* passionate, fervent. *(ant)* apathetic.

6 **siphon** *(v)* extract over a period. *(s)* draw off, drain. *(ant)* flood.

7 **soar** *(v)* climb or fly rapidly above usual levels. *(s)* ascend, rise. *(ant)* plummet.

8 **judgement** *(n)* the ability to make decisions or come to conclusions. *(s)* sense, intelligence. *(ant)* recklessness.

9 **disorder** *(n)* the breakdown of peaceful behaviour. *(s)* unrest, turmoil, disturbance. *(ant)* order.

10 **carnage** *(n)* the killing or injuring of people. *(s)* destruction, havoc, annihilation.

11 **retrieve** *(v)* bring or get something back. *(s)* reclaim, recover. *(ant)* lose, forfeit.

'Yes, he did,' replied Owain **gravely**[1]. 'It was cause for great concern and more so now.'

'Why?' But Cad had **surmised**[2] the answer and dreaded it coming.

'It was indeed a plan for a weapon. Unlike anything seen before, and they are constructing it now, beyond the reach of our **archers**[3].'

'What is it?'

'We suspect it to be some form of **trebuchet**[4]. They hauled it here on **wagons**[5] pulled by **oxen**[6]. They **heaved**[7] loads of **lead**[8] and **timber**[9] to construct it, and all beyond our **bowshot**[10] range.'

A trebuchet? Cad's mind whirled in a **maelstrom**[11] of questions.

'What do you suppose has happened to my father?' she asked, her voice cracking, her eyes watery.

'Callwen, I will not lie to you.' Owain's eyes met hers. 'Two **scenarios**[12] **exist**[13]. In the first, he is dead. In the second, he knows returning to Catrin will be futile, and he is hatching a plan. I pray it is the **latter**[14] over the **former**[15].'

Owain's words dropped on her like an **anvil**[16]. She'd faced them herself, but hearing the word *dead* uttered from his lips made the situation so real she froze inside.

'Why do you fear this trebuchet so? What is so different about it?' she asked, **vaguely**[17]

---

1 **gravely** *(adv)* in a serious manner. *(s)* solemnly. *(ant)* trivially, joyously.

2 **surmise** *(v)* suppose to be true with little or no evidence. *(s)* guess, deduce, infer, conclude. *(ant)* know.

3 **archer** *(n)* someone who shoots with bows and arrows.

4 **trebuchet** *(n)* a medieval siege machine used for hurling large stones and other missiles.

5 **wagon** *(n)* a vehicle used for moving and transporting goods, people or animals. *(s)* cart, trolley.

6 **oxen** *(n)* the plural of ox: a neutered bull used for pulling heavy things such as a plough or wagon.

7 **heave** *(v)* lift with great effort. *(s)* haul, pull, raise. *(ant)* push.

8 **lead** *(n)* a dense and heavy metal, but one that is soft.

9 **timber** *(n)* wood used for building and carpentry.

10 **bowshot** *(n)* the distance to which a bow can shoot an arrow.

11 **maelstrom** *(n)* a whirlpool or tumult. *(s)* commotion, turmoil, vortex, swirl.

12 **scenario** *(n)* a possible sequence of events. *(s)* situation, state, development, consequence.

13 **exist** *(v)* be. *(s)* be present.

14 **latter** *(n)* the second mentioned of two people or things. *(s)* last. *(ant)* former.

15 **former** *(n)* the first mentioned of two people or things. *(s)* previous, preceding. *(ant)* latter.

16 **anvil** *(n)* a heavy iron block used for hammering metal into shape.

17 **vaguely** *(adv)* in a vague (unclear) manner. *(s)* roughly, loosely. *(ant)* clearly, definitely.

remembering Dylan saying he'd read of dragons breathing fire when he'd first **cracked**[1] the cipher.

'The difference is, it is ten times larger than any constructed before, and could destroy a castle's wall with one **projectile**[2]. They seem to have **components**[3] hidden close to Catrin. We have rotting apples in our **barrel**[4]: someone from this castle aids the enemy.'

'Do you suspect my uncle Dewi is involved?'

'I have little doubt that he masters the Gwalch Gem bracelet in his dark ways.'

'Dark ways?' replied Cad, her eyes like **saucers**[5].

'He is **motivated**[6] by greed and uses the bracelet to gain power. If he learns to **manipulate**[7] time with it, then we may be doomed regardless.'

So Owain knows of its ***potential***[8] *time-altering abilities too*, realised Cad, unsurprised: he was, after all, her father's right-hand man.

'What will we do if we can't **reinstate**[9] a water supply?'

'The well is useless. We are boiling **vats**[10] of its water to see if that counters the poison. We hope boiling may **eradicate**[11] its **potency**[12]. Failing that, I fear we must surrender when the water is gone. We cannot hold out without water; looking at the skies and this **unseasonably**[13] warm weather, rain is unlikely. Let us hope Dewi has not learned to manipulate the skies, for if he has, there is little hope left.'

Digesting[14] his words, Cad now fully understood the **monumental**[15] powers of the Gwalch

---

1 **crack** *(v)* solve. *(s)* fathom, decipher, break, decode. *(ant)* encrypt.

2 **projectile** *(n)* a missile (object) that is forcibly fired from something.

3 **component** *(n)* a part of something. *(s)* piece, bit, element, portion.

4 **barrel** *(n)* a cylindrical container usually wider around the middle. *(s)* cask, butt, keg, vat, tub, drum.

5 **saucer** *(n)* a shallow dish on which a cup is placed, but in the Middle Ages was used for serving sauces.

6 **motivate** *(v)* provide a person with a reason for doing something. *(s)* drive, influence. *(ant)* demotivate.

7 **manipulate** *(v)* alter, control or influence. *(s)* direct, affect, change.

8 **potential** *(adj)* having the capacity to develop into something in the future. *(s)* possible, probable, likely. *(ant)* unlikely.

9 **reinstate** *(v)* restore. *(s)* renew, revive, return.

10 **vat** *(n)* a large tub used for holding liquid. *(s)* tank, drum, vessel, container.

11 **eradicate** *(v)* destroy or completely put an end to. *(s)* eliminate, remove. *(ant)* preserve.

12 **potency** *(n)* the power of something to impress or influence. *(s)* strength, force. *(ant)* impotence.

13 **unseasonably** *(adv)* (of the weather) unusual for the time of year. *(ant)* seasonably.

14 **digest** *(v)* take in and understand. *(s)* absorb, grasp, comprehend. *(ant)* misunderstand.

15 **monumental** *(adj)* of great extent. *(s)* huge, enormous, colossal. *(ant)* insignificant.

Gem bracelet and what **catastrophes**[1] it could **wield**[2] in the wrong hands.

'What was my mother thinking?' Cad shocked herself as the words left her mouth. Yet once they had, the **floodgates**[3] opened. 'Why did she do this? Why did she **annihilate**[4] our family and hurt my father so? And killing Gelert …'

Hot tears **gushed**[5] down Cad's cheeks. For the first time since Siân had left with Dewi and the stolen bracelet, Cad sobbed for her loss. She allowed herself to **grieve**[6], as for a death. Although Siân was her adoptive mother, Cad **mourned**[7] for this woman with overwhelming depth and **despondency**[8], for she'd not known her own birth mother who'd left her in the well as a baby.

A cruel agony stabbed at her chest, poked at her ribs, squeezed her heart. Unable to **discern**[9] if the pain was physical or emotional, like a two-year-old toddler, she sobbed **inconsolable**[10] **wails**[11] of **grief**[12] as the great Knight Hawk, Owain Glyn, cradled her head to his chest.

---

1 **catastrophe** *(n)* a terrible event. *(s)* disaster, crisis, calamity, tragedy. *(ant)* godsend.

2 **wield** *(v)* (of power) have and be able to use. *(s)* exert, exercise.

3 **floodgate** *(n)* something serving to restrain an outburst. *(s)* barrier, restraint.

4 **annihilate** *(v)* destroy completely. *(s)* obliterate, wreck, ruin. *(ant)* create, build.

5 **gush** *(v)* flow quickly. *(s)* pour, spill, stream. *(ant)* trickle.

6 **grieve** *(v)* feel intense sorrow. *(s)* mourn, lament, miss. *(ant)* rejoice, delight.

7 **mourn** *(v)* feel sadness or regret for. *(s)* grieve, miss, pine. *(ant)* rejoice.

8 **despondency** *(n)* low spirits. *(s)* sadness, sorrow, despair. *(ant)* cheer.

9 **discern** *(v)* understand. *(s)* recognise, identify. *(ant)* confuse.

10 **inconsolable** *(adj)* unable to be comforted. *(s)* heartbroken, despairing, desolate. *(ant)* ecstatic.

11 **wail** *(n)* a prolonged, high-pitched sound. *(s)* bawl, cry. *(ant)* laugh, giggle.

12 **grief** *(n)* intense sorrow. *(s)* anguish, desolation, distress. *(ant)* comfort.

CHAPTER NINE

Where Is Hugh Hughes?

'Master Cad, your face is **swollen**[1] and looks sore,' Goodwife Hughes **clucked**[2]. 'What in heaven happened?' she added, not one to let a good crisis go to waste.

'I think I was crying in my sleep,' Cad fibbed. 'And I'm so bored stuck here in my room all day. I want to scream.'

Cad had returned from Owain Glyn to find both boys absent. She couldn't reveal the real reason for her puffy face: she had sobbed inconsolably for the loss of a second mother and perhaps her father. But Cad refused to accept Llywelyn was dead. Until she saw him without breath, he would remain alive, forever. He would not leave her and John, nor would she leave them either. Callwen Cadwaladr would become a Knight Hawk, enjoy her **longevity**[3] and protect the **realm**[4] beside Llywelyn. They would retrieve the Gwalch Gem bracelet, and together they would try to understand and **reconcile**[5] Siân Cadwaladr's betrayal until it **maimed**[6] them no more.

'Oh, you poor lamb,' fussed Mrs Hughes, 'and what with the **frightful**[7] goings-on beyond the

---

1 **swollen** *(adj)* enlarged. *(s)* bloated, expanded. *(ant)* contracted.

2 **cluck** *(v)* fuss and make a noise like a chicken.

3 **longevity** *(n)* long life. *(s)* endurance, lastingness. *(ant)* impermanence, death.

4 **realm** *(n)* an area of responsibility or rule. *(s)* kingdom, domain, monarchy.

5 **reconcile** *(v)* accept, often reluctantly. *(s)* resign oneself to, come to terms with. *(ant)* reject.

6 **maim** *(v)* injure so as to be irreparably damaged. *(s)* hurt, disable, incapacitate. *(ant)* heal.

7 **frightful** *(adj)* very unpleasant. *(s)* ghastly, dire, grim. *(s)* mild, delightful.

castle walls,' she continued, with a cheery spring in her step.

Cad's eyebrow arched. Goodwife Hughes's apparent **nonchalance**[1] towards the siege surprised her. Perhaps the goodwife had not understood the castle's imminent lack of water. As she **pottered**[2] about Cad's room, sweeping and humming as if nothing **untoward**[3] **unravelled**[4] beyond the door, Cad dredged her mind for memories of before the poisoning. Perplexed, she pondered the night she'd fallen into the well. Mrs Hughes had administered her pain-killing draught that evening. Also, in the back of Cad's **bleary**[5] head she remembered that Mrs Hughes had seemed peculiar that day, especially when Cad had asked after her son, Hugh.

'Goodwife Hughes, how is your son after his ordeal of happening upon a marching army?' Cad used her **breeziest**[6] voice.

The goodwife continued her tasks, but Cad noticed a slight pause before she answered. 'Oh! He was most shaken on the night. **Petrified**[7]. But he's fine now. After all, we have plenty of food.'

Goodwife Hughes **waddled**[8] around Cad's room like a plump duck.

'I'm sorry to hear that,' Cad **consoled**[9], hoping for more.

The **stout**[10] woman stopped her **chores**[11] and regarded Cad. Then with a snort, she dropped her voice a **conspiratorial**[12] octave. 'I just hope Prince Llywelyn is safe somewhere beyond these castle walls. And something deep in my bones tells me he is.'

Does this woman know something about my father? Is Goodwife Hughes hiding something?

Cad **concealed**[13] the rush of emotion which **threatened**[14] to surface, nodding gravely instead. If

---

1 **nonchalance** *(n)* the state of being nonchalant (unemotional). *(s)* calmness, indifference. *(ant)* concern, anxiety.

2 **potter** *(v)* spend time aimlessly or work without much effort. *(s)* fiddle, doodle. *(ant)* toil.

3 **untoward** *(adj)* unanticipated, inappropriate or inconvenient. *(s)* troublesome, problematic. *(ant)* pleasant.

4 **unravel** *(v)* become apparent or happen. *(s)* unfurl, unwind.

5 **bleary** *(adj)* unfocused and dull. *(s)* hazy, blurry, unclear. *(ant)* lively, clear.

6 **breeziest** *(adj)* (of the voice) relaxed and cheery. *(s)* carefree, casual. *(ant)* serious.

7 **petrified** *(adj)* made so frightened as to be unable to move. *(s)* terrified, horrified. *(ant)* reassured.

8 **waddle** *(v)* walk with a clumsy swaying motion. *(s)* toddle, wobble, sway. *(ant)* stride, glide.

9 **console** *(v)* give comfort and reduce grief. *(s)* soothe, relieve, cheer. *(ant)* upset, distress.

10 **stout** *(adj)* heavily built. *(s)* strong, solid, sturdy, robust. *(ant)* thin, slight.

11 **chore** *(n)* a task, often a household one. *(s)* job, work, errand, duty, drudgery.

12 **conspiratorial** *(adj)* suggestive of or relating to something secret. *(s)* calculating. *(ant)* innocent.

13 **conceal** *(v)* hide or disguise. *(s)* cloak, veil, camouflage. *(ant)* reveal, uncover.

14 **threaten** *(v)* seem likely to happen. *(s)* promise, bode.

Cad spoke of Llywelyn now, she couldn't **guarantee**[1] the teary floodgates would remain closed. Instead, she sipped her cup of weak **ale**[2] and stroked Fishy's head. Cad would give Fishy ale to drink if the water dried up. She would not let her pets die.

Trying to sound **casual**[3], Cad said, 'Hugh seems to have taken a shine to riding Prince Dewi's destrier.'

Mrs Hughes didn't respond. Did Cad **detect**[4] another twitch from her?

'Midnight,' added Cad, changing **tack**[5] when the woman continued her duties in silence. 'He's a real **handful**[6], that horse.'

After **fluffing**[7] and fiddling in a corner, Goodwife Hughes said, 'I know nothing of the horse Hugh took that night; someone sent him out and he saw the army.'

Did Cad dare **probe**[8] further without raising the woman's suspicions or **irritating**[9] her more? Cad **fancied**[10] that the goodwife was vexed but trying to mask it, as the faint pink flush now hugging the woman's throat suggested.

Why is she ***irked***[11] *by my mentioning Midnight? Yet she bats not an eyelid at the siege beyond our walls.*

Something seemed off, and Cad was **determined**[12] to discover what. Flopping her head onto her pillow, Cad **feigned**[13] a sleepy face and turned onto her side. Without **preamble**[14], Fishy curled up beside her.

'I may sleep a while. The potion is working its magic,' she fibbed. 'Perhaps you should eat while

---

1 **guarantee** *(v)* promise with certainty. *(s)* vow. *(ant)* undermine.

2 **ale** *(n)* a type of beer.

3 **casual** *(adj)* casual (relaxed and informal) in manner or appearance. *(s)* nonchalant. *(ant)* formal.

4 **detect** *(v)* discern the presence of something. *(s)* notice, sense, perceive. *(ant)* miss, overlook.

5 **tack** *(n)* a direction or course of action.

6 **handful** *(n)* a person or animal that is difficult to handle or deal with. *(s)* bother, problem. *(ant)* blessing.

7 **fluff** *(v)* (informal) fiddle about. *(s)* mess, potter. *(ant)* toil.

8 **probe** *(v)* to enquire further. *(s)* explore, ask, dig.

9 **irritate** *(v)* make annoyed or slightly angry. *(s)* aggravate, vex. *(ant)* appease.

10 **fancy** *(v)* believe something to be the case. *(s)* suspect, imagine. *(ant)* know.

11 **irk** *(v)* irritate. *(s)* annoy, rattle, vex, aggravate. *(ant)* mollify, please.

12 **determined** *(adj)* having or displaying resolve. *(s)* resolute, firm, unwavering. *(ant)* irresolute.

13 **feign** *(v)* simulate or pretend. *(s)* affect, fake, bluff.

14 **preamble** *(n)* an introduction. *(s)* preliminary, preparation.

I sleep? Fishy will stay with me. She'll raise the alarm if something arises,' Cad added sweetly, knowing the minuscule amount of medicine she'd **quaffed**[1] would barely dull her painful ribs. But she cared not. She understood how quickly one could become **accustomed**[2] to pain and **discomfort**[3] when all choice was **wrenched**[4] from you. Her **tolerance**[5] for pain had risen **tenfold**[6] in a few days.

'If you are sure, Master Cad.' But Goodwife Hughes answered too quickly for Cad's comfort. From the woman's **demeanour**[7], Cad **gleaned**[8] that she aimed to avoid more probing questions.

Cad fingered the ring hidden in the hem of her tunic. Once she had written a letter to her father and **dispatched**[9] May to find him, Cad would take an invisible look at Catrin Castle, again starting in Sir Robert's private **quarters**[10].

As she hatched her plans, Cad remembered Evans had **vehemently**[11] **denied**[12] **creating**[13] the cipher she'd found **hosting**[14] the weapon's details. Maybe that was so, but she wouldn't take chances. **Furthermore**[15], with his current **demotion**[16] from commander of Catrin Castle, Sir Robert's **motivations**[17] to spy, and possibly betray her father, had just become twice as **compelling**[18].

---

1 **quaff** *(v)* drink with enthusiasm. *(s)* down, swig. *(ant)* sip.
2 **accustomed** *(adj)* used to something. *(s)* adapted, acclimatised. *(ant)* unaccustomed.
3 **discomfort** *(n)* unease or pain. *(s)* irritation, disquiet, upset, displeasure. *(ant)* comfort.
4 **wrench** *(v)* pull suddenly. *(s)* jolt, yank, wrest, heave.
5 **tolerance** *(n)* the ability to endure something undesirable. *(s)* endurance, forbearance. *(ant)* intolerance.
6 **tenfold** *(adj)* ten times greater than.
7 **demeanour** *(n)* outward bearing or behaviour. *(s)* appearance, attitude, disposition, air, conduct.
8 **glean** *(v)* get information from a source. *(s)* obtain, draw, gather, garner.
9 **dispatch** *(v)* send to a place for a purpose. *(s)* consign.
10 **quarters** *(n)* accommodation. *(s)* chambers, rooms, apartment.
11 **vehemently** *(adv)* in a vehement (forceful) manner. *(s)* strongly, emphatically. *(ant)* weakly.
12 **deny** *(v)* refuse to admit the truth or existence of. *(s)* contest, oppose. *(ant)* accept, confirm.
13 **create** *(v)* make or bring something into existence. *(s)* produce, design. *(ant)* destroy.
14 **host** *(v)* hold or store. *(s)* contain, house.
15 **Furthermore** *(adv)* in addition. *(s)* moreover, also, further.
16 **demotion** *(n)* a reduction in status or rank. *(s)* relegation, downgrade. *(ant)* promotion.
17 **motivation** *(n)* an incentive for acting or behaving in a certain way. *(s)* motive, reason. *(ant)* deterrent.
18 **compelling** *(adj)* causing great conviction. *(s)* powerful, strong. *(ant)* weak.

CHAPTER TEN

Tap, Tap, Tap

Cad, having not told the boys of her **intentions**[1], and **engaging**[2] her ring the moment Mrs Hughes had left, was surprised by the castle's **normality**[3] given an unknown army held them under siege.

Maybe it was due to the **abundance**[4] of food **coupled**[5] with an **obliviousness**[6] to the water situation. Most **inhabitants**[7] believed the vats in the bailey were boiling to **thwart**[8] an imminent main gate's **breach**[9]. Kept in the dark, even the folks stirring the vats believed that the steaming liquid might be poured through Catrin's murder holes inside the **drawbridge**[10] and **portcullis**[11]. The high **vantage**[12] points from where soldiers tipped hot sand, **quicklime**[13] and, on the rare occasion, bubbling oil onto the heads of invading soldiers. But that was not why folks stirred

---

1 **intention** *(n)* purpose or plan. *(s)* aim, objective, goal, desire.

2 **engage** *(v)* put into use. *(s)* employ, appoint, involve. *(ant)* disengage.

3 **normality** *(n)* the condition of being normal or usual. *(s)* ordinariness, routine. *(ant)* abnormality.

4 **abundance** *(n)* a large quantity of something. *(s)* wealth, bounty. *(ant)* lack, deficiency.

5 **couple** *(v)* combine or link together with something else. *(s)* pair, team. *(ant)* separate.

6 **obliviousness** *(n)* the state of being unaware. *(s)* ignorance, unawareness. *(ant)* awareness.

7 **inhabitant** *(n)* a person or animal that lives in a particular place. *(s)* dweller, resident, occupant.

8 **thwart** *(v)* successfully oppose. *(s)* foil, counter, stop, impede, defeat, overpower. *(ant)* aid, facilitate.

9 **breach** *(n)* a break or gap in something, often made by an attacking enemy. *(s)* hole, opening. *(ant)* repair.

10 **drawbridge** *(n)* a bridge that can be raised to prevent access, especially one over the moat of a castle.

11 **portcullis** *(n)* a heavy and strong grating that can be lowered to block a gateway.

12 **vantage** *(n)* a position or place offering a good view of something. *(s)* viewpoint.

13 **quicklime** *(n)* a chemical compound that burns and irritates the skin on contact.

the boiling liquid. Unknown to them, their central well was **polluted**[1], and a fresh water supply must be found.

Cad pondered the term 'murder hole', which turned her stomach. She must toughen to become a Knight Hawk. She wondered if Dewi were out there, beyond the castle's **boundaries**[2], camping with his fellow soldiers, but she doubted that. If Dewi had stolen from his brother to gain power, he was a craven man, and not one who would risk the **front line**[3]. No, she guessed he was elsewhere, **plotting**[4] and planning in **luxurious**[5] comfort.

Now in the high keep, and invisible, thanks to her ring, Cad had **conducted**[6] a thorough search of Sir Robert's rooms. To her **chagrin**[7] and disappointment, she'd found nothing of interest. Caught between the sharp horns of a decision, Cad rested a while, sitting in a window seat, **chewing over**[8] her next move. On her way to Evans's rooms, she'd been sorely tempted to call in on Flash, but, being invisible and **thus**[9] spooky to the horses, she'd decided against it. She would have to wait to see her pony.

Thinking of the stables brought to mind the cloaked figure she'd seen the night of the well ordeal. Memories flashed back, individual scenes filling blanks in her head, when a thought burst **forth**[10]. Rhys had said he'd found the monk's **habit**[11] he'd worn in the underground room where they'd hidden Fishy as a pup. Searching Sir Robert's rooms just now had proved completely **fruitless**[12]; it was as if he'd **vacated**[13] them.

'I wonder,' she whispered, back on the move and causing the guard she now passed to frown

---

1 **pollute** *(v)* contaminate with hazardous substances. *(s)* poison, taint, foul. *(ant)* purify, clean.

2 **boundary** *(n)* a line that marks the limit or border of an area. *(s)* confines, perimeter, frontier, edge.

3 **front line** *(n)* the closest proximity to the enemy.

4 **plot** *(v)* devise a harmful or secret plan (often as a group). *(s)* conspire, connive, contrive, scheme.

5 **luxurious** *(adj)* extremely comfortable and often expensive. *(s)* opulent, extravagant. *(ant)* meagre.

6 **conduct** *(v)* carry out. *(s)* do.

7 **chagrin** *(n)* annoyance or distress. *(s)* disappointment, exasperation, irritation. *(ant)* delight, joy.

8 **chew over** *(v)* (informal) think about. *(s)* ponder, mull over. *(ant)* decide.

9 **thus** *(adv)* as a result of this. *(s)* so, consequently, therefore, hence, ergo.

10 **forth** *(adv)* forward in direction (or time). *(s)* onward, ahead. *(ant)* back.

11 **habit** *(n)* a long, loose overgarment (item of clothing) worn by someone religious such as a monk or nun.

12 **fruitless** *(adj)* not achieving the desired results. *(s)* useless, pointless, futile. *(ant)* fruitful.

13 **vacate** *(v)* leave empty. *(s)* abandon, evacuate, desert. *(ant)* occupy, inhabit.

in confusion. The **confounded**[1] man twirled on his heel, **glaring**[2] in all directions, but eventually **cursed**[3] and resumed his **post**[4]. Cad noticed that hardly any men guarded the castle's inner areas. The **majority**[5] were positioned atop the castle walls, **crouched**[6] behind **crenels**[7], armed with bows to **fend off**[8] ladder and **siege-tower**[9] attacks. Thus, **roaming**[10] the castle invisibly would prove easier than before. Yet she'd noticed the ring's **declining**[11] **efficacy**[12] with every passing moment that Dewi **possessed**[13] the Gwalch Gem bracelet. With good reason, Cad feared that the ring and hairpin's powers would **wane**[14] until they **ceased**[15] completely.

Despite the fact that she could **potentially**[16] reappear, Cad decided her hunch was worth a try. Instead of heading back, she turned towards the underground **dungeons**[17], her hairpin in hand as she sidestepped the rats **scurrying**[18] underfoot. The deeper she descended, the more the memories of the **oubliette**[19] **ascended**[20], flooding her mind with a vivid terror that threatened to send her back up to the keep. But today, she need not enter the oubliette. She need not go that far.

Moving swiftly, Cad **navigated**[21] the last few **dingy**[22] twists and turns until she reached the

---

1 **confounded** *(adj)* surprised or confused. *(s)* puzzled, baffled, perplexed. *(ant)* enlightened.

2 **glare** *(v)* stare angrily or fiercely. *(s)* scowl, glower, frown. *(ant)* grin, smile.

3 **curse** *(v)* speak bad words or blaspheme (speak disrespectfully about God). *(s)* swear.

4 **post** *(n)* a position from where a person can guard or lookout for someone or something. *(s)* station.

5 **majority** *(adj)* the greater number of. *(s)* most. *(ant)* minority.

6 **crouch** *(v)* to lower the body by bending one's knees. *(s)* squat, shrink, huddle. *(ant)* stand.

7 **crenel** *(n)* the indentation at the top of a castle wall through which arrows or missiles are shot.

8 **fend off** *(v)* defend oneself from something. *(s)* stop, repel, parry. *(ant)* encourage, invite.

9 **siege-tower** *(n)* a siege engine constructed to protect ladders and fighters while approaching the walls of a fortification.

10 **roam** *(v)* move about. *(s)* prowl, wander.

11 **decline** *(v)* become less. *(s)* reduce, decrease, wane. *(ant)* increase.

12 **efficacy** *(n)* the ability to give an intended or desired result. *(s)* usefulness, effectiveness. *(ant)* inefficacy.

13 **possess** *(v)* have or own a characteristic or thing. *(s)* hold. *(ant)* lack.

14 **wane** *(v)* become weaker. *(s)* decrease, lessen, decline, dwindle, diminish. *(ant)* grow, increase.

15 **cease** *(v)* stop, end or finish. *(s)* halt, quit, discontinue. *(ant)* start, continue.

16 **potentially** *(adv)* with the ability to happen or develop in the future. *(s)* possibly, likely. *(ant)* unlikely.

17 **dungeon** *(n)* a cell or room where prisoners are held. *(s)* prison, jail, oubliette, donjon.

18 **scurry** *(v)* move quickly with short, hurried steps. *(s)* scamper, scuttle. *(ant)* saunter, amble.

19 **oubliette** *(n)* an underground dungeon, often in a medieval castle, with access only through a trapdoor in the ceiling.

20 **ascend** *(v)* rise up. *(s)* arise. *(ant)* descend.

21 **navigate** *(v)* find the way, guide or steer. *(s)* negotiate.

22 **dingy** *(adj)* drab and gloomy. *(s)* dim, dark. *(ant)* bright, clean.

corridor, off which the storage room **housing**[1] old **armaments**[2], **armour**[3] and battle **miscellany**[4] stood. Thankfully, a flickering lamp hung inside the passage, **illuminating**[5] her way. Many torches remained unlit in the castle; folks were busy elsewhere with the siege.

With care, Cad lifted the lamp from its **housing**[6] and made to pick the lock with her hairpin when she saw the door was already cracked open. A pain suddenly **seized**[7] her chest, yet it wasn't her ribs playing up, and her heart pounded so hard it beat in her ears. Why was the door open? She **squatted**[8], her hand **trembling**[9] as she checked the narrow gap for hairs, wax, **booby traps**[10], anything *she* might well attach to a door to monitor activity.

However, she saw nothing other than a fat-legged spider crawling up the **jamb**[11]. She **shuddered**[12]. Normally beetles, bugs and insects didn't bother her, but since her poisoned stupor, and her dreams of cockroach **infestations**[13], her skin bristled at the thought, let alone the sight of them. Both phobias must be **conquered**[14] if she were to become a Knight Hawk. How could a knight be afraid of bugs?

'Get a grip of things, Cad,' she whispered, mortified, as pimples rose on her arms like those of a freshly plucked goose.

With a shiver, she grimaced as she flicked the creature off the doorjamb, taking care not to kill it, when a sound behind her caused her blood to freeze.

Stock-still[15] and holding her breath, she listened. *Tap … tap … tap.*

---

1 **house** *(v)* provide space for or accommodate (keep in a certain place). *(s)* hold, contain. *(ant)* expose.

2 **armament** *(n)* military equipment and weapons. *(s)* arms, munitions.

3 **armour** *(n)* the metal plates worn to protect the body in battle. *(s)* covering, shield.

4 **miscellany** *(n)* a group or mixture of different items. *(s)* assortment, variety. *(ant)* uniformity.

5 **illuminate** *(v)* light up. *(s)* brighten, lighten. *(ant)* darken, dim.

6 **housing** *(n)* a casing that protects or holds something else. *(s)* covering, container.

7 **seize** *(v)* (of a feeling) affect suddenly and severely. *(s)* grip, grasp. *(ant)* relinquish.

8 **squat** *(v)* crouch down with bent knees. *(s)* sit. *(ant)* stand, straighten.

9 **tremble** *(v)* shake involuntarily (automatically) from fear or excitement. *(s)* quake, quiver. *(ant)* still.

10 **booby trap** *(n)* a trap or device appearing to be innocent when it is not. *(s)* ambush, trip wire, snare.

11 **jamb** *(n)* a post at the side or surface of a doorway. *(s)* frame, pillar.

12 **shudder** *(v)* tremble unwittingly. *(s)* shiver, shake, quiver, convulse.

13 **infestation** *(n)* the existence of an unusually large number of insects in a place, typically causing problems.

14 **conquer** *(v)* successfully overcome. *(s)* master, defeat, beat, control. *(ant)* surrender.

15 **stock-still** *(adj)* without motion. *(s)* immobile, unmoving. *(ant)* mobile, moving.

What in heaven?

Unable to **verify**[1] the sound's **source**[2], she **angled**[3] her head towards it. *Click … click … click.*

Crouched, her leg muscles on fire, she screwed up her eyes, ignored her pounding heart and waited. Nothing. It had stopped. She slowly stood, about to enter, when she heard it again, a slight scratching on the stone floor. Something was heading her way. She must get into that room or face the consequences.

Whatever it was, it was nearing. *Tap … tap … tap.* Its peculiar clickety, click, click creeping closer, echoing off the passageway's **dank**[4] walls, and it was loudening. Cad moved to push open the door, to dive through it, when a flash of white caught her eye. She froze again, ears pricked, breath held.

Silence. Nothing but silence. With her face **furrowed**[5], she **exhaled**[6] to hear another had replaced the tapping sound. Liquid fear flushed through her veins, her heart racing along with it. Something was there behind her, watching her. It was still. Very still and waiting for her to move. She heard its breathing. Fast, rapid, almost panting. Without moving her head, and **poised**[7] to either pounce on her **pursuer**[8] or dive **headlong**[9] through the door, she **swivelled**[10] her eyes as far towards the white flash as she could.

Had what she seen not shocked her so much, she might have burst out laughing at the situation's **absurdity**[11]. Instead she lowered her hairpin, and releasing a huge breath, her shoulders softening, she said, 'Well, hello little fella. I haven't seen you in a while.'

---

1 **verify** *(v)* make sure something is true. *(s)* prove, confirm. *(ant)* refute.

2 **source** *(n)* from where something originates. *(s)* creator, root, cause.

3 **angle** *(v)* incline or tilt. *(s)* move, turn.

4 **dank** *(adj)* cold and damp. *(s)* musty, unaired, fusty. *(ant)* warm, dry.

5 **furrowed** *(adj)* (of the face or forehead) marked with wrinkles or lines. *(s)* creased. *(ant)* smooth.

6 **exhale** *(v)* breathe out. *(s)* expire, respire. *(ant)* inhale, breathe in.

7 **poised** *(adj)* prepared. *(s)* primed, placed, positioned, ready, set. *(ant)* unprepared.

8 **pursuer** *(n)* something or someone that pursues (chases) another. *(s)* follower, stalker, hunter. *(ant)* prey.

9 **headlong** *(adv)* head first. *(s)* head foremost. *(ant)* feet first.

10 **swivel** *(v)* turn around a point. *(s)* rotate, pivot, spin.

11 **absurdity** *(n)* the quality or state of being ridiculous or unreasonable. *(s)* illogicality, irrationality. *(ant)* sensibleness.

CHAPTER ELEVEN

Skippy the Second Dog

'You've got a great nose, boy.' Cad crouched to stroke the tri-coloured **terrier**[1]. 'Because you can't see me, can you, fella?' she said, noting she was still invisible. The dog's tail swept the floor like a broom as he sat on his **haunches**[2], panting. He **cocked**[3] his ears, his head moving from side to side as he tried to work out **whence**[4] came the voice and the light touch he felt atop his head as Cad stroked it.

'What brings you down here?' she asked **rhetorically**[5]. 'There's nobody's backside to bite but mine.'

Cad chuckled, surprising herself, and glad of the company this **canine**[6] **companion**[7] now **proffered**[8]. 'I wonder who you belong to.'

The dog's head turned, his eyes searching the air for the voice's invisible source. 'Don't worry. If you stick around long enough, you'll soon see me; if that happens, I'm in trouble.'

---

1 **terrier** *(n)* a small breed of dog typically used for controlling perceived verminous animals (pests).

2 **haunches** *(n)* the thighs and bottom together. *(s)* buttocks, hindquarters, rump, rear, backside.

3 **cock** *(v)* tilt in a particular direction. *(s)* angle, tip, incline.

4 **whence** *(adv)* from where. *(s)* wherefrom, from what place.

5 **rhetorically** *(adv)* in a rhetorical (not seeking information or answer) way.

6 **canine** *(adj)* relating to or like a dog. *(s)* doggy, doggish.

7 **companion** *(n)* a person or animal one spends time with. *(s)* friend, acquaintance, ally. *(ant)* foe, enemy.

8 **proffer** *(v)* put forward or hold out to someone. *(s)* offer, give, present. *(ant)* withdraw.

Cad knew it was vital to act fast, or she'd be seen **wandering**[1] about the castle. She mustn't **incur**[2] the **wrath**[3] of Owain Glyn, who would put her under lock and key.

'Come on, let's go in.' She clicked her tongue between her teeth and **beckoned**[4] the dog to follow her. With a huge effort, she pushed open the door, whose **hinges**[5] protested with an **eerie**[6] creak, bringing goosebumps to her body again. The lamp she held **aloft**[7] added to the **sinister**[8] **ambiance**[9], its flame **casting**[10] Physician Jordan's **demons**[11] and **devils**[12] onto the shadowy walls.

Since her poisoning, Cad's imagination had run wild, often dredging up dark images, night terrors she struggled to ignore. Right now, she must remain calm despite a storm **brewing**[13] in her stomach.

'What's your name, little fella?' she whispered, **distracting**[14] her mind as they entered the **musty**[15] room. Why they stored things down here seemed odd, for it was **damp**[16] and below the **moat's**[17] level; some of its water **seeped**[18] through the castle's **foundations**[19] and into its **bowels**[20], where she currently stood holding an oil lamp, looking for what, she did not know.

While deciding whether to search the room or head back before she reappeared, something

---

1 **wander** *(v)* move in an aimless or leisurely way. *(s)* amble, dawdle, potter. *(ant)* march, stride.

2 **incur** *(v)* become subject to (often something unwelcome) because of one's own behaviour *(s)* cause. *(ant)* avoid.

3 **wrath** *(n)* anger. *(s)* fury, rage, outrage, vexation. *(ant)* happiness.

4 **beckon** *(v)* make a gesture with the hand, arm or head to instruct someone. *(s)* signal, sign.

5 **hinge** *(n)* a movable joint or mechanism that a gate or door is hung upon. *(s)* link, pivot.

6 **eerie** *(adj)* strange and scary. *(s)* spooky, creepy, weird, peculiar. *(ant)* familiar, normal.

7 **aloft** *(adv)* overhead. *(s)* high, upwards. *(ant)* low, down.

8 **sinister** *(adj)* giving a feeling that something bad may happen. *(s)* menacing, threatening. *(ant)* innocent.

9 **ambiance** *(n)* the feel and character of a place. *(s)* atmosphere, air, tone.

10 **cast** *(v)* cause shadow or light to appear on a surface. *(s)* form, make, create.

11 **demon** *(n)* a bad spirit. *(s)* devil, fiend. *(ant)* angel.

12 **devil** *(n)* in some religions and beliefs only, a bad entity or spirit.

13 **brew** *(v)* begin to develop in an unwanted way. *(s)* materialise, loom.

14 **distract** *(v)* deflect attention from something or someone. *(s)* divert, sidetrack. *(ant)* focus.

15 **musty** *(adj)* having a stale, mouldy, or damp and dank smell. *(s)* stuffy, fusty. *(ant)* fresh.

16 **damp** *(adj)* a little wet. *(s)* moist, dank. *(s)* dry.

17 **moat** *(n)* a defensive, water-filled trench surrounding a castle or town.

18 **seep** *(v)* slowly leak through. *(s)* ooze, bleed, trickle, permeate. *(ant)* pour.

19 **foundation** *(n)* an underground, weight-bearing part of a building. *(s)* base, footing, substructure.

20 **bowels** *(n)* the depths, the deepest part. *(s)* core, recesses, interior. *(ant)* peak, summit.

caught her eye. Something she'd not noticed when caring for Fishy because it wasn't there then. Holding the lamp out at arm's length, Cad made her way to the back, **weaving**[1] between piles of old barrels, **rusting**[2] armour and **rotting**[3] bows and arrows.

As she moved, she **combed**[4] the **locale**[5] for signs of the monks' habits Rhys had said he'd seen. Even though she **delved**[6] beneath the miscellany, she found no **evidence**[7] of clothing anywhere.

She and Dylan had since **dismantled**[8] Fishy's **makeshift**[9] kennel that they'd **obscured**[10] beneath the **trapdoor.**[11] Nothing seemed untoward apart from what she'd spotted along one wall of the cave-like place.

None the wiser[12], Cad watched the **wiry**[13]-haired terrier sniffing Fishy's old home, recognising one of his own and seeming quite happy down here.

'Who *is* your master?' she asked him, but he carried on snuffling the **filthy**[14] floor, cobwebs collecting in his ears.

The air seemed to sing with **tension**[15] and, taking tentative steps, Cad shuffled towards a dark shadow in the furthest corner. What was causing the **silhouette**[16] she saw against the wall? The black outline she'd never spotted before, even though she'd spent hours in the hidden **dugout**[17] beneath this dingy place when secretly feeding Fishy. Nothing could cast a shadow here: there

---

1 **weave** *(v)* twist and turn while moving to avoid obstructions. *(s)* wind.

2 **rust** *(v)* be affected by rust (the reddish flaking coating of iron oxide).

3 **rot** *(v)* cause to decay (break down). *(s)* degrade, decompose.

4 **comb** *(v)* search thoroughly. *(s)* scour, sweep.

5 **locale** *(n)* a place. *(s)* area, location, setting, position.

6 **delve** *(v)* reach inside something and search. *(s)* rummage, dig, root. *(ant)* withdraw.

7 **evidence** *(n)* facts or information presented to support the truth. *(s)* proof, confirmation.

8 **dismantle** *(v)* take something apart. *(s)* disassemble, deconstruct. *(ant)* build, construct.

9 **makeshift** *(adj)* acting as a temporary or make-do measure. *(s)* improvised. *(ant)* permanent.

10 **obscure** *(v)* prevent from being seen. *(s)* conceal, hide, mask. *(ant)* reveal.

11 **trapdoor** *(n)* a (often hidden) hinged or removable panel in a floor, ceiling or roof.

12 **be none the wiser** (phrase) to not understand something even though one perhaps should.

13 **wiry** *(adj)* resembling wire in texture or form. *(s)* coarse, rough, bristly. *(ant)* soft, sleek.

14 **filthy** *(adj)* extremely dirty. *(s)* grimy, mucky. *(ant)* clean.

15 **tension** *(n)* stress or unrest. *(s)* agitation, unease, apprehension. *(ant)* calmness.

16 **silhouette** *(n)* a visible, dark shape and outline. *(s)* contour, form, shadow, figure.

17 **dugout** *(n)* an underground shelter. *(s)* den.

was no light. That meant only one thing to Cad as she **inched**[1] closer, stepping over piles of junk, **antiquated**[2] weapons and broken jousting **lances**[3] – it wasn't a shadow, but something else.

Why bother keeping this **clutter?**[4] she wondered, tripping over a pile of pots and slipping so badly she almost ended up in the splits. In a **heap**[5] on the floor and in agony, she yelped as her ribs reminded her again of their broken state.

At once, the dog stopped its **foraging**[6] and trotted over, sniffing the air, its tail dropping between its legs on hearing Cad's **yowls**[7]. Cad wriggled onto her bottom and sat for a time, recovering on a pile of old **sackcloth**[8] and wondering if she'd bitten off too big a mouthful in coming down to the dungeons alone. Fatigue, a foggy mind and now screaming ribs all urged her to go back and **heed**[9] Owain Glyn's orders. Common sense said she should return later with Rhys or Dylan to help her search.

Considering whether to stand, she cracked a smile as she wiped her face; the little fella was licking it.

'What's your name?' she asked him, guessing she'd probably never find out. She'd lived in this castle for years and seen this dog only once before, when he'd saved her skin by biting Sir Robert's rear outside his rooms. She understood dogs, and this terrier was no pup, nor was he old either. **Gauging**[10] his **physique**[11], she guessed him to be four or **thereabouts**[12]. The **toil**[13] of the last few days now dogged Cad. Exhausted, she stroked the terrier's head, **mustering**[14] the

---

1 **inch** *(v)* move along carefully and slowly. *(s)* budge, edge, shuffle. *(ant)* rush, leap.

2 **antiquated** *(adj)* old-fashioned or outdated. *(s)* ancient, archaic. *(ant)* modern.

3 **lance** *(n)* a long wooden weapon with a pointed steel tip, used in middle-aged jousting and battle.

4 **clutter** *(n)* things lying about in an untidy state. *(s)* mess, jumble, muddle.

5 **heap** *(n)* an untidy pile. *(s)* bundle.

6 **forage** *(v)* search widely for (often food). *(s)* look for, seek, rummage.

7 **yowl** *(n)* a loud cry. *(s)* wail, howl.

8 **sackcloth** *(n)* a course fabric. *(s)* sacking, hessian.

9 **heed** *(v)* take notice of. *(s)* pay attention to, consider. *(ant)* disregard, ignore.

10 **gauge** *(v)* measure or estimate. *(s)* judge, assess, evaluate.

11 **physique** *(n)* a person's (or animal's) body shape. *(s)* build, form, figure.

12 **thereabouts** *(adv)* approximately. *(s)* or so. *(ant)* exactly.

13 **toil** *(n)* extremely hard work, especially physically so. *(s)* effort, exertion, labour.

14 **muster** *(v)* summon up (a response, attitude or feeling). *(s)* raise, call on. *(ant)* disperse.

energy to get to her feet and so **grateful**[1] for his **presence**[2].

'I'm calling you Skip,' she said, 'because you skip along and join me whenever I need you. You just appear. I didn't know I needed you, but it seems I do. You're my friend, Skippy.' Cad smiled as the dog's tail whirled.

Maybe you can see me? she thought. Nothing would surprise her in this castle. *Perhaps I'm not invisible to animals?*

'So now we have a Fishy the dog, Slippy the snake, May the hawk, and you, Skippy the second dog.'

Still in pain and taking time to recover from her tumble, Cad reclined, resting on the pile of sacks, her new friend Skippy by her side.

*I wonder how May **fared**[3] with my father's note?* she thought, her eyes leaden and scratchy, as though filled with **grit**[4]. She blinked furiously, but they fought her.

I'll just close them for a few minutes while they clear ...

---

1 **grateful** *(adj)* feeling or showing appreciation for something. *(s)* thankful, glad, appreciative. *(ant)* ungrateful.

2 **presence** *(n)* the state of being present or occurring. *(s)* existence, appearance, attendance. *(ant)* absence.

3 **fare** *(v)* perform. *(s)* progress, manage, cope, do.

4 **grit** *(n)* dirt. *(s)* dust, soil.

CHAPTER TWELVE

Rotten Eggs

'Stop it!' Cad mumbled. 'Stop it!'

She swiped at her face; it tickled. Her eyes flickered open, struggling to focus in the dark.

'Fishy, stop that,' she snapped, irritated by her friend.

Heaven above, it's cold and so dark.

She shivered. Where were her blankets? She leaned across her bed, **groping**[1] to find them. As her eyes adjusted to the inky blackness, horrified, she saw a white outline next to her head. Cad **vaulted**[2] to her feet with a shriek as she remembered where she was, and why she was there. Fishy hadn't woken her; Skippy had.

'Saints save us all!' she yelled. 'What a nonny I am.'

She ran her hands over her thighs; she was now visible. Her limbs were well and truly where they should be. In a **tizzy**[3], she **fished**[4] around the floor beside her and located the now dead oil lamp. If she could just make her way to where they'd kept Fishy, she might find some candles left here by her and Dylan. But she wasn't hopeful, and how in heaven would she light them? She must feel her way out, but then the corridors would be dark until she found a lamp or a lit torch.

That damn potion! I cannot gauge its potency. Or is it the poison's dregs still affecting me?

---

1 **grope** *(v)* feel or search about for blindly with the hands. *(s)* fumble, scrabble, fish. *(ant)* withdraw.

2 **vault** *(v)* leap or spring by supporting or propelling oneself with one's hands. *(s)* jump, bound.

3 **tizzy** *(n)* nervous excitement or agitation. *(s)* flap, state, panic. *(ant)* calm.

4 **fish** *(v)* search by feeling. *(s)* scrabble, fumble. *(ant)* find.

She could answer neither question; right now, she needed light to return to her quarters before Owain Glyn found her missing.

Then she remembered the shadow she'd seen before nodding off. It was too dark in here to make out anything now, but even so, how could a shadow exist when no light cast it? The **measly**[1] lamplight hadn't caused it, for it shone in the wrong direction. Still, something had, and she must find out what.

As she grappled with her thoughts, Cad stood, stuck both arms straight out in front and, **fumbling**[2] her way, decided it **prudent**[3] to head back. She hoped she could dodge Owain on the way. Later, she'd return with one of the boys and decent **lanterns**[4], and **inspect**[5] what had caused that sinister shadow to be there. Something here didn't add up. Rhys wouldn't lie about the monk's habit. Why would he? The door had been open when she'd arrived. Something appeared odd at the rear that she'd not noticed before, even though she'd spent hours down here **weaning**[6] Fishy.

'It is *fishy* indeed,' said Cad to the little dog, pleased she could muster some humour, when suddenly the most **ungodly**[7] sound screeched. Although still **woozy**[8], Cad jumped so hard she **collided**[9] with a stack of barrels, knocking them flying and dodging away just in time. Thank goodness the terrier was **fleet of foot**[10], leaping aside with ease and disappearing off to safety.

Her **perception**[11] now blade-sharp, panting and regaining her **composure**[12], Cad **nigh on**[13] had heart failure when she first saw the two yellow-green lantern-shaped eyes glowing at her feet.

---

1 **measly** *(adj)* small, few or little. *(s)* inadequate, insufficient. *(ant)* large, sufficient, adequate.

2 **fumble** *(v)* move the hands about clumsily. *(s)* scrabble, search, root, dig, rummage.

3 **prudent** *(adj)* acting with care. *(s)* cautious, careful. *(ant)* imprudent, careless.

4 **lantern** *(n)* a portable (moveable) lamp with a handle. *(s)* light.

5 **inspect** *(v)* look at something closely and with care. *(s)* examine, scrutinise, check.

6 **wean** *(v)* introduce to food rather than a mother's milk.

7 **ungodly** *(adj)* without religion or morality. *(s)* unholy, immoral, godless. *(ant)* godly, holy, moral.

8 **woozy** *(adj)* unsteady, dazed or dizzy. *(s)* light-headed, groggy. *(ant)* clear-headed, lucid.

9 **collide** *(v)* come into contact with (usually forcefully). *(s)* bump, crash, ram, run into. *(ant)* miss.

10 **fleet of foot** (phrase) be able to move fast. *(s)* quick, speedy, swift. *(ant)* slow.

11 **perception** *(n)* the ability to understand something by using the senses. *(s)* judgement.

12 **composure** *(n)* the feeling of being calm and in control. *(s)* self-control, poise. *(ant)* agitation.

13 **nigh on** *(adv)* almost. *(s)* nearly, just about.

'Lord!' she cursed, realising at once it was the **soot**[1]-black cat who had guided her through those hideous tunnels weeks back.

'What are *you* doing here?' she said, knowing how **ridiculous**[2] she sounded but so pleased to see him. 'How do your eyes glow in the dark?' she asked, not caring a jot, for they would light her way out. It would be tricky **negotiating**[3] the dark corridor if the cat vanished, but she'd manage somehow.

'Come on, Sooty,' she said, naming the cat and fumbling towards the exit. 'Come on,' she called, but 'Sooty' didn't budge.

'Cat, this way,' she snapped, heading off and tripping again. But the cat sat mannequin-like, its **ghoulish**[4]-green eyes gazing at Cad.

'Cat, this way!' hissed Cad, her **irritation**[5] rising like a fire's heat. *Dogs are so much more* ***compliant***[6], she thought, wondering where Skip had gone.

The cat, or its eyes, for that's all Cad saw, twirled its **customary**[7] **figure of eight**[8], and headed into darkness.

'Wait! Come back!' she cried. 'I can't see you. Your eyes are facing the other way.'

Just before the cat managed to **slink**[9] further off, Cad lurched and grabbed its tail, knowing that was the only way she'd keep up with him.

'You little **villain**[10],' she muttered, as she stumbled into the darkness, almost bent double, one arm out in front and the other holding on to the cat's tail. How her ribs **objected**[11]!

For one moment, Cad **toyed**[12] with **yanking**[13] the cat's tail and pulling him in the opposite

---

1 **soot** *(n)* a black powdery residue left over from burning organic matter.

2 **ridiculous** *(adj)* something deemed to be silly. *(s)* absurd, laughable. *(ant)* sensible.

3 **negotiate** *(v)* find a way through, around or over a difficult obstacle or route. *(s)* navigate. *(ant)* fumble.

4 **ghoulish** *(adj)* like a ghoul (an evil spirit). *(s)* ghastly, scary. *(ant)* wholesome.

5 **irritation** *(n)* the state of feeling impatient, annoyed or slightly angry. *(s)* exasperation, chagrin. *(ant)* delight.

6 **compliant** *(adj)* one who agrees with or obeys others, sometimes excessively so. *(s)* biddable. *(ant)* disobedient.

7 **customary** *(adj)* usual or typical. *(s)* expected, habitual, characteristic. *(ant)* unusual, uncharacteristic.

8 **figure of eight** *(n)* something that is shaped like the number 8.

9 **slink** *(v)* move smoothly and quietly in a stealthy way. *(s)* slip, steal. *(ant)* stomp.

10 **villain** *(n)* a person or thing responsible for a wrongdoing or a term for cheeky behaviour. *(s)* devil, scamp. *(ant)* goodie.

11 **object** *(v)* complain. *(s)* oppose. *(ant)* approve.

12 **toy** *(v)* consider an idea or proposal casually or indecisively. *(s)* play with. *(ant)* decide.

13 **yank** *(v)* pull with a sudden, hard movement. *(s)* tug, jerk, wrench. *(ant)* push, shove.

direction, but **tolerance**[1] and **prudence**[2] **prevailed**[3] as she **lumbered**[4] on after him. Clueless as to the cat's intentions, she followed, when a **pungent**[5] smell, unlike anything she'd **encountered**[6] before, hit her nostrils, making her **retch**[7]. Coughing, Cad **floundered**[8] and thank goodness the cat stopped moving. Then, like a **phantom**[9] in the dark, it turned to face her, its eerie eyes lighting the locale.

You're ghoulish, thought Cad, fanning her nostrils as a **putrid**[10], fart-like smell wafted by. What on earth was going on here? This rotten-egg **stench**[11] wasn't present when she'd weaned Fishy. She and Dylan wouldn't have chosen this place if so, for it was **intolerable**[12].

'What is it, Sooty?' asked Cad, the egg-like **odour**[13] **overriding**[14] any pain or fear she may have felt. 'Show me,' she added, realising she must never underestimate these animals. They were clearly *special* and here to help her.

As the cat turned away, he moved towards the back wall, where she'd seen the shadow earlier. On approaching it, she no longer saw the darker patch, but she was sure of one thing as they neared the room's rear: the smell's intensity threatened to make her vomit. Cad **gagged**[15] as Sooty abruptly stopped again, miaowed, pawed the wall, and sat staring straight at it. Without hesitating, Cad knelt.

'Stay right there,' she said. 'I need your lantern eyes on this wall.'

Cad knew if the cat stopped, he was signalling something, just as he had before. What was it?

---

1 **tolerance** *(n)* the ability to endure something undesirable. *(s)* restraint. *(ant)* intolerance.

2 **prudence** *(n)* wisdom or cautiousness. *(s)* judgement, sense. *(ant)* folly, carelessness.

3 **prevail** *(v)* succeed or win. *(s)* triumph. *(ant)* fail, lose.

4 **lumber** *(v)* move in an awkward, heavy and slow way. *(s)* shamble, plod, galumph. *(ant)* glide.

5 **pungent** *(adj)* strong and sharp in smell. *(s)* powerful, pervasive, overpowering. *(ant)* bland, plain.

6 **encounter** *(v)* be faced with an experience.

7 **retch** *(v)* make the motion and sound of vomiting. *(s)* heave, gag, convulse.

8 **flounder** *(v)* struggle physically or mentally. *(s)* falter, blunder, stumble.

9 **phantom** *(n)* a ghost. *(s)* apparition, spirit, spook, wraith.

10 **putrid** *(adj)* repulsive. *(s)* rancid, foul, bad, rotten, stinking. *(ant)* fresh, perfumed.

11 **stench** *(n)* a strong and horrid smell. *(s)* stink, reek, malodour. *(ant)* perfume, fragrance.

12 **intolerable** *(adj)* not able to be endured. *(s)* unbearable, insufferable. *(ant)* bearable, tolerable.

13 **odour** *(n)* a distinctive, often unpleasant, smell. *(s)* aroma, stink, stench.

14 **override** *(v)* become more important or noticeable than something else. *(s)* overpower, supersede. *(ant)* balance.

15 **gag** *(v)* threaten to vomit. *(s)* heave, retch, choke.

Weeks back, he'd nosed open a flap in the wooden **wainscoting**[1]. With that in mind, she assumed if he could **replicate**[2] that ability here, then he would. She waited, but Sooty simply sat, staring.

You want me to look?

Cad forced her mind to order, realising she must find what he was trying to show her. As she thought, it struck her that she'd not seen Skip, the second dog, for a while.

Where are you, little fella? she wondered.

On her knees, she began **scouring**[3] the wall at the same level as the cat's eyes, when a sudden cough led to a **heave**[4] as the foul stench filled her nose and irritated her lungs. It was the strangest smell: a mixture of rotten eggs, lamp oil and, most oddly, pine trees!

The wall rose before her. At first, Cad patted it, pushing and scraping, achieving nothing but **grazing**[5] her palms and **snagging**[6] fingernails. Impatience and **vexation**[7] **loomed**[8] as she told herself, 'Calm, Cad, calm.'

Somehow, talking and singing to herself in times of trouble **soothed**[9] her, and now, thanks to Rhys, she knew she often did this whilst sleeping and fending off nightmares.

As she searched, Sooty pawed the wall again. Now balanced on her haunches, Cad explored a little higher, scratching and scraping away, but to no **avail**[10].

Keep going!

After a slight pause, she prepared to begin again, when to her alarm, Cad remembered she was still wearing the emerald invisibility ring and might damage it digging **thus**[11]. It was too tricky to hide it on her person here. She dared not risk dropping it – she'd never find it in this light.

---

1 **wainscoting** *(n)* panels (often wooden) that decorate the walls of a room, especially the lower parts.

2 **replicate** *(v)* copy or repeat. *(s)* duplicate, reproduce, recreate.

3 **scour** *(v)* look or search thoroughly. *(s)* scrutinise, study, inspect. *(ant)* overlook.

4 **heave** *(v)* threaten to vomit. *(s)* gag, retch, choke.

5 **graze** *(v)* cause a slight injury to the skin. *(s)* scrape, abrade, scuff.

6 **snag** *(v)* catch or tear on something. *(s)* rip, gash.

7 **vexation** *(n)* the state of being irritated or worried. *(s)* annoyance, exasperation. *(ant)* ease.

8 **loom** *(v)* about to happen. *(s)* approach, threaten.

9 **soothe** *(v)* gently calm or quieten. *(s)* pacify, mollify. *(ant)* aggravate, exacerbate.

10 **avail** *(n)* benefit or use. *(s)* advantage, reward. *(ant)* uselessness.

11 **thus** *(adv)* in this way. *(s)* like so, like this.

She must be careful to protect its stone because grappling with earth and rock would damage it. With **caution**[1], she removed it and placed it onto her right thumb, where it fitted **snugly**[2] and it wouldn't **activate**[3] accidentally as it **remotely**[4] refilled with power from the distant Gwalch Gem. Then, one-handed, she continued to search. She must not **jeopardise**[5] her ring.

Time **trickled**[6] away, and Sooty miaowed again. Cad saw she must continue, that she would find something here if she persisted. But with the remains of poison **coursing**[7] through her veins, weakness crippling her body, and with the smell so rotten, Cad's resolve began to crumble and her temper rise. She must keep a grip of herself.

'Calm, Cad, calm,' she **chanted**[8]. *She who tries wins!*

Despite her efforts, her clawing, her scraping and however much she pulled at the wall, all proved futile. As the red mist of anger descended, Cad jumped to her feet. Without thought, and with the **heft**[9] of an **incensed**[10] bull, ignoring her ribs, she let out an **almighty**[11] shriek, punching so hard her knuckles crunched as they met the wall. The second they made contact, the regret hit her. She had broken ribs, and her fist had probably joined them now.

Cad stifled a squeal of **remorse**[12], jigging on the spot, and shaking her wrist so hard she noticed nothing at first. It was only when the stench overpowered her, and Sooty trotted off, that Cad looked up, her jaw dropping open with disbelief at what she saw.

---

1 **caution** *(n)* care. *(s)* vigilance, wariness. *(ant)* recklessness.

2 **snugly** *(adv)* in a snug (well-fitting) way. *(s)* tightly, comfortably. *(ant)* loosely.

3 **activate** *(v)* make active. *(s)* start, trigger. *(ant)* deactivate, switch off.

4 **remotely** *(adv)* from a distance and without physical contact.

5 **jeopardise** *(v)* to risk or put into a dangerous situation. *(s)* endanger, imperil. *(ant)* safeguard.

6 **trickle** *(v)* come, go, appear or pass by gradually or slowly. *(s)* flow, seep. *(ant)* gush.

7 **course** *(v)* move through without obstruction. *(s)* flow, gush, race, surge, stream. *(ant)* trickle.

8 **chant** *(v)* say or shout repeatedly in a sing-song tone. *(s)* chorus, repeat.

9 **heft** *(n)* weight or heaviness. *(s)* bulk, size, mass, immensity. *(ant)* lightness.

10 **incensed** *(adj)* incredibly angry. *(s)* enraged, infuriated, annoyed. *(ant)* placated, calm.

11 **almighty** *(adj)* great or enormous. *(s)* massive, tremendous. *(ant)* weak, feeble.

12 **remorse** *(n)* guilt or regret. *(s)* shame, repentance, ruefulness. *(ant)* remorselessness.

CHAPTER THIRTEEN

Alchemy at Play

Cad stared ahead, sucking her knuckles. A coppery taste **tingled**[1] her tongue as she **squinted**[2] through the hole she'd punched in the wall. Only she now realised it wasn't a wall, but thin strips of wood, **caked**[3] with earth, like **wattle and daub**[4], constructed to **camouflage**[5] whatever lay on the other side. Had this been the unusual shadow she'd seen earlier?

Having spent much time in this den-like place with Fishy, Cad had spotted the **subtle**[6] difference, yet the putrid stench was new. She coughed and spluttered, turning her head away as the **malodorous**[7] **whiff**[8] rushed through the hole she'd **inadvertently**[9] created.

With both hands, but being careful to protect the ring on her right, Cad clawed at the surrounding hole. The earth crumbled away **relatively**[10] easily. This was neither exit nor entrance:

---

1 **tingle** *(v)* experience a prickling sensation. *(s)* prick.

2 **squint** *(v)* look with one's eyes screwed up or partly closed.

3 **cake** *(v)* cover and become crusted or hard. *(s)* coat, smother, plaster.

4 **wattle and daub** *(n)* interwoven twigs and sticks covered with clay or mud, formerly used in building walls.

5 **camouflage** *(v)* hide or disguise by means of camouflage. *(s)* conceal, mask. *(ant)* reveal, show.

6 **subtle** *(adj)* delicate or difficult to detect. *(s)* slight. *(ant)* obvious.

7 **malodorous** *(adj)* smelling terribly. *(s)* fetid, stinking, reeking. *(ant)* fragrant.

8 **whiff** *(n)* a smell that is only smelled briefly or faintly. *(s)* waft. *(ant)* saturation.

9 **inadvertently** *(adv)* in an inadvertent (unintended) manner. *(s)* accidentally, unwittingly. *(ant)* purposely.

10 **relatively** *(adv)* in comparison to something else. *(s)* fairly, somewhat, comparatively.

if so, why hide it thus? Cad assumed it to be an emergency **egress**[1] or secret **route**[2], one known to a few, yet hidden from most folks privy to what existed beyond.

The hole sat at the shoulder-punch height where Cad had lashed out in **rage**[3]. To get a better view, she poked her head through the gap, but gulping, quickly withdrew it. Several oil lamps flickered inside, and from her **hindered**[4] vantage point, she could see that the room **yonder,**[5] **fortuitously**[6] seemed **devoid**[7] of people.

For a moment Cad wondered if she should replace the earth, leave and return later with the boys, or at least one of them. But with no means of light, she couldn't see. Sooty and his glowing eyes had vanished along with Skippy, and from what Cad made out, lamps were **abundant**[8] behind the wall. She must take one to get out of here and back up to the castle.

Cad pulled away at the earth in a snap decision, yanking at the thin wooden planks until she'd created an opening wide enough to wriggle through, but it was high. Should she risk the time to make it bigger, and thus more noticeable?

No! She'd need to go head first, allowing her torso and legs to follow. Her ribs would protest but she'd learned to ignore them, and maybe the **meagre**[9] potion she'd licked from the vial had taken the edge off her pain after all.

As she pulled, the hole **expanded**[10] and Cad saw that the area beyond was some kind of workshop. From where she stood, she made out rows of shelves holding what resembled myriad tools. To the centre lay tables **strewn**[11] with **apothecaries'**[12] equipment: a **complex**[13]

---

1 **egress** *(n)* way out. *(s)* exit. *(ant)* entrance.

2 **route** *(n)* the course taken to get from one place to another. *(s)* way, passage.

3 **rage** *(n)* extreme anger. *(s)* wrath, fury, outrage. *(ant)* calmness.

4 **hinder** *(v)* make difficult, hamper, obstruct or slow down. *(s)* impede. *(ant)* help.

5 **yonder** *(adv)* over there. *(s)* in the distance.

6 **fortuitously** *(adv)* in a fortuitous (by chance) way. *(s)* luckily, serendipitously.

7 **devoid** *(adj)* free of. *(s)* without, lacking. *(ant)* full.

8 **abundant** *(adj)* in plentiful supply. *(s)* ample. *(ant)* scarce.

9 **meagre** *(adj)* inadequate or scant. *(s)* measly, paltry, insufficient. *(ant)* plentiful.

10 **expand** *(v)* make or become larger. *(s)* enlarge. *(ant)* shrink.

11 **strew** *(v)* scatter or spread things untidily (past participle: strewn). *(s)* throw, cast, toss, litter. *(ant)* gather.

12 **apothecary** *(n)* (archaic) a person who mixed and sold medicines.

13 **complex** *(adj)* consisting of different and connected parts. *(s)* complicated, intricate. *(ant)* simple.

assembly[1] of pipes, tubing, jars and **receptacles**[2], objects **alien**[3] to her.

The gap she'd created in the wall sat at the end of a short passageway, leading into the place housing the **apparatus**[4]. The passage seemed to have tunnels feeding off it but, from where Cad stood, it was too **dim**[5] to discern fully.

Cad **braced**[6] herself and pushed her head through the opening. Then, sucking in lungfuls of the **foul**[6] air, she leaped up and through the gap, landing on her hands, her **hips**[7] balanced on the hole. She paused a moment, see-sawing on the hole's rim and hoping the room beyond was empty.

She'd avoided bashing her ribs as planned, and her legs rested on the hole she'd **fashioned**[8]. Then as carefully as her position allowed, she walked her hands forward and pulled her hips through, her legs following with a plop onto the floor. When her legs landed, her ribs **howled**[9] as if **skewered**[10] by a lance, and she lay in **brutal**[11] pain until it **abated**[12] enough to allow her to stand.

After a little while, Cad recovered enough to struggle to her feet. Persistent pain poked her sides as she hobbled down the short cave-like corridor, **scanning**[13] the space, taking it in. Cad **reckoned**[14] that if the lamps remained lit, whoever toiled here wouldn't be absent long. Given this, she had little time to search before she must **flee**[15], taking a lamp with her.

---

1 **assembly** *(n)* something consisting of separate parts that have been fitted together. *(s)* construction.

2 **receptacle** *(n)* a hollow object for containing something. *(s)* holder, container, vessel.

3 **alien** *(adj)* unfamiliar. *(s)* unusual, strange. *(ant)* familiar, usual.

4 **apparatus** *(n)* the equipment needed for a specific purpose. *(s)* gear, kit.

5 **dim** *(adj)* (of a light or colour) not bright or clear. *(s)* dull, dingy. *(ant)* bright, light, airy.

6 **brace** *(v)* prepare for something difficult or unpleasant. *(s)* prime, fortify, ready. *(ant)* weaken.

6 **foul** *(adj)* offensive to one's senses. *(s)* disgusting, revolting. *(ant)* pleasant.

7 **hip** *(n)* the protruding pelvis bones of a human being.

8 **fashion** *(v)* make into a specific form. *(s)* create, construct, fabricate. *(ant)* destroy.

9 **howl** *(v)* make a howling (crying) sound. *(s)* yowl, groan, wail, shriek.

10 **skewer** *(v)* pierce with something sharp. *(s)* lance, stab.

11 **brutal** *(adj)* cruel or unpleasant. *(s)* vicious, harsh, callous, ruthless. *(ant)* gentle, humane.

12 **abate** *(v)* become less severe. *(s)* subside, lessen, ease, decrease, diminish. *(ant)* increase, intensify.

13 **scan** *(v)* look carefully or quickly. *(s)* study, inspect, glance.

14 **reckon** *(v)* work something out. *(s)* figure, gauge.

15 **flee** *(v)* run away. *(s)* depart, abscond, leave. *(ant)* linger, remain.

Honing[1] her **concentration**[2], Cad ignored the tool-**laden**[3] shelves and moved to inspect the apothecary contraption whence the putrid smell **emanated**[4]. Almost vomiting as the stink **intensified**[5], she gagged again, fanning her nose in **vain**[6], for the stench **dominated**[7] the entire space. On high alert, Cad grasped a lamp and inspected further. She'd read of **devices**[8] like this. This place was no apothecary workshop; this was **alchemy**[9] at play. Whoever ran this workroom was **formulating**[10] something unusual, and with what little knowledge she had, Cad now realised the **fetid**[11] smell **issued**[12] from the mixtures brewing here.

Whilst trying to ignore the stench, taking great pains to avoid the equipment, Cad inspected the table as best she could. Parchments lay strewn between various **crocks**[13] and containers filled with coloured powders, all placed **adjacent**[14] to the set-up. **Intrigued**[15], Cad inspected the parchments. She was **proficient**[16] in Latin, and most contained instructions she could read, but their content **flummoxed**[17] her. Numbers and **symbols**[18], signs and codes, all rhubarb apart from one word, **brimstone**[19], which explained the rotten-egg pong.

To her right, a piece of parchment caught her eye: medium-sized, the **vellum**[20] contained

---

1 **hone** *(v)* refine, sharpen or perfect. *(s)* improve, enhance. *(ant)* impair.

2 **concentration** *(n)* the act of focusing all attention. *(s)* awareness, attentiveness. *(ant)* inattention.

3 **laden** *(adj)* heavily loaded or weighed down. *(s)* overloaded. *(ant)* unburdened.

4 **emanate** *(v)* come or spread out from. *(s)* arise, derive, issue, emerge. *(ant)* absorb, withdraw.

5 **intensify** *(v)* become more intense (stronger). *(s)* increase, strengthen. *(ant)* abate, lessen.

6 **vain** *(adj)* producing no result. *(s)* useless, pointless, futile. *(ant)* productive, successful.

7 **dominate** *(v)* be the most conspicuous (stand out most) thing. *(s)* command.

8 **device** *(n)* a thing made or adapted for a specific purpose. *(s)* tool, mechanism, apparatus.

9 **alchemy** *(n)* medieval chemistry.

10 **formulate** *(v)* make in a methodical way. *(s)* prepare, create, develop.

11 **fetid** *(adj)* smelling extremely unpleasant. *(s)* putrid, rank, malodorous. *(ant)* fresh.

12 **issue** *(v)* produce or give off. *(s)* emit, discharge. *(ant)* absorb.

13 **crock** *(n)* a jar or pot made from clay. *(s)* vessel, container, receptacle.

14 **adjacent** *(adj)* next to or adjoining. *(s)* beside, alongside. *(ant)* distant from.

15 **intrigue** *(v)* arouse curiosity or interest. *(s)* fascinate. *(ant)* bore, disenchant.

16 **proficient** *(adj)* able and skilled. *(s)* adept, capable, competent. *(ant)* inept, incompetent.

17 **flummox** *(v)* perplex or bewilder. *(s)* baffle, puzzle, mystify. *(ant)* clarify, demystify.

18 **symbol** *(n)* a mark or character that represents something. *(s)* sign, ideogram.

19 **brimstone** *(n)* (archaic) sulphur, a yellow strong smelling substance.

20 **vellum** *(n)* quality parchment made from the skin of a calf.

drawings and pictures, plans and a code, like the document she'd taken from Sir Robert's rooms when she'd searched for John weeks back. Cad **gingerly**[1] folded it, for it would not otherwise fit into her secret pocket. Then she replaced the parchments as she'd found them, knowing that whoever had listed their contents thus, would notice at least this sheet was missing.

Investigating further, Cad couldn't fathom whether the bowls' powdered substances had been created here or whether they were the **ingredients**[2] for other **compounds**[3] and potions not yet made. Uncertain, she lifted one dish to her nose and **recoiled**[4]. She recognised the smell of a **vermifuge**[5]-type substance, often doled out by the castle's physicians to rid folk of the **parasitic**[6] worms **lodging**[7] in their **guts**[8]. The source of the hideous stench was now so **apparent**[9]: it was clearly brimstone. Yet, why make it down here secretly if it was worming potion? It didn't make square. The castle's vermifuge draught for treating worms was as common as cow **dung**[10].

Curious[11], Cad picked up another pot of whitish-grey powder and gently sniffed. As she exhaled, a cloud of light dust **dispersed**[12] into the air and, as fine as **pollen**[13] from a flower, flew into Cad's face. Within seconds, Cad's eyes burned, tears bursting **forth**[14] like a winter **brook**[15]. Stunned, she blindly replaced the bowl, almost spilling its entire contents and coughing so hard

---

1 **gingerly** *(adv)* in a careful manner. *(s)* cautiously, delicately, gently. *(ant)* boldly, rashly.

2 **ingredient** *(n)* a part of something that makes a whole. *(s)* component, constituent. *(ant)* whole.

3 **compound** *(n)* a mixture of several elements. *(s)* blend, mix.

4 **recoil** *(v)* suddenly spring or flinch back in horror or disgust. *(s)* withdraw, retreat. *(ant)* confront.

5 **vermifuge** *(n)* a medicine used for clearing worms from the gut.

6 **parasitic** *(adj)* living off something or someone else as a parasite. *(s)* dependent.

7 **lodge** *(v)* live or become embedded in a place. *(s)* remain. *(ant)* remove.

8 **gut** *(n)* the stomach. *(s)* belly, abdomen, tummy.

9 **apparent** *(adj)* obvious, visible or understood. *(s)* evident, discernible, perceptible. *(ant)* unclear.

10 **dung** *(n)* animal poo. *(s)* muck, droppings, faeces, excrement.

11 **curious** *(adj)* keen to know or learn something. *(s)* inquisitive, interested. *(ant)* indifferent.

12 **disperse** *(v)* distribute, spread or scatter over a wide area. *(s)* separate, dissipate. *(ant)* assemble.

13 **pollen** *(n)* a fine powder discharged from the male part of a flower.

14 **forth** *(adv)* forward in direction (or time). *(s)* ahead. *(ant)* back.

15 **brook** *(n)* a small stream. *(s)* streamlet, rill, rivulet, runnel, beck.

she feared such noise would draw attention. But her spluttering spread the dust further **afield**[1], filling the room with its minuscule **motes**[2] of **misery**[3].

Cad coughed, choking and springing away from the powder rapidly **infiltrating**[4] the air. Like a hunted **hare**[5], she leaped and crouched into a dark corner, sheltering from the swirling motes beneath a shelf as far from the **facilities**[6] as possible. In no time, the pain in her eyes **superseded**[7] that of her knuckles and ribs, and the more she rubbed them, the worse they became.

What a fool I am, sniffing the substance. What was I thinking? she **scolded**[8] herself, furious at her curiosity and lack of sense.

Cad tried to open her eyes but found it impossible. She pushed herself tightly into the corner, **longing**[9] for the agony to subside, battling the urge to scrub away tears with her fists.

Immobile[10] and blinded, Cad waited, her heart pounding so loudly she feared it was **reverberating**[11] around the walls. What had she done? Rivers of tears rushed from her eyes and snot gushed from her nose, which she wiped on her sleeve.

She blinked over and over, yet saw nothing but a grey blur; her eyes **smarted**[12] so much, she squeezed them shut, willing her vision to return. **Stricken**[13], unable to **stem**[14] her coughs, Cad **wheezed**[15] and **rasped**[16], **expelling**[17] the dust from her lungs with great heaves, when she heard voices approaching in the distance.

---

1 **afield** *(adv)* to or at a distance. *(s)* away.

2 **mote** *(n)* a tiny piece of something. *(s)* particle, speck, spot, fleck.

3 **misery** *(n)* distress or discomfort. *(s)* unhappiness, suffering, anguish. *(ant)* cheer, happiness, joy.

4 **infiltrate** *(v)* gain access to or pass into unobtrusively. *(s)* invade, penetrate, enter.

5 **hare** *(n)* a fast-running mammal that resembles a large rabbit.

6 **facility** *(n)* a space provided for a specific purpose. *(s)* place.

7 **supersede** *(v)* take the place of. *(s)* replace, overthrow, overtake. *(ant)* submit to.

8 **scold** *(v)* tell someone off angrily. *(s)* reprimand, admonish, chastise. *(ant)* praise.

9 **long** *(v)* to have great want. *(s)* yearn, ache, desire. *(ant)* hate, despise.

10 **immobile** *(adj)* not moving. *(s)* motionless, static, still. *(ant)* mobile, moving.

11 **reverberate** *(v)* repeat as an echo or pulsating vibration. *(s)* resonate, resound.

12 **smart** *(v)* feel a sharp, stinging pain. *(s)* burn, hurt. *(ant)* soothe.

13 **stricken** *(adj)* gravely affected by a disagreeable feeling or unwanted condition. *(s)* afflicted, troubled. *(ant)* unaffected.

14 **stem** *(v)* restrict or stop something. *(s)* halt, check, staunch, curb. *(ant)* increase.

15 **wheeze** *(v)* make a whistling or rattling sound in the chest. *(s)* gasp, rasp, cough.

16 **rasp** *(v)* make a harsh sound. *(s)* croak, grate. *(ant)* soothe.

17 **expel** *(v)* force something out. *(s)* spit out, eject, issue.

Her heart almost stopped. Horrified, she shrank further into the dark corner, her hand clamped over her mouth as she swallowed and swallowed to **stave off**[1] the persistent coughs. Had the owners of the advancing voices heard her, or simply returned to work? Cad hoped for the latter as she tried to make out the passageway whence she'd entered. She reckoned that unless the approaching folks went down there, they should not easily notice the hole she'd made. It was gloomy and unlit where she'd entered via the gap in the wall.

Cad gasped for air, breathing as softly as her condition allowed, her choking **reflex**[2] almost **victorious**[3]. Taking deep but hushed breaths, she quickly tucked the stolen cipher away in the most secret pocket of her **undergarments**[4], **stowing**[5] it as close to her skin as her **attire**[6] would allow.

The voices neared; male voices, she thought. To her chagrin, they approached from a passageway that **muffled**[7] the sound, so she couldn't make out their words. Unable to face her **self-inflicted**[8] **predicament**[9], Cad cursed her **rashness**[10], and although not a God-fearing girl, she silently prayed and prayed.

Footsteps entered the room. No one spoke. Cad **prised**[11] open her eyes but saw only silhouettes, and the pain and **futility**[12] of the attempt to see, forced them closed again. Now cornered, Cad **channelled**[13] her energy into **checking**[14] the coughs that promised to **expose**[15] her at any minute.

---

1 **stave off** *(v)* put off or delay something (often something undesirable). *(s)* prevent, foil, halt. *(ant)* assist, encourage.

2 **reflex** *(n)* a reaction done without conscious thought. *(s)* impulse, response.

3 **victorious** *(adj)* having won a victory. *(s)* winning, triumphant. *(ant)* defeated.

4 **undergarment** *(n)* clothing worn beneath other clothing. *(s)* underwear, underclothes. *(ant)* overgarment.

5 **stow** *(v)* store, pack or keep neatly in a specific place. *(s)* stash, secrete. *(ant)* remove.

6 **attire** *(n)* clothes. *(s)* clothing, dress, outfit, garments.

7 **muffle** *(v)* cover or wrap to reduce sound. *(s)* dampen, deaden, suppress. *(ant)* amplify.

8 **self-inflicted** *(adj)* done to one's self.

9 **predicament** *(n)* a difficult situation. *(s)* dilemma, crisis, plight. *(ant)* walkover.

10 **rashness** *(n)* the state of acting without due thought. *(s)* haste, carelessness. *(ant)* care.

11 **prise** *(v)* use force to move. *(s)* push, pry.

12 **futility** *(n)* uselessness. *(s)* pointlessness, hopelessness. *(ant)* usefulness.

13 **channel** *(v)* direct towards a specific outcome, end or object. *(s)* focus, guide. *(ant)* diverge.

14 **check** *(v)* slow or stop something from happening. *(s)* arrest, halt, bar. *(ant)* encourage.

15 **expose** *(v)* make visible or reveal. *(s)* unveil, uncover. *(ant)* cover, hide.

Almost retching as she **suppressed**[1] the reflex clawing her throat, Cad hoped the people entering the **cavern**[2] would neither see nor hear her hiding beneath the shelf just feet away from where they now stood, preparing to continue their work.

1 **suppress** *(v)* force something to stop or end. *(s)* repress, quash. *(ant)* encourage.

2 **cavern** *(n)* a large cave or cave-like place. *(s)* cavity, hollow, dugout, underground chamber.

CHAPTER FOURTEEN

Lost

'I've searched everywhere for Cad,' said Rhys in frustration, having met Dylan back in their room.

'Me too, or at least as much as I could while **skivvying**[1] for Bryn.'

Rhys eyed his friend, now a **mite**[2] guilty for the irritation he felt towards him, but Dylan's recent **whining**[3] irked him. Cad had vanished, Catrin was under siege, and Dylan seemed more concerned with **carping**[4] on about his chores.

Prioritising[5] Cad, Rhys brushed aside his **exasperation**[6] and **contemplated**[7] the situation. 'Something's clearly wrong,' he murmured, thinking aloud.

Dylan fiddled by his bed, untying his boots as though finished for the evening. Rhys watched, his fair brows **knitted**[8], his full lips pulled into thin lines.

'Dylan?' questioned Rhys, eyeing the boots, his voice firm with **wonderment**[9].

---

1 **skivvy** *(v)* work doing tasks that are thought to be unimportant. *(s)* toil, slave, slog.

2 **mite** *(n)* a small amount. *(s)* little, touch, tad. *(ant)* lot, loads.

3 **whine** *(v)* moan or carp on about things. *(s)* grouse, whinge, complain. *(ant)* enthuse.

4 **carp** *(v)* complain in a whining way. *(s)* moan, whinge. *(ant)* enthuse.

5 **prioritise** *(v)* make the most important. *(s)* prefer, put first. *(ant)* disregard.

6 **exasperation** *(n)* a feeling of annoyance. *(s)* irritation, vexation, *(ant)* delight.

7 **contemplate** *(v)* think about. *(s)* ponder, consider, deliberate. *(ant)* disregard.

8 **knit** *(v)* come together. *(s)* unite. *(ant)* separate.

9 **wonderment** *(n)* a state of admiration or respect. *(s)* amazement. *(ant)* indifference.

'*What*?' Dylan raised his hands at Rhys, shaking his head. 'We've searched high and low for her. **Busybody**[1] Hughes will swoop soon, honking as she does. Then Cad's completely **scuppered**[2]. Mrs Hughes will waddle straight to Owain Glyn and **bleat**[3] on about Cad.'

Dylan removed his boots and began changing for supper.

Rhys hid his **indignation**[4] at Dylan's **indifference**[5] towards the situation, but something he'd said **resonated**[6] in Rhys's brain. But what it was, Rhys couldn't quite catch, but if he chased it hard enough, he would.

'I've bought us some time with the goodwife,' said Rhys. 'Hugh, Mrs Hughes's son, plays chess for **coin**[7]. I told him of a **covert**[8] **tourney**[9] in which he now plays, and I gave her the nod to take the night off to attend. She couldn't resist. I promised her we'd look after Cad this evening.'

'Well, we can't even *find* her, let alone look after her,' snapped Dylan.

Rhys bit back, **rattled**[10] now. 'Dylan, Cad's missing. She likely used her ring, has become visible and is hiding somewhere ...' Rhys stopped mid-sentence and **glowered**[11] at Dylan, who shifted uncomfortably at the sudden **outburst**[12].

Then the realisation that had **eluded**[13] Rhys just a moment ago came to him like the dawning of day. 'You said "high and low".'

Dylan's face creased at Rhys's comment as he muttered a confused, 'Huh?'

Rhys paused, **deliberating**[14]. 'We've not searched high and low; we've searched only high. We've not searched below the keep. We've not searched the dungeons.'

---

1 **busybody** *(n)* a person who meddles in the affairs of others. *(s)* gossip, nosy parker.

2 **scupper** *(v)* prevent from working or succeeding. *(s)* ruin, thwart, foil. *(ant)* help.

3 **bleat** *(v)* complain in a whining manner. *(s)* grumble, groan, grouch. *(ant)* enthuse.

4 **indignation** *(n)* anger caused by something unfair. *(s)* resentment, distress. *(ant)* contentment.

5 **indifference** *(n)* lack of interest, concern or sympathy. *(s)* disinterest, coldness. *(ant)* care, heed.

6 **resonate** *(v)* evoke (bring or recall) an emotion, image or feeling.

7 **coin** *(n)* a flat disc with an official stamp used as money.

8 **covert** *(adj)* not openly displayed or acknowledged. *(s)* secret, clandestine. *(ant)* obvious, overt.

9 **tourney** *(n)* a tournament, especially jousting set in medieval times. *(s)* contest, bout.

10 **rattled** *(adj)* nervous or irritated. *(s)* perturbed, disturbed, flustered, agitated. *(ant)* comforted.

11 **glower** *(v)* scowl angrily or sullenly (glare daggers at). *(s)* stare, frown. *(ant)* beam, smile.

12 **outburst** *(n)* an abrupt release of emotion. *(s)* eruption, outpouring, explosion.

13 **elude** *(v)* avoid, escape or fail to achieve. *(s)* evade. *(ant)* embrace, pursue.

14 **deliberate** *(v)* consider carefully. *(s)* ponder, contemplate. *(ant)* rush.

Face blank, Dylan **gawked**[1] at Rhys.

'Dylan, put your boots back on. We're going underground.'

'What?' groaned Dylan, clearly picturing the food waiting in the great hall as he now reached for his boots again instead of his evening shoes.

'If Cad's hiding somewhere or in trouble, she's not up in the castle and cannot leave the grounds because of the siege. Thus, we search beneath Catrin, starting with the most obvious of places.'

Dylan screwed his face into a question. 'The most obvious of places?'

'There are two,' replied Rhys, alarmed at Dylan's lack of **insight**[2].

'The room in which you and Cad spent hours raising Fishy.'

Rhys stopped to stroke the dog, whose tail now beat at the mention of her name.

'And if Cad's not there,' he continued, 'then the place she and I would both rather forget.'

Dylan said nothing but regarded Rhys blankly, who, exasperated, eventually said, 'If we can't find Cad in the most likely places, then we search the place I would rather we forget: the oubliette.'

*

At the same time as the boys readied to search, but deep in the bowels of Catrin Castle, Cad's sticky eyes struggled to stay open. Statue-still, she lay curled like a comma beneath the shelving. Blinking furiously, she forced her streaming eyes to focus on the silhouettes that swished around where she hid. Oddly, when they'd entered, neither person had spoken – she assumed there were only two of them, but she could scarcely see.

Now **ruing**[3] her rash decision to enter the room, Cad, sweating like a hog, hoped neither would notice her crouched in the corner. More important, she hoped the cipher, now **secreted**[4] close to her body, would not be immediately missed. If they noticed it gone, it would be no time before they discovered the hole in the passageway – then her.

So close to capture, Cad wished she had never started this. The constant sneaking and hiding was all too much for her recovering state, and now she'd nigh on blinded herself.

---

1 **gawk** *(v)* stare stupidly. *(s)* gape, gaze, gawp. *(ant)* ignore.

2 **insight** *(n)* understanding. *(s)* awareness. *(ant)* unawareness.

3 **rue** *(v)* regret something you wish you could undo. *(s)* lament. *(ant)* celebrate.

4 **secrete** *(v)* hide. *(s)* conceal, stash, stow. *(ant)* display, reveal.

Even though Cad had her ring, sling and hairpin, all were useless while she was **blighted**[1] by what she now knew was powdered **lime**[2]. Quicklime, another nasty siege weapon, often scattered onto the enemy from castles' murder holes. A fine white powder that burned and maimed, **scorching**[3] through clothes and blinding those in its wake. Cad hoped little had entered her eyes, and that the damage might be **minimal**[4]. Still, to halt further **impairment**[5], she must bathe them with water soon. If she was stuck here for too long, she may never see again.

As Cad's eyes smarted and her ribs ached, stabbing their daggers of pain with each breath, she **debated**[6] **submission**[7]. After all, whoever worked here might be creating weapons for Owain Glyn's **defence**[8] of the castle – they may be friend not foe, yet there was no proof either way. What if they toiled thus for hours? How long could Cad stay in this **cramped**[9] space, her eyes untreated?

The more Cad considered her **plight**[10], the more she grasped that little choice remained but to reveal her presence and hope these folks worked for Sir Owain. What other options had she? Hitherto, it seemed neither of them had detected the missing cipher. If so, they would have raised an alarm, or at least mentioned it. If she revealed herself now, feigning goodness knows what, she may even get away with keeping the cipher.

Cad shifted her position, restraining the cough which constantly fought to heave up the **particles**[11] polluting her lungs. She prised open her eyelids again, **compelling**[12] them to stay thus. Even so, just **murky**[13] shadows swam into view. With her resolve rapidly melting, Cad

---

1 **blight** *(v)* have an extremely bad effect on. *(s)* disrupt, wreck, devastate.

2 **lime** *(n)* a white substance that irritates the skin.

3 **scorch** *(v)* burn the surface of something. *(s)* sear.

4 **minimal** *(adj)* of the smallest degree, quantity or amount. *(s)* slight. *(ant)* great.

5 **impairment** *(n)* the state of having a problem that hinders one. *(s)* disablement.

6 **debate** *(v)* consider or discuss something before reaching a decision. *(s)* ponder, contemplate. *(ant)* decide.

7 **submission** *(n)* the action of acceptance or yielding (surrender). *(s)* capitulation, resignation. *(ant)* rebellion.

8 **defence** *(n)* the action of defending or resisting an attack. *(s)* protection, resistance, security. *(ant)* offence, attack.

9 **cramped** *(adj)* uncomfortably small or restricted. *(s)* confined, tight, limited. *(ant)* comfortable.

10 **plight** *(n)* a difficult or dangerous situation. *(s)* predicament, bind, dilemma.

11 **particle** *(n)* a minute (tiny) piece of matter. *(s)* speck, mote.

12 **compel** *(v)* force or oblige someone to do something. *(s)* impel, drive.

13 **murky** *(adj)* gloomy and dark. *(s)* dim, shadowy, obscured. *(ant)* bright, light, clear.

rehearsed[1] the excuses she might give these strangers, none of which rang true.

In a **bind**[2], Cad toyed with various choices she might try: perhaps crawling on all fours from beneath the shelf like an **innocent**[3] playing hide-and-seek; maybe speaking first to **avert**[4] alarm; or pretending the potion had addled her mind and **purporting**[5] to having no memory of getting here. All scenarios were dire, but she must pick the best from a bad bunch.

As it turned out, they spared her the difficulty of choosing which **lurid**[6] lie might work best. For what happened next settled all Cad's uneasy **qualms**[6] for her.

---

1 **rehearse** *(v)* practise or prepare (sometimes mentally). *(s)* recite. *(ant)* improvise.

2 **bind** *(n)* a difficult situation. *(s)* dilemma, plight, predicament.

3 **innocent** *(n)* a pure or inexperienced person. *(s)* child, novice.

4 **avert** *(v)* prevent or ward off something undesirable. *(s)* stop, avoid. *(ant)* welcome.

5 **purport** *(v)* appear to do or be something, often falsely so. *(s)* claim, pretend. *(ant)* deny.

6 **lurid** *(adj)* presented in a shocking or sensational way. *(s)* exaggerated, vivid. *(ant)* pleasant.

6 **qualm** *(n)* a feeling of doubt or unease. *(s)* concern, worry. *(ant)* ease.

CHAPTER FIFTEEN

A Raptor Swoops

Astounded by what she heard, Cad listened to the voices that now spoke in the room. *It can't be!* So shocked, she almost cried out.

'Did you hear that?' said a male voice for the second time.

'Hear what?' replied a woman's, with a swish of what sounded like skirts.

Cad's heart felt like it **lodged**[1] in her throat. She forced open her eyes, but even though light, she discerned but blurred images.

Maybe my ears **deceive**[2] *me?* thought Cad, desperate to poke them and reminding herself she'd not long since woken from a drug-induced stupor and almost blinded herself. *My mind is still addled.*

'There, I hear it again,' said the man, **apprehension**[3] creeping into his tone.

Once more, a stillness **befell**[4] the room.

'I hear nothing,' snapped the woman. 'Continue as required, you **godforsaken**[5] **clod pate**[6],' she added, **blatantly**[7] **insulting**[8] him.

---

1 **lodge** *(v)* firmly wedge, embed or stick in a place. *(s)* fix, plant, jam. *(ant)* dislodge.

2 **deceive** *(v)* give the wrong impression. *(s)* mislead, hoodwink, dupe, trick. *(ant)* be honest.

3 **apprehension** *(n)* fear that something bad may happen. *(s)* worry, unease, anxiety. *(ant)* confidence.

4 **befall** *(v)* happen to (past tense: befell). *(s)* occur, arise.

5 **godforsaken** *(adj)* lacking any attraction. *(s)* miserable, wretched, grim. *(ant)* charming.

6 **clod pate** *(n)* a fool. *(s)* nitwit, blockhead, idiot. *(ant)* genius.

7 **blatantly** *(adv)* in an obvious way, with no shame. *(s)* flagrantly. *(ant)* furtively.

8 **insult** *(v)* make a rude or unkind remark. *(s)* dig, jibe, abuse. *(ant)* compliment.

Cad couldn't believe their conversation, nor could she believe it was who she suspected it might be. The man ignored the woman's insults. A lengthy silence ensued, and he remained still as the woman moved across the room.

On hearing these voices, Cad couldn't reveal herself. So, blinking furiously, she focused on the cloudy shapes working the apparatus and prayed for **miracles**[1]. After hearing these folks speak, she would need one.

Can it really be Peggy and Goodwife Hughes working this equipment? That **notion**[2] seemed so **outlandish**[3] as to be **utterly**[4] absurd. Until she saw them properly with her own two eyes, it **beggared belief**[5].

I'm losing my mind. It's Jordan's potion.

'There it is again!' cried the man. 'Surely you hear it now?'

Almost certain that was Peggy's voice, Cad held her breath. Even if plagued by hungry fleas, she must not budge now.

Goodwife Hughes with Peggy. Down here? she **marvelled**[6].

The woman stilled her **labours**[7]. Cad assumed she was listening for whatever concerned the man so much.

Curled like a **hibernating**[8] hedgehog, Cad lifted her shoulder and lowered her chin, wiping away a slush of tears and snot on her tunic. Hitherto, she'd made not a murmur. She'd barely breathed, swallowing back the constant tickle in her throat as they'd carried out their tasks. But now, with her face dried, she **cocked**[9] her ears, listening intently for what the man had heard.

Silence fell again. Something slithered across Cad's cheek; had it been an **adder**[10], she'd have ignored it. Over and over Cad blinked, not daring to scratch her face. In this grave-like silence

---

1 **miracle** *(n)* an extraordinary event often attributed to religious beliefs.

2 **notion** *(n)* an idea or something imagined. *(s)* thought, concept, desire.

3 **outlandish** *(adj)* unfamiliar and bizarre. *(s)* peculiar, weird. *(ant)* normal.

4 **utterly** *(adv)* to an extreme degree. *(s)* absolutely, completely, totally. *(ant)* somewhat.

5 **beggar belief** (phrase) something so extraordinary it is unbelievable.

6 **marvel** *(v)* be filled with amazement and wonder. *(s)* admire, applaud. *(ant)* deride.

7 **labour** *(n)* work. *(s)* toil, industry. *(ant)* rest, leisure.

8 **hibernate** *(v)* (of an animal) sleep through the winter months. *(s)* overwinter.

9 **cock** *(v)* tilt in a particular direction. *(s)* angle, tip, incline.

10 **adder** *(n)* the only poisonous snake found in Britain.

they might hear her. As she **batted**[1] her eyelids, the two shapes standing by the table took further **form**[2], their outlines slightly more solid than before. It seemed that Cad's eyes were clearing. **Frantically**[3] she blinked them into focus, until what she eventually saw chilled her to the bone.

It cannot be! Cad's jaw **slackened**[4]. Peggy and Goodwife Hughes stood side by side next to the table. Cad's breaths roared in her ears. The brimstone flame burning on the table **pattered**[5] like moths' wings beating above a candle. Yet despite her **heightened**[6] hearing, Cad could not glean what **perturbed**[7] Peggy so. Utter silence filled the room, nothing more.

Then a moment later, Cad heard it, faint but nearing: the unmistakable sound of beating wings.

Wily[8] Peggy had heard it, Goodwife Hughes not, and neither would **predict**[9] what came next. But Cad knew. Cad knew that sound and what was coming next. With her recovering eyes wide open, she prepared to sprint back to the hole whence she came before Peggy and Mrs Hughes would know what had hit them.

*'**Raptors**[10] – taken from the Latin,* rapere, *to seize – are diurnal (active by day) **predatory**[11] birds. In many animal **species**[12] the males are larger and stronger, but in hawks the difference in size between the genders is **reversed**[13] and females are larger.'*

Why this incongruous Latin lesson burst into Cad's mind as she prepared to spring, she neither fathomed nor cared. Cad knew what was coming, for she had trained her pet to do this as a last resort if necessary. Both Rhys and Dylan had been there each time she had done so.

A few beats passed and the flapping sound ceased. Both confused voices had quietened. But

---

1 **bat** *(v)* (of the eyes) open and close in fluttering movements. *(s)* flicker, blink.

2 **form** *(n)* the visible shape of something or someone. *(s)* formation.

3 **frantically** *(adv)* in a frantic (urgent) way. *(s)* desperately, madly. *(ant)* calmly.

4 **slacken** *(v)* become or make slack (without tension). *(s)* loosen, relax. *(ant)* tighten.

5 **patter** *(v)* make a repeated tapping noise. *(s)* beat, pitter-patter.

6 **heighten** *(v)* increase. *(s)* intensify, strengthen, amplify, enhance. *(ant)* lessen, reduce.

7 **perturb** *(v)* make uneasy or anxious. *(s)* worry, concern. *(ant)* reassure, calm.

8 **wily** *(adj)* clever and sharp, sometimes deceitfully so. *(s)* shrewd, astute, crafty, cunning. *(ant)* guileless.

9 **predict** *(v)* say or guess that something will happen in the future. *(s)* foresee, forecast, expect, anticipate.

10 **raptor** *(n)* a bird of prey.

11 **predatory** *(adj)* (of an animal) hunting another for food. *(s)* raptorial, predacious.

12 **species** *(n)* a specific type of living thing. *(s)* kind, class, variety.

13 **reverse** *(v)* make the opposite of what it was. *(s)* alter, change. *(ant)* uphold.

Cad wasn't confused. She knew her raptor had soared to the heights of the cave, **primed**[1] to dive on its prey.

Two living things stood in this room **bar**[2] Cad, and May would view both as **quarry**[3] when commanded. May was blind, so her **acute**[4] hearing **compensated**[5] for that loss. And if Cad were right, then May would have been told what to do when guided into this **dome**[6]-roofed cavern.

When not hunting, May was a **docile,**[7] gentle bird, perhaps grateful to live after being blinded by the heartless **falconers**[8]. Yet when she hunted, or if anything jeopardised her **offspring**[9], she was like any other **bird of prey**[10] – a killer. Hawks kill with their claws. May saw Cad as hers – her **kin**[11]. Cad had trained May to protect her family when necessary. In ordinary flight a hawk is **nimble**[12], yet not especially **outstanding**[13]. However, they achieve **spectacular**[14] speeds when diving or swooping on prey, slicing the air like the swiftest of arrows.

Neither Peggy nor Goodwife Hughes, who now pottered about their labours again, would **foretell**[15] their **dilemma**[16]. Their undoing would be too rapid for any human to **divine**[17].

As Cad's eyesight improved, she seized her opportunity the moment it came. Before Peggy had chance to cry in shock, his hands flew to his face. But May had since risen, dived again

---

1 **primed** *(adj)* made ready for use or action. *(s)* prepared, poised. *(ant)* unprepared.

2 **bar** *(prep)* except for. *(s)* besides. *(ant)* including.

3 **quarry** *(n)* an animal pursued by a hunter or predator for food. *(s)* prey, victim, target. *(ant)* hunter.

4 **acute** *(adj)* highly developed (on the ball). *(s)* keen, sharp. *(ant)* poor.

5 **compensate** *(v)* neutralise an effect. *(s)* rectify, offset. *(ant)* exaggerate.

6 **dome** *(n)* a rounded space forming part of a structure. *(s)* arched roof, hemisphere.

7 **docile** *(adj)* accepting of control or instruction. *(s)* passive, obedient, pliant. *(ant)* wilful, disobedient.

8 **falconer** *(n)* someone who keeps, trains or hunts with falcons or other birds of prey.

9 **offspring** *(n)* an animal's young or a person's child. *(s)* babies, youngsters.

10 **bird of prey** *(n)* a bird that hunts and feeds on other animal flesh. *(s)* raptor.

11 **kin** *(n)* a person's family. *(s)* flesh and blood, clan, tribe.

12 **nimble** *(adj)* light and quick in movement. *(s)* agile, deft. *(ant)* awkward, clumsy.

13 **outstanding** *(adj)* exceptionally good. *(s)* distinguished, stupendous. *(ant)* abysmal, dire.

14 **spectacular** *(adj)* impressive. *(s)* amazing, staggering, dramatic. *(ant)* dull.

15 **foretell** *(v)* see something coming in the future. *(s)* anticipate, predict.

16 **dilemma** *(n)* a difficult situation where a decision must be made. *(s)* predicament, plight. *(ant)* breeze, cinch.

17 **divine** *(v)* work out by guessing, or using insight or intuition. *(s)* foresee, predict.

and hit Goodwife Hughes at speed. May saw her targets and **executed**[1] perfect strikes on both occasions.

Both adults, now **caterwauling**[2], **flailed**[3] around the cave, crocks and pots crashing to the floor. The **sulphuric**[4] stench of brimstone filled the cave. Powders and dust **flurried**[5] through the air, their particles irritating, attacking the throat, burning the eyes, stinging the skin.

None of it hurt Cad. The moment May had struck Peggy, causing Mrs Hughes to gaze at him **agog**[6], Cad, like a deer, had **darted**[7] from beneath the shelves. Now, still half-blind, she **pelted**[8] down the passageway to the hole whence she'd entered. Pain battered her body but, mustering her **mettle**[9], she dived at the high gap. With one leap, she was through and finishing with a forward roll in the other room. May, as silent as a shadow, sped through the hole after Cad, leaving Peggy and Goodwife Hughes reeling with bewilderment behind her.

---

1 **execute** *(v)* put an order, plan or action into effect, carry out. *(s)* implement. *(ant)* fail.

2 **caterwaul** *(v)* make a shrill noise like that of a crying cat. *(s)* wail, screech, howl.

3 **flail** *(v)* swing or wave wildly. *(s)* whirl, flap, lash.

4 **sulphuric** *(adj)* containing sulphur (a yellow smelly substance).

5 **flurry** *(v)* (of small particles or things) move in small swirling masses. *(s)* swirl, whirl.

6 **agog** *(adj)* keen or curious. *(s)* anxious, intrigued. *(ant)* uninterested.

7 **dart** *(v)* run suddenly and quickly. *(s)* bolt, charge, bound. *(ant)* walk, dawdle, amble.

8 **pelt** *(v)* (informal) run quickly. *(s)* race, dash, streak. *(ant)* dawdle.

9 **mettle** *(n)* someone's ability to deal with difficulties. *(s)* strength, tenacity, fortitude.

CHAPTER SIXTEEN

The Knock

'You have Fishy to thank for your swift discovery,' said Rhys to Cad, who sat tightening the strapping that held her ribs in place. Thanks to Dylan's endless bathing of them with water, Cad's eyes had rapidly improved but remained red and sore.

'Fishy took us to her childhood hideaway. Didn't you, girl?' said Rhys, **ruffling**[1] the dog's coat. 'She followed your **scent**[2] straight there, and good old May did the rest.'

Since returning to their room with Rhys and Dylan, Fishy and May had not left Cad's side. May insisted on perching **comically**[3] on Fishy's back, even when Fishy **padded**[4] about the room. Even though **beleaguered**[5] by their experiences, all three friends had chuckled at that, and did so now.

'It won't be long before someone raps on that door,' said Cad, lifting her chin towards it, and bringing them back to earth with a bump.

All eyes swivelled towards the door, the air **bearing down**[6] as Dylan returned to

---

1 **ruffle** *(v)* mess up something or someone's hair (or fur). *(s)* tousle, dishevel. *(ant)* smooth, straighten.

2 **scent** *(n)* a distinctive smell (often a pleasant one). *(s)* trace. *(ant)* stench, stink.

3 **comically** *(adv)* in a comical (funny or amusing) way. *(s)* hilariously. *(ant)* seriously, solemnly.

4 **pad** *(v)* walk making a soft, dull sound. *(s)* patter. *(ant)* stomp, march, stride.

5 **beleaguered** *(adj)* in a difficult situation. *(s)* plagued, tormented. *(ant)* assisted.

6 **bear down** (phrase) move in a purposeful or threatening manner. *(s)* close in on.

interpreting[1] the new cipher Cad had snatched from the cave.

'How close are you to cracking it?' asked Cad as Rhys peered over Dylan's shoulder to help.

'It's coded similar to the weapon cipher,' Dylan said. 'Yet not **identical**[2]. I think it's a recipe of some sort.'

'What? Like for baking bread?' asked Cad with genuine surprise.

'No! Clod pate!' Dylan's eyes rolled before returning to study the vellum before him. 'I think it to be some sort of alchemy. A list of mixtures, powders and potions. **Elements**[2], quantities, **et cetera**[3]. But exactly what, I can't yet **unravel**[4].'

'Do you think Peggy and Goodwife Hughes had any notion you were in that room?' asked Rhys.

'No. Definitely not. But we're in trouble once they discover the hole, and I trust they will. Even though we camouflaged it, they'll put two and two together and come looking.'

'Is there anything that ties us to that room?' asked Dylan, looking up from the cipher.

'No. We cleared all **traces**[5] of Fishy after we found Prince John. Neither Peggy nor the goodwife knows of May. At least, I *think* they don't.'

Though deep down, it bothered Cad that Mrs Hughes might, and that **rather**[6] worried her, but she kept it to herself for now.

'Then perhaps they won't suspect us,' said Dylan. 'I doubt either will be in any state to come running. Their scratches might take weeks to heal.'

Cad suffered **ghastly**[7] guilt for the hurting of Goodwife Hughes, who could, after all, be working for Owain Glyn. Peggy was a different story though. Surely he wasn't working for Owain? Cad's mind whirled with unanswered questions and doubt. Peggy had been in that room, and he *must* be entangled with her uncle, Dewi.

---

1 **interpret** *(v)* understand the meaning of. *(s)* comprehend, decipher. *(ant)* misinterpret.

2 **identical** *(adj)* similar in every way. *(s)* equal, duplicate, matching. *(ant)* different.

2 **element** *(n)* a part of something that makes up the whole. *(s)* component, bit. *(ant)* whole.

3 **et cetera** *(adv)* used at the end of a list of something to indicate that similar or further items are included. *(s)* and so on.

4 **unravel** *(v)* investigate and solve. *(s)* fathom, decipher. *(ant)* complicate.

5 **trace** *(n)* a mark or object indicating the passing or existence of something. *(s)* evidence, sign.

6 **rather** *(adv)* to a degree. *(s)* somewhat, quite, slightly. *(ant)* significantly.

7 **ghastly** *(adj)* extremely unpleasant. *(s)* grim, frightful, hideous. *(ant)* pleasant.

Cad remembered Sir Robert telling her he had gained Peggy's **confidence**[1] in case Dewi or Siân contacted him from their shadowy **lairs**[2]. Sir Robert and Peggy were on first-name terms. Most **incongruously**[3], Cad had heard Sir Robert **address**[4] Peggy as Hari.

Cad despised **unprovoked**[5] violence. **Nonetheless**[6], she must now seek solace from knowing that Rhys and Dylan had commanded May into the cave as a **last resort**[7]. Regardless, the **conundrum**[8] Cad struggled to **comprehend**[9] was **twofold**[10]: when she had observed Mrs Hughes and Peggy working the apparatus in that room, the former had been in charge. Goodwife Hughes had **supervised**[11] Peggy, even insulting him at times. Her **character**[12] had seemed **transformed**[13]. Gone was the **pleasant**[14] woman who fussed, tidying Cad's room, clucking and honking like a nesting goose. If Peggy was under Dewi's command, was Goodwife Hughes working for him too? If not Dewi, then who?

That puzzle remained unsolved, but the second part of the conundrum – their attire, worried Cad more, filling her with **disquiet**[15]. Why in heaven had Mrs Hughes and Peggy been wearing monks' habits in that godforsaken cave? When Cad had dived out from her hidey-hole, that horror is what she'd seen: Peggy and Goodwife Hughes **enshrouded**[16] in the habits of monks,

---

1 **confidence** *(n)* trust. *(s)* faith. *(ant)* distrust.

2 **lair** *(n)* a secret hideaway, or a place where a wild animal lives. *(s)* hideout.

3 **incongruously** *(adv)* in a way that is out of keeping. *(s)* oddly, inappropriately. *(ant)* appropriately.

4 **address** *(v)* name someone. *(s)* label, identify, call.

5 **unprovoked** *(adj)* something (often bad) caused or occurring without justification. *(s)* unfounded. *(ant)* provoked.

6 **nonetheless** *(adv)* but. *(s)* in spite of, still, regardless.

7 **last resort** *(n)* the last action after all else has failed.

8 **conundrum** *(n)* a difficult or confusing question or problem. *(s)* puzzle, mystery.

9 **comprehend** *(v)* understand. *(s)* get, fathom, grasp. *(ant)* misunderstand, misinterpret.

10 **twofold** *(adj)* twice as great or as numerous.

11 **supervise** *(v)* watch over and control. *(s)* direct, handle, organise. *(ant)* neglect.

12 **character** *(n)* a person's qualities and ways. *(s)* personality, temperament, nature.

13 **transform** *(v)* markedly change something. *(s)* alter, modify. *(ant)* preserve, sustain.

14 **pleasant** *(adj)* (of a person) friendly. *(s)* amiable, affable, genial. *(ant)* unpleasant, unfriendly.

15 **disquiet** *(n)* a feeling of worry or unease. *(s)* anxiety, distress. *(ant)* contentment.

16 **enshroud** *(v)* cover completely and hide from view. *(s)* veil, cloak, swathe. *(ant)* uncover, reveal.

their faces obscured from view, draped in the **coarse**[1] **cowls**[2] of the **pious**[3]. Could Mrs Hughes be **colluding**[4] with such a traitor as Dewi? It was **unthinkable**[5], but think of it she must, for the web of lies and **deceit**[6] spinning through Catrin's corridors became stickier with each passing day.

'Cad?' said Rhys, tearing her back to the present. 'Are you well?'

Cad's mind **wheeled**[7] and, exhausted beyond belief after two days of non-stop **anguish**[8], she accepted she must rest a while lest she crumble completely.

'Goodwife Hughes will not come tonight or any night soon, and now we know she wasn't watching her son playing chess—' Cad abruptly stopped, pieces, like a puzzle, taking shape in her mind.

After a long pause, Cad said, 'We know Hugh Hughes works with Sir Robert, yet on two separate occasions he's taken Dewi's destrier at Sir Robert's **behest**[9]. Now, **unbeknown**[10] to most, Hugh's mother is an underground **alchemist**[11] in charge of Peggy, Dewi's old **henchman**[12].'

Dylan and Rhys **gaped**[13] at Cad.

'We have a web of lies, treachery and betrayal at Catrin Castle and we must find its culprits. I suspect things are far from what they seem here.'

'What do you **propose**[14]?' said Dylan, with a huge yawn.

'That you stop yawning,' snapped Cad.

Rhys **eyeballed**[15] Dylan, who raised an eyebrow.

---

1 **coarse** *(adj)* rough or abrasive in texture. *(s)* wiry, scratchy, prickly. *(ant)* smooth, sleek, silky.

2 **cowl** *(n)* a large and loose hood, especially as part of a monk's habit.

3 **pious** *(adj)* deeply religious. *(s)* devout, devoted. *(ant)* impious, irreligious.

4 **collude** *(v)* work together in a secret or unlawful way to gain advantage. *(s)* conspire, plot.

5 **unthinkable** *(adj)* too horrid to be thought possible. *(s)* unimaginable, inconceivable. *(ant)* desirable.

6 **deceit** *(n)* the action of deceiving (lying to) someone by concealing the truth. *(s)* deception. *(ant)* honesty.

7 **wheel** *(v)* turn. *(s)* rotate.

8 **anguish** *(n)* severe mental suffering. *(s)* distress, despair, woe. *(ant)* happiness.

9 **behest** *(n)* someone's orders or command. *(s)* bidding, direction, instruction.

10 **unbeknown** *(adj)* without knowing something. *(s)* unknown, unrealised. *(ant)* known.

11 **alchemist** *(n)* someone who practises alchemy (medieval chemistry).

12 **henchman** *(n)* a follower prepared to engage in criminality. *(s)* supporter, underling. *(ant)* leader.

13 **gape** *(v)* stare with one's mouth open wide in astonishment or wonder. *(s)* gawk, gawp.

14 **propose** *(v)* suggest a plan. *(s)* present, offer, recommend. *(ant)* withdraw.

15 **eyeball** *(v)* look at someone closely. *(s)* eye.

'Dylan Rogers, if you want to be a Knight Hawk, then **brace**[1] yourself. Tonight may be long,' she said, knowing that her much-needed rest must wait.

Mired[2] in such **turmoil**[3], Cad considered **confiding**[4] in Owain Glyn, but could she trust him? Even if she could, without cracking the new cipher she had nothing, and would face dreadful **embarrassment**[5] and **shame**[6] should Peggy turn out to be working for Sir Owain. No, they must **decode**[7] the cipher first, and take things from there.

Cad made her decision, and turned to share her thoughts, when a hard rap on the door stopped her.

---

1 **brace** *(v)* prepare for something difficult or unpleasant. *(s)* steel, prime, fortify, ready. *(ant)* weaken.

2 **mire** *(v)* involve in a difficult situation. *(s)* entangle, embroil.

3 **turmoil** *(n)* a state of confusion, disturbance or uncertainty. *(s)* chaos, disorder. *(ant)* order.

4 **confide** *(v)* trust someone enough to tell them about a private or secret matter. *(s)* entrust, disclose. *(ant)* withhold.

5 **embarrassment** *(n)* a feeling of shame or awkwardness. *(s)* disgrace, humiliation. *(ant)* esteem.

6 **shame** *(n)* a feeling of distress and humiliation caused by one's own wrongdoing. *(s)* embarrassment. *(ant)* pride.

7 **decode** *(v)* convert a coded message into understandable language. *(s)* decipher, unravel. *(ant)* code.

CHAPTER SEVENTEEN

Clandestine Intelligence

The knocking persisted. All three froze, their eyes wide, breaths held. Here it was, the visit they'd expected. The rapping on the door that would take them to Sir Robert's court and then to the tower. No Prince Llywelyn was on hand to lighten the **sentences**[1], to help her friends out of the **mire**[2] into which she had **plunged**[3] them. It was her fault. She'd dropped them in this **stew**[4]. Catrin Castle was under siege, her father was missing, and she had no idea whether May's note, which she'd dispatched on her return, would reach him or not: May might never find him. The water within the walls would soon dry up, and Catrin would collapse as they turned on each other like **savages**[5], or surrendered to the enemy.

In that **instant**[6], Cad's world **imploded**[7], and her shattered brain and body **relented**[8] to the

---

1 **sentence** *(n)* the punishment given for a person found guilty of a crime. *(s)* time, stint. *(ant)* freedom, liberty.

2 **mire** *(n)* a challenging situation from which it is difficult to escape. *(s)* predicament. *(ant)* bliss.

3 **plunge** *(v)* suddenly bring into a specified condition or state. *(s)* thrust, force, throw.

4 **stew** *(n)* a state of difficulty. *(s)* mess, muddle, predicament. *(ant)* boon, benefit.

5 **savage** *(n)* a brutal person. *(s)* brute, beast, animal.

6 **instant** *(n)* a short period of time. *(s)* a moment.

7 **implode** *(v)* fail or end suddenly. *(s)* cave in, fold. *(ant)* explode.

8 **relent** *(v)* give in to something. *(s)* capitulate, yield, concede. *(ant)* stand firm.

recent **trauma**[1]. Her mind blanked out the hearing of the **harsh**[2] raps at the door. Her reflexes refused to respond.

'Put away the cipher,' said Rhys to Dylan. 'Cad, get into bed and look as though you've **lain**[3] there for days.'

Cad blinked, unable to understand Rhys, her mind **spent**[4].

'Cad, please, bed now.'

Like a compliant child, Cad crawled into bed. Dylan **whipped**[5] away the cipher and Rhys moved towards the door. He glimpsed back once, his **profile**[6] **taut**[7] with tension as he turned to face the music.

Rhys inhaled and, shoulders squared, he yanked open the door. In unison, all three friends exhaled. Their faces softened, their shoulders **drooped**[8], their minds easing with relief; that is, until they **clocked**[9] the colour of Ellis Williams's face.

'What's wrong?' asked Cad, her alarm **reignited**[10] at his expression, her nerves crackling with foreboding. She sat bolt upright in bed, her ribs proffering **sabre**[11]-like jabs. 'Is it Flash?'

'No. No. I'm sorry to alarm you, Master Cad. Flash is fine. She's stabled with Midnight, although we are running a little low on water. Apparently there's a problem with the central well.'

The three friends said nothing, but Cad perceived the **strain**[12] rippling between them.

'But that's not why I came.' Ellis's eyes darted everywhere as if in search of secret **assassins**[13]. 'I knew not in whom to confide.' His face seemed filled with anxiety.

---

1 **trauma** *(n)* a distressing occurrence or experience. *(s)* agony, anguish, hurt, upset. *(ant)* benefit.

2 **harsh** *(adj)* unpleasant to the senses. *(s)* jarring, discordant. *(ant)* soft.

3 **lie** *(v)* assume a horizontal position on something that supports the weight (past participle: lain). *(s)* recline. *(ant)* stand.

4 **spent** *(adj)* used up. *(s)* exhausted, depleted, drained. *(ant)* replete.

5 **whip** *(v)* snatch suddenly and quickly. *(s)* tear, grab.

6 **profile** *(n)* an outline, especially of a person's face. *(s)* side view.

7 **taut** *(adj)* tight, with no slack. *(s)* stiff, rigid, tense. *(ant)* slack, loose.

8 **droop** *(v)* hang or slump down loosely. *(s)* sag, hang, drop.

9 **clock** *(v)* notice or watch. *(s)* see, discern, detect. *(ant)* overlook, ignore.

10 **reignite** *(v)* ignite (burn or flare up) or cause to ignite again. *(s)* rekindle. *(ant)* extinguish.

11 **sabre** *(n)* a heavy sword.

12 **strain** *(n)* a demand on the strength, abilities or resources. *(s)* stress, pressure. *(ant)* comfort.

13 **assassin** *(n)* someone who murders another for political or religious reasons or payment.

'Ellis, what is it?' Cad swung her legs out of bed, then remembered she must be boy-like now Ellis was here.

'Go on,' urged Rhys, casting a frown at Cad, who'd wriggled back beneath her covers.

'I had … I had tended Midnight. I was bedding him and Flashy down late, as I had been on siege duties. I must have been very tired, for I didn't reach the groom's bed and woke curled up in the straw inside the **crook**[1] of Flash's belly.'

On hearing her name, Cad **pined**[2] for Flash, her heart longing to see her pony. **Alas**[3], she must wait.

'Ellis, continue. You can tell us,' urged Cad, seeing that Ellis appeared to trip over his words.

Rhys and Dylan plonked down onto Cad's bed, and Fishy sat at their feet.

'When I heard hushed voices, I dared not breathe lest they heard me. I guessed by their tones that they met in secret, for they whispered, but I couldn't see them from where I lay. Because the horses weren't spooked, I knew they found the voices and smells familiar. I tried to recognise them. It was only when they slunk past the stall to leave that I saw their faces, or at least I think I did. Perhaps I was mistaken. It was dark, and a lantern lit their way, throwing shadows across their features.'

Cad's heart thudded, her eyes meeting those of her friends.

'Whose faces do you think you saw?' asked Rhys.

'I think one was that long-shanked son of gossipy Goodwife Hughes; the boy who takes Midnight out on late-night **jaunts**[4].'

'And the other?' asked Cad.

'Well, that's the peculiar part. I think he was talking to Sir Robert, who was holding something. They seemed to study an **article**[5] of some sort. I couldn't see exactly what.'

The three friends wore similar expressions, Cad's chest tightening all the time.

'I caught but a glimpse, so I might be mistaken.'

'That matters not,' Cad reassured him. 'Just tell us what you can, exactly as you saw and heard

---

1 **crook** *(n)* a bend in something. *(s)* curve, bend, curvature.

2 **pine** *(v)* miss and long for. *(s)* ache, yearn, crave, hanker. *(ant)* dislike.

3 **alas** *(int)* used to express pity, regret, grief, disappointment or concern.

4 **jaunt** *(n)* a short journey or outing. *(s)* trip, tour.

5 **article** *(n)* an item or object. *(s)* piece, thing, entity.

it.' Cad **appreciated**[1] none of this made sense to Ellis, for he knew nothing of the **intrigue**[2].

'I think he held a parchment. It wasn't large, and I saw not its contents. I caught parts of their conversation, but I made head nor tail of it. Still, nothing is normal in this siege,' he added, a tear escaping his eye.

'What did they say?' asked Dylan, clearly pondering the new cipher he'd just **squirrelled away**[3].

'Lots of it was as a **foreign tongue**[4] to me, but I'm sure they spoke of fire.'

'Fire?' Cad straightened.

'Yes. I'm sure that's what they said. I heard it mentioned several times. They discussed ingredients, and needing more, and debated mixtures and amounts. Then they were gone. Out of my **range**[5].'

'And you are certain they spoke of fire?'

Ellis nodded, his eyes finding each of the friends in turn.

'Is there anything else?' Cad changed the subject of fire. One look at Ellis and she knew not to alarm him further.

'I don't think so.' Ellis screwed up his face in **contemplation**[6]. 'Nothing more than I've already told you.'

'You did the right thing in telling us.' Cad's voice was soft. 'We must evaluate this information before acting upon it **heedlessly**[7].'

She smiled to reassure a grim-looking Ellis, but her mind **waltzed**[8].

'You look exhausted.' Cad realised the late hour. 'Go. Rest, and care for my pony,' she said with another smile, but not feeling the least bit **jovial**[9]. 'Don't share this conversation, what with the siege and everything.' She nodded at Rhys to see Ellis out. Her ribs still hurt and her head swam

---

1 **appreciate** *(v)* understand or see the full worth of. *(s)* recognise, perceive, realise. *(ant)* disregard.

2 **intrigue** *(n)* secret goings on. *(s)* plotting, planning, conspiracy.

3 **squirrel away** (phrase) hide away something of value or importance. *(s)* stash, secrete.

4 **foreign tongue** *(n)* a language not native to a person or place.

5 **range** *(n)* the area included or covered by something. *(s)* reach, scope.

6 **contemplation** *(n)* deep thought. *(s)* reflection, consideration.

7 **heedlessly** *(adv)* in a heedless (careless) manner. *(s)* recklessly, carelessly. *(ant)* carefully.

8 **waltz** *(v)* dance a waltz. *(s)* swirl, whirl.

9 **jovial** *(adj)* happy and cheerful. *(s)* jolly, genial, amiable. *(ant)* miserable, surly.

with fatigue. 'I think it best we ponder this a while, and if need be, we'll take this information to Owain Glyn.'

Now even more perturbed than before, Cad's mind danced as Ellis made to leave, her plans floating in **limbo**[1]. About to jump out of bed, she stopped. Rhys was closing the door behind Ellis, when Ellis turned and took a step back into the room.

'There is one thing I forgot to mention.' Ellis scratched his chin looking rather **vacant**[2].

'What is it?' Cad was now back on high alert.

Ellis seemed perturbed, pausing a moment before finally saying, 'It seemed strange to me that both Evans and Hughes were attired in such an odd way, for they were draped in the brown habits of monks.'

Cad said nothing, but nodded, swallowing hard, and as Rhys thanked Ellis and **shepherded**[3] him through the door, the eyes of all three friends met in consternation once more.

---

1 **limbo** *(n)* an uncertain or undecided state or condition.

2 **vacant** *(adj)* showing no interest or intelligence. *(s)* blank, deadpan. *(ant)* expressive.

3 **shepherd** *(v)* guide. *(s)* usher, direct, steer.

CHAPTER EIGHTEEN

Dragon Fire

'Monks' habits! What connects these damned monks' clothes?'

Silent, Rhys and Dylan shrugged their shoulders **in tandem**[1].

'I suppose the monks' habits don't mean **automatic**[2] guilt.' Cad looked at Rhys.

He tilted his head in agreement. After all, he'd worn the same disguise when rescuing Cad from the well.

'Though it's so **coincidental**[3] that Peggy and Hughes were wearing them too. A cowl-wearing figure trapped me in an oubliette, and I saw one slinking through the stables, spooking the horses.'

The boys nodded.

'And now Hugh and Sir Robert too,' added Rhys.

'It would seem there is more than a strong connection,' agreed Dylan, whose **analytical**[4] mind would be **churning**[5].

---

1 **in tandem** *(adv)* in the manner of one following or behind the others.

2 **automatic** *(adj)* occurring with certainty. *(s)* inevitable, assured. *(ant)* uncertain.

3 **coincidental** *(adj)* occurring by chance. *(s)* accidental, random. *(ant)* intentional.

4 **analytical** *(adj)* relating to logic and reasoning. *(s)* inquiring, systematic. *(ant)* unsystematic.

5 **churn** *(v)* turn and move (often in an anxious or excited way). *(s)* whirl. *(ant)* abate.

'Or is it a **ruse**[1]? A **red herring**[2] to throw us,' said Rhys quietly.

Cad and Dylan gaped at him.

'I often dupe folks when playing chess, sending my **opponents**[3] one way then the other. They're **ignorant**[4] until I swoop and **blindside**[5] them. A bit like Peggy and Hughes when May appeared from nowhere.'

On hearing Rhys's words, Cad's mind snapped into clarity.

'Dylan, when we discovered the first cipher, the one Sir Robert took from me, I asked you to make a copy. Did you do it?'

Seemingly pleased to prove his worth, Dylan knelt and fiddled beneath his bed, retrieving a folded parchment from between the wooden **slats**[6].

'I took pains to **transcribe**[7] it as **accurately**[8] as possible.' Dylan waved it, wearing a proud grin.

But before he could say anything else, Cad had already taken it from his hands and was unfolding it gingerly lest she tear the **precious**[9] vellum. In her **haste**[10], she missed the disappointment scudding across Dylan's face.

Cad **devoured**[11] the parchment, **absorbing**[12] its contents, her mind **galloping**[13].

'Dylan, read this aloud,' she bossed. Alas, she didn't trust her deciphering skills enough to rely on her interpretation of its symbols.

Dylan beamed, taking it from her with an eager nod while Rhys observed, silently stroking Fishy, who **nestled**[14] alongside.

---

1 **ruse** *(n)* an action intended to deceive (trick) someone. *(s)* con, ploy, dupe. *(ant)* truth.

2 **red herring** *(n)* a misleading clue. *(s)* ruse, deception, trick. *(ant)* truth, actuality.

3 **opponent** *(n)* a person competing with another. *(s)* contender. *(ant)* partner.

4 **ignorant** *(n)* lacking awareness or knowledge. *(s)* unaware, clueless, oblivious. *(ant)* aware.

5 **blindside** *(v)* shock unpleasantly. *(s)* stun, stupefy, astound, floor.

6 **slat** *(n)* a thin narrow piece of material such as wood, especially one that overlaps with another.

7 **transcribe** *(v)* put content into written form. *(s)* write, copy, rewrite, duplicate.

8 **accurately** *(adv)* in an accurate (correct) way. *(s)* exactly, precisely. *(ant)* inaccurately.

9 **precious** *(adj)* of great value or importance. *(s)* priceless, special. *(ant)* unimportant.

10 **haste** *(n)* speed or urgency. *(s)* swiftness, briskness, rapidity. *(ant)* slowness.

11 **devour** *(v)* read eagerly and quickly. *(s)* consume.

12 **absorb** *(v)* take in because of great interest. *(s)* assimilate, understand.

13 **gallop** *(v)* do something at great speed. *(s)* race, sprint. *(ant)* dawdle.

14 **nestle** *(v)* be situated. *(s)* lie, settle, sit.

'Yesterday, Owain Glyn confirmed they suspect the army's secret weapon to be a giant trebuchet. A machine able to destroy the castle's walls with one terrifying blow.'

Both boys listened, **rapt**[1], as Cad spoke.

'Dylan, please **corroborate**[2] the **pertinent**[3] facts. I must understand the cipher's words.'

'Yes, of course.' Dylan grinned as he studied the code.

'Do you read "dragon" and "fire" as I do?' asked Cad.

Dylan nodded, his eyes flitting from the cipher to Cad and back again.

'To be exact, I read it as "fire-breathing dragon".'

Dylan's shining eyes met Cad's.

'You're sure?'

'Yes. As sure as I can be.'

'Rhys, please check it too.'

'But Dylan is more skilled than I.'

'Check it,' insisted Cad. 'The more eyes on this cipher, the better. Why has Sir Owain not mentioned dragons and fires? Why just the trebuchet?'

'Maybe they aren't reading it properly,' said Dylan.

'Exactly! Rhys, read it.'

For a while, Rhys **pored**[4] over the cipher in silence, then slowly nodded.

'I **concur**[5]. I think what Dylan reads is correct. It speaks of dragons and fire, albeit poetically so.'

'I need to get to the top of the high keep,' Cad suddenly announced, catching both boys unaware. 'But in daylight and unseen,' she continued, as though to herself. 'Or better still …' But she didn't finish the sentence, and her voice trailed away.

The boys waited, knowing she would finish her thought soon enough. Fishy padded over to Cad, who automatically **petted**[6] her pup as she pondered her next move.

---

1 **rapt** *(adj)* fascinated by what one sees or hears. *(s)* riveted, captivated. *(ant)* uninterested, inattentive.

2 **corroborate** *(v)* confirm or support something. *(s)* verify, validate. *(ant)* contradict.

3 **pertinent** *(adj)* appropriate, applicable or relevant. *(s)* apt, suitable, fitting. *(ant)* irrelevant.

4 **pore** *(v)* be absorbed in reading or studying something. *(s)* examine, inspect, scrutinise.

5 **concur** *(v)* agree with. *(s)* approve. *(ant)* disagree.

6 **pet** *(v)* stroke. *(s)* pat.

Cad was exhausted, her ribs screamed and her mind **ailed**[1] as if **wading**[2] through mud.

With **slumping**[3] shoulders, Cad finally **conceded**[4] defeat, for now. 'I suppose there is little we can do tonight.'

'As you wish,' agreed Dylan too quickly for Cad's liking, and looking relieved.

'We must sleep or we will fail on the **morrow**[5].'

The boys exchanged puzzled looks.

'What do you mean?' mumbled Dylan through a huge yawn.

'I'm not sure.' Cad sighed, her face saying everything. 'My mind is sapped. I must think. But I fancy there's much more to the giant trebuchet than meets the eye, and tomorrow, we must prove it.'

Cad patted Fishy.

'*We?*' A look of shock slapped Dylan's face.

'Yes, *we*! Now, get some sleep, because I need to leave just before dawn.'

'Leave! For where?' Rhys looked **bemused**[6]. 'You can't leave, because of the siege.'

'Oh, but I can.' Cad waved her thumb which wore the emerald hawk ring. 'And I will,' she said, removing it.

Then with a swift **sleight of hand**[7], she hid it in her secret pocket. Tonight Cad would venture back out into the castle, meaning little sleep lay in store for her before tomorrow came.

---

1 **ail** *(v)* trouble or afflict. *(s)* pain, distress, bother, worry.

2 **wade** *(v)* walk with effort through water or such like. *(s)* wallow, paddle.

3 **slump** *(v)* fall or droop. *(s)* sag, slouch, collapse. *(ant)* lift, straighten.

4 **concede** *(v)* admit defeat. *(s)* capitulate, surrender, yield. *(ant)* deny, fight.

5 **morrow** *(n)* (archaic) the following day. *(s)* tomorrow.

6 **bemused** *(adj)* confused or muddled. *(s)* bewildered, perplexed, stumped. *(ant)* clear, definite.

7 **sleight of hand** (phrase) manual dexterity, especially in performing conjuring tricks. *(s)* skill.

CHAPTER NINETEEN

Proof

Now, in the early hours of the morning, Cad, still invisible, returned to her room after her **foray**[1] into the castle. As she crept in, Fishy's nose twitched. The dozing dog half opened one eye, and although she couldn't see Cad, her nose wriggled with recognition of her master's scent, and in an instant, Fishy was sound asleep and snoring.

Cad removed her boots, which became visible, then without waking either boy, who'd both evidently slept for hours in her **absence**[2], searched beneath the slats of Dylan's bed. She quickly found both ciphers, tucked them away on her person and slipped into bed.

Hitherto, her ring had never failed her, but now it dulled, becoming lifeless, and in dire need of more energy if she were to use it again later.

As she began to reappear, she hoped Dewi's grip on the ring's power source, the Gwalch Gem bracelet, was not yet too strong. The firmer his control, the weaker the connection to the ring, for the emerald hawk was taking longer to **replenish**[3] each time Cad used it.

As Cad stroked Fishy, she mulled over the situation and what she'd just learned in the castle's chapel. She'd been out a while and reckoned that she'd be lucky to snatch two hours' sleep before dawn broke.

---

1 **foray** *(n)* a sneak visit or attack. *(s)* sortie. *(ant)* retreat.

2 **absence** *(n)* the state of not being at an occasion or a place. *(s)* absenteeism. *(ant)* presence.

3 **replenish** *(v)* restore. *(s)* restock, recharge, reload. *(ant)* exhaust, empty.

Should I stay awake? she wondered, now so tired she was afraid her body's **rhythms**[1] wouldn't rouse her as they always did. Cad slept like a **bullfrog**[2] – barely – and able to wake on hearing a pin drop. But that was when she was well and not suffering from **torpor**[3] and exhaustion.

Fishy opened one eye, as Cad snuggled in close to her. Although physically drained, Cad's mind would need time to quieten as she deliberated her findings in the castle. Earlier, when re-reading the cipher with the boys, the words 'fire' and 'dragon' had sparked her thoughts, and she'd remembered a particular history lesson. Distant memories of studying seventh-century wars with the chapel's **priests**[4]. While thinking, it had struck Cad with sudden horror what had caused that memory to surface. To **confirm**[5] her suspicions before sharing them with Dylan and Rhys, she'd decided to visit the chapel. While there, poring over endless **historical**[6] **scrolls**[7], she'd seen the proof she needed. Now she was sure.

Despite the ring's power having been waning fast, Cad had risked one last **detour**[8] before returning to her room and headed back down to Fishy's room whence she'd fled earlier. With a flick of her hairpin, she'd opened its door, wondering who'd locked it, for she, Rhys, Dylan and May had left in quite a hurry.

Once inside, the room had still reeked of brimstone, and she'd quickly located where she'd slipped over earlier, before she'd **unwittingly**[9] dozed off. The odd little pots she'd **clattered**[10] into still lay scattered but unbroken. So she'd knelt and turned the tap of one, and a clear, strange-smelling liquid had trickled forth. Flummoxed, she'd closed the tap, then carefully gathered the oddly shaped pots into a sack and stowed them beneath the trapdoor where they'd once hidden Fishy. On her way out, Cad had stopped to check some of the **stacked**[11] barrels. They too, were

---

1 **rhythm** *(n)* a regularly recurring sequence of patterns, processes or events. *(s)* biorhythm.

2 **bullfrog** *(n)* a very large frog that does not sleep but does rest.

3 **torpor** *(n)* a state of mental or physical inactivity. *(s)* inaction, lethargy, fatigue. *(ant)* vigour.

4 **priest** *(n)* an ordained minister of a Christian religion.

5 **confirm** *(v)* establish that something is true. *(s)* prove, verify. *(ant)* confuse.

6 **historical** *(adj)* concerning history or past events. *(s)* ancient, old. *(ant)* modern.

7 **scroll** *(n)* a roll of paper or parchment for writing on. *(s)* document.

8 **detour** *(n)* an alternative route (course). *(s)* diversion, digression, deviation.

9 **unwittingly** *(adv)* in an unwitting (unintentional) way. *(s)* accidentally, inadvertently. *(ant)* wittingly, deliberately.

10 **clatter** *(v)* make or cause a continuous rattling noise. *(s)* clank, bang, clunk.

11 **stacked** *(adj)* arranged on top of each other in a stack or stacks. *(s)* piled up.

full – of what, she was unsure, but she'd **hazarded**[1] a good guess – the same strange liquid as was in the little pots.

Now, as she tossed and turned in her bed, she couldn't help wondering if Rhys, who lay still in his, had slept through her absence, or whether he'd replayed chess moves in his head, waiting for her return.

Who knows with Lord Nosy?

As her restless body twitched, unable to find comfort, she thought, *I will tell the boys in the morning.* Then in desperation, knowing little time remained left for sleep, she flushed all thoughts from her head, turned onto her side, and forced a stillness to her **frazzled**[2] bones. Eventually, she drifted away.

A short while later, as Cad snored lightly, a soft voice sounded from across the room. 'Fishy, come. Off that bed. Your mistress needs all the rest she can get.'

The ever-obedient Fishy quietly left her master's warm bed, and joined Rhys over in the corner of the room, on his.

---

1 **hazard** *(v)* say, do or think something in a tentative (uncertain) way. *(s)* proffer, volunteer.

2 **frazzled** *(adj)* presenting or feeling the effects of strain or exhaustion. *(ant)* shattered, exhausted. *(ant)* alert.

CHAPTER TWENTY

Cuffs

Cad hadn't needed to rely on her body's rhythms to wake her after all, for May had returned from her flight and **alighted**[1] on Cad's bed, **emitting**[2] such a high-pitched squawk that it threatened to wake even Dylan. To Cad's utter **dismay**[3], the note she'd tied to May's leg remained **in situ**[4] – May hadn't found Llywelyn. No matter what, though, Cad refused to believe her father dead.

With a leaden heart, Cad rose. Her eyes stung, but more **resolute**[5] than ever and still fully clothed from her foray into the castle, she forced her weary body onwards. Dylan snored like a pig with an **ague**[6]. She contemplated jabbing him with her hairpin, then decided to let him sleep. He could stay here with Fishy, May and Slippy, the toothless adder who slept among the **reeds**[7] by Rhys's bed. Dylan craved sleep and she would leave him be. He slept like the dead. Besides, she needed one of them to stay safe just in case her quest failed.

Cad went to wake Rhys, but found him lying in his bed, eyes wide open. Slippy, not sleeping either, was wriggling away in the leather pouch Cad had fashioned for him.

---

1 **alight** *(v)* (of a bird) descend from the air and settle somewhere. *(s)* land, arrive. *(ant)* fly off.

2 **emit** *(v)* make a sound. *(s)* issue, produce, utter, voice. *(ant)* silence.

3 **dismay** *(n)* concern or distress. *(s)* alarm, dread, trepidation. *(ant)* contentment.

4 **in situ** *(adv)* in the appropriate place or position. *(s)* in place.

5 **resolute** *(adj)* determined. *(s)* decided, adamant. *(ant)* irresolute, half-hearted.

6 **ague** *(n)* (archaic) a fever (high temperature). *(s)* illness, shivers.

7 **reed** *(n)* a tall, slim piece of grass, dried out and placed on the ground to adsorb waste or act as flooring.

'You're awake?' she whispered.

'I'm ready to join you.' Rhys jumped out of bed fully clothed.

On seeing Rhys's attire, Cad's eyes widened: he was **partially**[1] armoured.

'What in heaven!' she cried, eyeing Rhys.

'I fetched yours too.'

Rhys reached beneath his bed and pulled out a sack. 'Put it on. And drink this. I've measured it perfectly. It will kill your pain, but fortunately, not you.'

'Where did you get *that*?' Cad stared at the vial Rhys held.

He flushed. 'I snuck it from your doses when I felt you were taking too much. It made you sleep too heavily, and I feared you'd not wake.'

Dumbfounded[2], Cad gaped in amazement at Rhys. 'How on earth do you know of my plans?' she asked, now feeling a little **disgruntled**[3].

'Remember, you talk in your sleep.'

It was Cad's turn to **redden**[4].

'Like I say, you must never share your room with another. Not with the secrets you keep.' Rhys's voice came with a serious tone.

'Dylan may sleep like a **sozzled**[5] guard, but I don't. And your ring **exudes**[6] a mighty bright flash of green just before you vanish. I stayed awake until you returned, and whilst you slept.'

'So you haven't slept at all?' asked Cad, stunned.

'Not yet.' Rhys flapped his hand at a fly. 'There'll be time to sleep later. I'm used to sleeplessness. It's a lifelong **affliction**[7], **hence**[8] I play chess in my head instead.'

Again, Cad **gawped**[9] at this boy, realising her mouth might just catch the fly he'd wafted away.

---

1 **partially** *(adv)* to a partial (limited) extent. *(s)* partly. *(ant)* completely.

2 **dumbfound** *(v)* greatly astonish. *(s)* stagger, startle, amaze, flabbergast. *(ant)* underwhelm.

3 **disgruntled** *(adj)* displeased or angry. *(s)* discontented, dissatisfied. *(ant)* pleased, contented.

4 **redden** *(v)* (of a person) blush. *(s)* colour, flush. *(ant)* pale.

5 **sozzled** *(adj)* (informal) very drunk. *(s)* drunken, intoxicated. *(ant)* sober.

6 **exude** *(v)* display a quality or characteristic strongly and openly. *(s)* radiate, emit. *(ant)* absorb.

7 **affliction** *(n)* a cause of harm or pain. *(s)* complaint, trouble. *(ant)* wellness, contentment.

8 **hence** *(adv)* for this reason. *(s)* therefore, consequently, thus, so.

9 **gawp** *(v)* (informal) stare in a rude or silly manner. *(s)* gawk, gape.

Then when she thought he couldn't stun her further, he said, 'Before you **don**[1] your armour, stand still a moment. You look like a girl.'

And as quick as a **cutpurse**[2], he wielded Cad's sewing **shears**[3], **lopping**[4] away **inches**[5] of hair.

'There we are.' He stepped back to admire his **handiwork**[6]. 'You look a little more **laddish**[7] now, albeit a pretty one.'

Speechless, Cad turned **puce**[8]. Without a word, she tightened up the strapping supporting her ribs, quaffed the potion as if commanded by a parent, and donned her armour.

Then something struck her. 'Rhys, why are *you* dressed in armour? I must leave alone. It's dawn. I must gather evidence of what I fear to be true. You can't join me.'

'Actually, I think I can.' Rhys took something else from Cad's secret sewing box.

He's found my box too, thought Cad as her eyes followed him.

'You don't call me Lord Nosy for nothing.' It was as if he'd read her thoughts.

'Pass me your ring,' he said **nonchalantly**[9].

Cad opened her mouth to object, but it closed again as her hand reached inside her tunic to retrieve her prized piece.

Rhys took it from her, pricked his thumb with a sewing needle and allowed two drops of blood to fall into the glittering emerald in its centre.

Again, Cad's mouth opened to ask how he knew to drop his blood onto the ring, but she closed it, and vowed that she would never share a room with anyone other than Rhys, Dylan and the animals.

'But we only have one ring.'

'I've thought of that too.' Rhys reached beneath his bed.

---

1 **don** *(v)* put on or get dressed in. *(s)* throw on, slip on, change into. *(ant)* take off, remove.

2 **cutpurse** *(n)* a thief, especially one that steals from a person's pocket. *(s)* pickpocket, dipper, finger.

3 **shears** *(n)* large scissors. *(s)* snippers.

4 **lop** *(v)* cut off. *(s)* chop, shear.

5 **inch** *(n)* a unit of measurement which is equal to one twelfth of a foot.

6 **handiwork** *(n)* something made or done by someone. *(s)* creation, work, craft.

7 **laddish** *(adj)* having the characteristics of a young man or boy. *(s)* boyish. *(ant)* girly.

8 **puce** *(adj)* dark red or purple-brown in colour.

9 **nonchalantly** *(adv)* done in a nonchalant (relaxed) way. *(s)* casually. *(ant)* emotionally.

Cad's eyes were the size of **ducats**[1]. 'Where in heaven did you get those?'

'I won them from a **gaoler**[2] playing chess. He was rubbish, but **arrogance**[3] blinds men. I let him win, for a while. Fed him lots of those juicy red herrings, and when the worm was on its hook, the **pike**[4] bit. I took his **handcuffs**[5] as a prize. Easy really.'

Agog, Cad stared in silence.

'There is no chance I am letting you roam alone half blinded with broken ribs and an addled **pate**[6].' Rhys grinned at his insulting **quip**[7].

Cad couldn't help but grin back. 'We don't know if it works for two.'

'There's only one way to find out,' said Rhys, as he pulled Cad closer, handcuffed his wrist to hers and placed the key in the pouch with Slippy.

---

1 **ducat** *(n)* a gold coin formerly used for trading in Europe from the Middle Ages.

2 **gaoler** *(n)* a person who locks prisoners in jail. *(s)* keeper, captor, turnkey. *(ant)* liberator.

3 **arrogance** *(n)* a sense of self-importance. *(s)* ego, pride, hubris. *(ant)* humility.

4 **pike** *(n)* a long predatory fish with large teeth and a pointed snout.

5 **handcuffs** *(n)* a pair of lockable linked metal rings for securing a person's wrists. *(s)* irons, restraints.

6 **pate** *(n)* (archaic) someone's head.

7 **quip** *(n)* a witty (humorous or sharp) remark. *(s)* witticism, retort, jibe.

CHAPTER TWENTY-ONE

Slippy Does it Again

Not only had Rhys handcuffed himself to Cad, but he'd armed them both with daggers – real daggers, 'borrowed' from the knights' **armoury**[1]. Both had sheathed the weapons at their belts. Now invisible, they crept across the bailey towards the tunnel which would lead them under the gardens and moat and out to the tilt yard. There they could spy on the army forcing Catrin under siege.

Cad's **sole**[2] mission was to find the true machine **depicted**[3] on the cipher's plans. It was not the trebuchet it purported to be. The trebuchet itself **posed**[4] a **harrowing**[5] threat, and it seemed near to **completion**[6]. But far worse: if Dewi's army possessed what Cad had **deduced**[7] it might, the giant trebuchet was the least of their worries. If Cad was right, the giant **catapult**[8] was a

1 **armoury** *(n)* a place where weapons are stored. *(s)* arsenal.

2 **sole** *(adj)* one and only. *(s)* single, singular. *(ant)* many, numerous.

3 **depict** *(v)* represent in some form. *(s)* portray, show, describe, illustrate. *(ant)* misrepresent.

4 **pose** *(v)* present or be (often a problem). *(s)* cause, constitute.

5 **harrowing** *(adj)* very upsetting. *(s)* distressing, agonising, traumatic. *(ant)* pleasant.

6 **completion** *(n)* the state of being completed (finished). *(s)* conclusion.

7 **deduce** *(v)* reach a conclusion (realisation) by thinking and reasoning. *(s)* infer, conclude, judge.

8 **catapult** *(n)* a device that uses stored potential energy to launch a projectile (such as a stone). *(s)* sling, trebuchet.

charlatan[1]. A **decoy**[2] for the real weapon – their weapon of **mass**[3] **devastation**[4].

'You brought cheese!' whispered Cad, once out of earshot of folks **milling about**[5] the bailey. Rhys had scattered the sniffing dogs with one throw of the stinky stuff, sending them scurrying in all directions.

Rhys's idea to rid the dogs had worked a treat, and the two friends now headed to the gate adjacent to the keep. The gate opened to a tunnel that ran under the gardens and moat, out into the tilt yard. This covert exit was **purposely**[6] camouflaged from view to any onlookers outside the castle's walls. It had been built as a **discreet**[7] and speedy way to bring **necessities**[8], and often physicians, from the castle and into the tilt yard during tourneys.

'Do you suppose Sir Robert has secret tunnels leading out of Catrin? I do,' said Cad, before Rhys had chance to speak.

'Who knows?' Rhys yanked Cad sideways to avoid a dung pile. 'Probably.'

To their left, oblivious women **oversaw**[9] huge vats of bubbling poisoned water, their children **grubbing**[10] in the dirt at their feet.

'I wonder if they've tested the boiled water on anyone yet,' said Cad, thinking Bryn Davis would be a good place to start.

'Shush,' snapped Rhys, halting as that very squire marched from the keep, Jack Jones **in tow**[11]. Both looked incredibly grave.

Cad grinned. It was as if she'd **conjured**[12] up the boy. But quickly taken aback, she froze as Owain Glyn marched out after them, accompanied by an unfamiliar knight. The men spoke in hushed tones.

---

1 **charlatan** *(n)* someone or something falsely claiming to have a certain skill or knowledge. *(s)* impostor, cheat. *(ant)* expert.

2 **decoy** *(n)* something used to mislead or lure into a trap. *(s)* distraction, smokescreen. *(ant)* repellent.

3 **mass** *(adj)* involving a large number of things or people. *(s)* widespread, extensive. *(ant)* meagre.

4 **devastation** *(n)* great destruction. *(s)* ruin, suffering, desolation. *(ant)* creation.

5 **mill about** *(v)* move around. *(s)* rove, wander.

6 **purposely** *(adv)* done with intention. *(s)* deliberately, wilfully. *(ant)* unintentionally, accidentally.

7 **discreet** *(adj)* intending to be unobtrusive. *(s)* subtle, inconspicuous. *(ant)* obtrusive.

8 **necessity** *(n)* something that is needed absolutely. *(s)* essential, prerequisite. *(ant)* luxury.

9 **oversee** *(v)* watch over (past tense: oversaw). *(s)* supervise, manage.

10 **grub** *(v)* poke or dig about in the soil (often in search of food). *(s)* rummage, forage. *(ant)* plant, bury.

11 **in tow** (phrase) following or accompanying a person or thing. *(s)* in convoy.

12 **conjure** *(v)* make something appear unexpectedly or from nowhere. *(s)* summon, raise. *(ant)* dispel.

'From what we see from the highest **battlements**[1], their trebuchet readies to fire. Time runs short. Water levels are not yet **critical**[2], but this machine is,' muttered Owain as he passed by and out of earshot.

Rhys made to follow them, but Cad dragged him back saying, 'There's no time. We must find the contraption that **propels**[3] the liquid, for I'm sure that's what Peggy and Mrs Hughes were attempting to **manufacture**[4] in the dungeons – the liquid. But I can't be certain. Either way, we must be decided before sharing this with *anyone*. We **deem**[5] even Owain Glyn a traitor until we have proof to the **contrary**[6]. How I wish my father was here. He's the only person I trust apart from you and Dylan.'

They neared the gate, and Cad hadn't bargained on how difficult being cuffed to Rhys would be. The two of them had almost tumbled several times, and they'd only crossed the bailey.

'We'll get better,' Rhys had whispered each time.

Once they reached the gate, dancing past dung piles again, Cad said, 'We now wait for an **opportune**[7] time to move. If folks see a gate swing open unaided, their hearts will stop.'

'Good point,' agreed Rhys.

The two huddled away, hiding from the **bustle**[8] of the bailey, which had assumed an **air**[9] of **impending**[10] doom. They watched as women stirred the boiling **drums**[11], sweat – or was it steam? – **drenching**[12] their faces. No children played; even the castle's **fowl**[13] seemed **subdued**[14], sensing

---

1 **battlement** *(n)* the top of a wall, such as a castle's, that has openings (often rectangular) through which projectiles are shot.

2 **critical** *(adj)* potentially disastrous. *(s)* grave, dangerous, perilous. *(ant)* safe.

3 **propel** *(v)* drive or push into a specific direction. *(s)* thrust, shoot, force, launch. *(ant)* pull.

4 **manufacture** *(v)* make, often on a large scale. *(s)* produce, create. *(ant)* destroy.

5 **deem** *(v)* consider, judge or regard in a specified way. *(s)* assume, suppose. *(ant)* misjudge.

6 **contrary** *(n)* the opposite or reverse of. *(s)* converse. *(ant)* same.

7 **opportune** *(adj)* (of a time) appropriate or convenient for an action or event. *(s)* advantageous. *(ant)* disadvantageous.

8 **bustle** *(n)* noisy and excited activity. *(s)* busyness, liveliness. *(ant)* inactivity.

9 **air** *(n)* a portrayal, quality, manner or impression. *(s)* appearance, aura, tone.

10 **impending** *(adj)* about to happen. *(s)* imminent, looming, approaching. *(ant)* receding.

11 **drum** *(n)* a cylindrical container. *(s)* barrel, vat.

12 **drench** *(v)* wet thoroughly. *(s)* soak, saturate. *(ant)* dry.

13 **fowl** *(n)* birds such as chickens, turkeys and ducks. *(s)* poultry.

14 **subdued** *(adj)* quietened, overcome or controlled. *(s)* sombre, downcast. *(ant)* encouraged.

peril. The dogs certainly did. Cad noticed folks' faces **awash**[1] with fear. If only they knew what Cad suspected, that fear would turn to terror.

'What do you understand of my night-time foray into the castle? What did I **spout**[2] in my sleep?' whispered Cad into Rhys's ear, the handcuffs rendering their proximity somewhat close.

'You spoke of fire. But most was garbled, and I couldn't grasp detail.'

Cad thought, then said, 'I hid the cipher I took from the alchemy room. I'm counting on only one existing and that *they* don't fully understand its meaning. If the recipe for the liquid is accurate, and the enemy understand how to make it, then we're truly doomed.'

Cad looked at Rhys, who couldn't see her. Even so, her face was grave. 'I suspect they are attempting to recreate **Greek fire**[3].'

'Greek what?' Rhys's voice squeaked. 'What in God's name is that?' he asked, lowering it again.

'I learned of it from the pious priest who drums history into Dylan and me in the chapel. He first spoke of it when discussing the early Crusades. It's said it caused enemies to quake in terror, for it burns on water.'

The cuffs pulled at Cad's wrists as Rhys tensed.

'It was deemed to be magic and spews from the heads of dragons. It **reduced**[4] entire **naval**[5] **fleets**[6] to ashes in minutes.'

'And you imagine busybody Hughes and Peggy are creating *that* in Catrin's cellars?' Rhys sounded **incredulous**[7]. 'I doubt either of them can read, let alone decode an intricate cipher.'

'One thing I have learned,' said Cad, thinking how **ironic**[8] it was that Rhys could not see her face, yet she was referring to him, 'is never to judge a **pearl**[9] by its shell. We don't know their **capabilities**[10]. And although my eyes were smarting with quicklime, Peggy, and

---

1 **awash** *(adj)* containing a large amount of. *(s)* swamped, overwhelmed, drenched.

2 **spout** *(v)* express one's views without thinking about them. *(s)* declaim, rant.

3 **Greek fire** *(n)* a combustible (something that burns) liquid used centuries ago which ignited on top of water.

4 **reduce** *(v)* bring something or someone to a worse condition or situation. *(s)* disable, cripple.

5 **naval** *(adj)* relating to a navy (a fleet of military ships) or navies.

6 **fleet** *(n)* a group of ships sailing together for the same reasons and under the same ownership. *(s)* flotilla, armada.

7 **incredulous** *(adj)* not able to believe. *(s)* doubtful, unconvinced. *(ant)* believing.

8 **ironic** *(adj)* happening in an unexpected and often amusing way. *(s)* paradoxical. *(ant)* expected.

9 **pearl** *(n)* the hard but small spherical mass formed within the shell of a bivalve mollusc and prized as a gem.

10 **capability** *(n)* someone's or something's abilities. *(s)* competence, proficiency. *(ant)* inability.

especially Goodwife Hughes, seemed quite **adept**[1].'

Rhys said not a word, and Cad wished she could see his expression.

'I can't fathom where they got the recipe from, which I am sure is on this cipher.' Cad patted her invisible tunic. 'Or whether they've concocted an **imitation**[2],' muttered Cad, to herself.

'Tell me more of this liquid that burns atop water.' Rhys sounded lost.

'Greek fire was first used in **Byzantine**[3] **warfare**[4] in the seventh century and was a most devastating weapon. In fact, it was so **lethal**[5], its **imperial**[6] **creators**[7] vowed it must never reach the hands of foreigners for fear of **retribution**[8]. And it never did. The Byzantines manufactured it in different **stages**[9] and **locations**[10]. Separate producers who never saw the others' methods. Yet, there is no recent record of its usage. The secret of Greek fire is said to be lost forever – until now, perhaps.'

Rhys said nothing, but Cad sensed the **cogs**[11] **grinding**[12].

'Come!' Cad hissed, seeing the perfect opportunity to leave, and yanking at the cuffs. 'Run!' She feared that if anyone saw the gate open and close unaided, **mayhem**[13] would ensue.

The invisible pair pelted towards the small gate, pulled it open and dived headlong. With a clumsy **lunge**[14], and falling through, Cad, Rhys in tow, closed it as soundlessly as their situation permitted.

'Well, that wasn't pretty.' Cad listened for impending footsteps.

---

1 **adept** *(adj)* skilful or proficient. *(s)* competent, adroit, deft. *(ant)* inept.

2 **imitation** *(n)* something intended to be the same as something else. *(s)* copy, simulation. *(ant)* original.

3 **Byzantine** *(adj)* relating to the Byzantine Empire, which is now Istanbul in Turkey.

4 **warfare** *(n)* the activity or engagement in conflict or war. *(s)* combat, fighting. *(ant)* peace.

5 **lethal** *(adj)* able to cause death, hugely harmful or destructive. *(s)* deadly, fatal. *(ant)* life-giving.

6 **imperial** *(adj)* relating to an empire (many countries ruled by one). *(s)* royal, regal.

7 **creator** *(n)* someone or something that brings an object into being. *(s)* maker, inventor. *(ant)* destroyer.

8 **retribution** *(n)* punishment inflicted as an act of revenge for a wrongdoing. *(s)* redress. *(ant)* forgiveness.

9 **stage** *(n)* a period, step or point in the process or making of something. *(s)* phase, time.

10 **location** *(n)* a specific position or place. *(s)* site, setting.

11 **cog** *(n)* a bar or wheel with edge projections, which when engaged with another transfers motion.

12 **grind** *(v)* rub or grate together. *(s)* gnash, grit.

13 **mayhem** *(n)* extreme disorder. *(s)* confusion, chaos, havoc, tumult. *(ant)* order.

14 **lunge** *(n)* a forward thrust. *(s)* pounce, leap, spring, jump.

'I'm sick with fear now we're almost there,' Rhys confessed, his voice **quavering**[1].

'**Likewise**[2],' Cad replied. Because now, they stood just **yards**[3] away from an invading army – an army poised to attack at any time.

'Remember, no one can see us. At least, not for now. It's easy to forget that,' said Cad, willing the ring's effect to last long enough to see them through this mission. 'Once we're beyond the moat, we must be silent and swift. I know what I'm looking for, so be led by me.'

Cad heard Rhys gulp.

'Hurry! Now!' She yanked Rhys along. 'And be set to **chuck**[4] cheese if need be. They'll have hunting dogs. Soldiers must eat.'

Within no time, they were through the tunnel beneath the gardens and moat, then into the **occupied**[5] tilt yard. Cad's heart hammered, then her mouth dropped open. Men built like mountains strode between tents and makeshift huts. Many carried swords, and most had daggers sheathed at their waists. Some hauled wood, while others wheeled carts **heaped**[6] with timber, metals and **indiscernible**[7] substances. There was not a woman in sight. All labours pointed towards one thing – the wooden monster **looming**[8] above Catrin Castle. The monster just out of reach of Catrin's archers. The **behemoth**[9], whose **fodder**[10] of lethal-sized rocks lay in wait beside it. **Boulders**[11] bigger than Cad had ever seen. This **ravenous**[12] beast lay **dormant**[13], waiting to be fed those massive rocks.

Why is Dewi doing this? Cad agonised. *Why does he seek to destroy his castle thus? Why does he seek to ruin his brother?*

---

1 **quaver** *(v)* shake or tremble. *(s)* quiver, tremor. *(ant)* steady.

2 **likewise** *(adv)* in the same way. *(s)* the same, similarly. *(ant)* differently.

3 **yard** *(n)* a unit of linear measurement equal to three feet.

4 **chuck** *(v)* (informal) throw casually. *(s)* fling, hurl, lob, launch.

5 **occupied** *(adj)* (of a place) taken over by a military conquest. *(s)* invaded, captured. *(ant)* free.

6 **heap** *(v)* collect in a pile or bundle. *(s)* clump, lump, arrange.

7 **indiscernible** *(adj)* difficult to see or distinguish. *(s)* indistinguishable, indefinite. *(ant)* discernible.

8 **loom** *(v)* appear over someone or something as a large, often threatening presence. *(s)* tower, rise. *(ant)* recede.

9 **behemoth** *(n)* a monstrous or huge creature or thing. *(s)* beast, giant.

10 **fodder** *(n)* food, especially for livestock. *(s)* feed.

11 **boulder** *(n)* a large rock. *(s)* stone.

12 **ravenous** *(adj)* very hungry. *(s)* famished, starving. *(ant)* full, sated, satiated.

13 **dormant** *(adj)* temporarily inactive. *(s)* quiet, latent, idle, inert. *(ant)* active.

Her heart clenched, but this was no time for emotion. The trebuchet was not her target. The Greek-fire-breathing dragon was.

'Are you all right?' she whispered in Rhys's ear, terrible doubts **spiralling**[1] in her own head. Cad felt him nod, but the trembling handcuffs gave him away.

Quashing a **host**[2] of unspeakable thoughts, Cad braced herself.

Her **keen**[3] eyes scoured the **plethora**[4] of tents before **alighting on**[5] one that stood out to her. She doubted Dewi was here, yet this tent had a whiff of the **regal**[6] to it. Her uncle was nothing if not **ostentatious**[7] and would provide well for his **generals**[8].

Without thinking, Cad yanked Rhys towards it and straight into the path of a **cantering**[9] destrier. Its fully armoured rider thundered **blithely**[10] by, oblivious to having narrowly missed **trampling**[11] two children beneath his mount's giant hooves.

Rhys gasped, his breaths **ragged**[12], but neither spoke. Feeling **appalled**[13] by her **reckless**[14] move, Cad froze, struck by the reality: if they became visible now, the soldiers would feed them to their pigs. **Haunted**[15] by that image, Cad tugged at Rhys to speed up. They weaved between the tents, the huts, the fires roasting fowl, the cooks boiling broths and baking bread for the fighters. Cad wondered if her bravery – or was it stupidity? – was **fuelled**[16] by the **nip**[17] of potion

---

1 **spiral** *(v)* increase dramatically. *(s)* soar, rocket. *(ant)* decrease, abate.

2 **host** *(n)* a large number of things or people. *(s)* myriad, multitude. *(ant)* few, scant.

3 **keen** *(adj)* sharp and intense. *(s)* astute, deep, bright, responsive. *(ant)* dull.

4 **plethora** *(n)* a large or excessive amount of something. *(s)* abundance. *(ant)* lack, dearth, deficiency.

5 **alight on** *(v)* notice something (sometimes by chance). *(s)* arrive upon.

6 **regal** *(adj)* fit for a ruler. *(s)* royal, grand, majestic. *(ant)* humble.

7 **ostentatious** *(adj)* fancy and showy. *(s)* pretentious, flamboyant. *(ant)* plain, modest.

8 **general** *(n)* a commander or high ranking military officer.

9 **canter** *(v)* run at the pace of a horse or other quadruped between a trot and a gallop.

10 **blithely** *(adv)* in a blithe (carefree) manner. *(s)* casually, carelessly, unthinkingly. *(ant)* anxiously, warily.

11 **trample** *(v)* tread on and crush underfoot. *(s)* stamp, flatten.

12 **ragged** *(adj)* (of sound) uncontrolled. *(s)* uneven, irregular. *(ant)* regular, controlled.

13 **appalled** *(adj)* greatly dismayed or shocked. *(s)* horrified, mortified. *(ant)* pleased.

14 **reckless** *(adj)* heedless of danger or the consequences of an action. *(s)* irresponsible, wild, rash. *(ant)* cautious.

15 **haunt** *(v)* always be present in the mind but in a negative way. *(s)* torment.

16 **fuel** *(v)* power or inflame. *(s)* feed, provoke, stimulate, encourage. *(ant)* deplete.

17 **nip** *(n)* a small sip or quantity. *(s)* drop, mouthful. *(ant)* slurp.

administered by Rhys. Too late for such questions though, Cad **cast**[1] them aside.

In such tense times as this, Cad constantly forgot she was invisible, fearing capture in the next breath. She sensed that Rhys felt the same, but neither dared utter a sound. Relieved that the camp seemed devoid of stray dogs, they arrived at the **majestic**[2]-looking tent, **flanked**[3] by a sturdy hut. Two gigantic men guarded its **canvas**[4] mouth. Cad pulled Rhys around to the rear.

'We can crawl underneath at the back. Perhaps you should unlock me and I'll go in alone.'

'I'm not leaving you. If we part, one of us may reappear. I have a better idea.' Rhys reached for the invisible pouch at his belt. 'It's a risk, but one I'm willing to take.'

Rhys fiddled, Cad's hands wiggling along with him, when she realised what he was about to do.

'You're risking Slippy?' whispered Cad, remembering how **reluctant**[5] he'd been to let the adder loose beneath Mrs Hughes's skirts in the great hall.

'Yes. Those guards will dance a **merry**[6] jig and we'll be in.'

'Are you sure?' Cad was thinking of her own beloved pets, but Rhys jerked her towards the entrance. Without warning, he **stooped**[7], taking Cad with him. Cad **smothered**[8] a gasp and, as fast as a fox, Rhys released an invisible Slippy at the feet of the largest soldier. Cad held her breath. It took but a beat for Slippy to reappear and the giant man to leap, yell, swipe at his legs and scare the **wits**[9] out of his **comrade**[10], who dived sideways, grappling for the dagger at his belt.

Rhys scooped Slippy up, shoved him into the pouch, saw him vanish, then **wrangled**[11] Cad

---

1 **cast** *(v)* (often used figuratively) throw. *(s)* toss, fling.

2 **majestic** *(adj)* showing or having great beauty or size. *(s)* awesome, splendid. *(ant)* pathetic, pitiful.

3 **flank** *(v)* be on each side or on one side of.

4 **canvas** *(n)* a strong, coarse pale-coloured cloth used to make items such as tents and sails.

5 **reluctant** *(adj)* unwilling or hesitant. *(s)* opposed, grudging, resistant. *(s)* eager, willing.

6 **merry** *(adj)* cheerful. *(s)* lively, jolly, joyous. *(ant)* gloomy, miserable.

7 **stoop** *(v)* bend one's head or body forward and downwards into a hunch. *(s)* crouch. *(ant)* straighten.

8 **smother** *(v)* suppress an action or feeling. *(s)* stifle, gag, suppress.

9 **wits** *(n)* sense.

10 **comrade** *(n)* a colleague or a friend. *(s)* co-worker, companion. *(ant)* enemy, foe.

11 **wrangle** *(v)* round up and take charge of. *(s)* guide, herd, shepherd.

into the tent before the soldier **cited**[1] his dance as **cramp**[2] and his puce face had **paled**[3]. Left outside the tent to lick their wounded pride, both guards swiftly **rallied**[4], looking for the adder that had slithered between their calves then vanished.

Once inside, as Rhys rearranged a now invisible Slippy back safely in his pouch, Cad **surveyed**[5] the tent. But **unbeknownst**[6] to her, what she was about to see next would scar her forever.

---

1 **cite** *(v)* refer to as evidence for or justification of something. *(s)* name, specify.

2 **cramp** *(n)* a painful tightening of a muscle or muscles, often caused by strain or fatigue.

3 **pale** *(v)* lose colour in one's face from fear or shock. *(s)* blanch, blench, whiten. *(ant)* flush.

4 **rally** *(v)* recover. *(s)* improve, revive. *(ant)* deteriorate.

5 **survey** *(v)* look closely at or examine. *(s)* study, inspect, assess, evaluate. *(ant)* overlook.

6 **unbeknownst** *(adj)* without knowing something. *(s)* unknown, unrealised. *(ant)* known.

CHAPTER TWENTY-TWO

Grim Realisation

Cad froze, her feet glued to the spot. She sensed Rhys was staring at the scene in the tent, then back at her. If Cad could have seen his face, she would have seen his eyes were wide with sympathy and **pity**[1]. Mortified, Cad now relied on her own tears being invisible.

The tent's **occupants**[2] had clearly halted their work when hearing the sudden **commotion**[3] outside. But, after the guards had reassured their masters with **abashed**[4] tones and lies of cramp, the superiors had returned to their **observations**[5]. They inspected a grim-looking apparatus at the back of the tent, poking and prodding, admiring it and **cooing**[6]. The two obvious leaders grinned **smugly**[7], yet spoke of a 'slight **setback**'[8] that they would soon overcome.

Cad couldn't move. She felt like a wet rag. Like someone had stolen her heart from her chest. Rhys waited for her, his body trembling through the handcuffs. For Cad, time had stopped.

---

1 **pity** *(n)* the feeling of sadness for the suffering of others. *(s)* compassion, sorrow. *(ant)* indifference.

2 **occupant** *(n)* a person who resides (exists) in a place. *(s)* incumbent, inhabitant, resident.

3 **commotion** *(n)* a noisy disturbance and confusion. *(s)* uproar, tumult. *(ant)* calm, peace.

4 **abashed** *(adj)* embarrassed, ashamed or disconcerted. *(s)* deflated, mortified. *(ant)* undaunted.

5 **observation** *(n)* the action or process of observing (watching) closely. *(s)* examination, inspection.

6 **coo** *(v)* make soft murmuring sounds. *(s)* mutter, murmur.

7 **smugly** *(adv)* in a smug (self-satisfied) way. *(s)* arrogantly, conceitedly. *(ant)* humbly.

8 **setback** *(n)* a problem with the progress of something. *(s)* difficulty, hitch. *(ant)* breakthrough.

Now **suspended**[1] in this moment, a lifetime flashed before her eyes, the same as when she'd been poisoned in the well and she'd feared drowning. The **joyous**[2] years living at Cadwaladr Castle with her parents before Prince John's birth; the laughter, dancing and feasting; the stunning summers riding through flower-filled **meadows**[3]; **cosy**[4] winters before roaring fires; and then the baby's **cherished**[5] arrival after Siân's **barren**[6] years. Had her mother changed so much after John's birth?

Cad, frozen in thought, and despairing, knew she must act, and quickly.

Think Cad, think.

Neither friend spoke, for they would be heard. What Cad had **speculated**[7] about, and searched for, stood before them like a sleeping savage. A dormant **fiend**[8] preparing for battle. A demon which stared **willingly**[9] into the eyes of death.

Yet it wasn't the discovery of this deadly **invention**[10] that appalled Cad so. It wasn't the tangle of pipes, pumps and **bellows**[11], the forged metal and the wheels for legs that sickened her. It wasn't its **ferocious**[12] head, that of a dragon. Nor its **drooling**[13] jaws, teeth bared and a devil's **forked**[14] tongue, from where the **catastrophic**[15] liquid that blazed atop water would spout. It was not the fact that one of the men circling the **appliance**[16] was the **brute**[17] from whom she'd

---

1 **suspended** *(adj)* in an immobile state. *(s)* hanging, held, static.

2 **joyous** *(adj)* full of joy and happiness. *(s)* jolly, cheery, blissful. *(ant)* sad.

3 **meadow** *(n)* open grassland. *(s)* field, pasture.

4 **cosy** *(adj)* giving a feeling or air of comfort and warmth. *(s)* snug, homely. *(ant)* uncomfortable.

5 **cherish** *(v)* hold dear and protect. *(s)* treasure, adore, appreciate, value. *(ant)* neglect.

6 **barren** *(adj)* (of a female) not being with child (pregnant) and unable to become so. *(s)* childless.

7 **speculate** *(v)* form a theory without firm proof. *(s)* guess, surmise. *(ant)* confirm.

8 **fiend** *(n)* a cruel or wicked person or thing. *(s)* baddie, monster. *(ant)* hero, angel.

9 **willingly** *(adv)* in a willing (ready) manner. *(s)* readily, voluntarily. *(ant)* unwillingly.

10 **invention** *(n)* something made for the first time or an improvement upon. *(s)* innovation, creation.

11 **bellows** *(n)* squeezable airbags used for blowing a stream of air into a fire.

12 **ferocious** *(adj)* fierce. *(s)* vicious, aggressive, brutal, savage. *(ant)* gentle, mild.

13 **drool** *(v)* drop saliva (spit) from the mouth. *(s)* slobber, salivate.

14 **forked** *(adj)* having a divided or pronged end. *(s)* V-shaped, branched.

15 **catastrophic** *(adj)* extremely unfortunate and damaging. *(s)* calamitous, ruinous. *(ant)* beneficial.

16 **appliance** *(n)* a piece of equipment designed for a specific task. *(s)* machine, apparatus.

17 **brute** *(n)* a violent person. *(s)* barbarian, thug, savage, bully.

saved Bryn Davis those weeks back. The **stocky**[1], unknown **assailant**[2] she'd left for dead on the oubliette's floor.

Cad had expected to see the worst when entering the tent. To see her uncle Dewi, **parading**[3] his power. To see him wield the **might**[4] of the Gwalch Gem bracelet, and preparing for all-out annihilation. All of this she'd dreaded, yet expected. But nothing could have prepared her for the scenario **unfurling**[5] before her now – nothing.

Cad felt Rhys's tension **vibrate**[6] through their joined arms. He waited, quaking. He could do nothing more. The decision lay firmly at his friend's feet.

As a heat rose in Cad's chest, **resentment**[7] burning her throat, the **heavy-set**[8] man began to speak.

'Although the cipher is missing, our people believe the **blend**[9] to be correct; thus, the composition will work. We will test it today at the **secluded**[10] lake, so as not to attract attention, for its fire rages and its noise petrifies.'

He paused, **engaging**[11] his rapt audience, ensuring they listened to his every word.

'Then we will position it by the moat, within breathing range of the castle. The trebuchet will blow the wall to **smithereens**[12], then our **fiery**[13] friend here will rain **hell**[14] down upon them all.'

One listener, clearly in charge, eyes like those of an **executioner**[15], said nothing, but

---

1 **stocky** *(adj)* broad and heavily built. *(s)* stout, chunky, burly, hefty. *(ant)* slight, slender.

2 **assailant** *(n)* a person who physically harms or attacks another. *(s)* assaulter, aggressor. *(ant)* ally.

3 **parade** *(v)* display in order to attract attention or impress. *(s)* show off, flaunt.

4 **might** *(n)* impressive power. *(s)* strength, force, vigour. *(ant)* weakness, feebleness.

5 **unfurl** *(v)* reveal and become apparent. *(s)* unfold, present. *(ant)* end.

6 **vibrate** *(v)* shake. *(s)* tremble, quiver, quaver, tremor.

7 **resentment** *(n)* a feeling of indignation (anger) at unfair treatment. *(s)* hatred, bitterness. *(ant)* satisfaction.

8 **heavy-set** *(adj)* a broad and strongly built person or thing. *(s)* thick-set, stocky, sturdy. *(ant)* slight.

9 **blend** *(n)* a mixture of things. *(s)* combination, mix.

10 **secluded** *(adj)* private and sheltered. *(s)* isolated, quiet. *(ant)* public, busy.

11 **engage** *(v)* attract and occupy the attention of. *(s)* capture, seize, grab. *(ant)* lose.

12 **smithereens** *(n)* small pieces. *(s)* bits, fragments. *(ant)* whole, completeness.

13 **fiery** *(adj)* like fire. *(s)* hot, burning, scorching. *(ant)* cold.

14 **hell** *(n)* (of a religious belief) a place of suffering depicted by fire.

15 **executioner** *(n)* a person who carries out a death sentence on someone who is condemned.

smiled like a skull. The cold, **arresting**[1] eyes revealing nothing.

'Our spies continue to search for the cipher stolen from the imbeciles creating the liquid in the basement. We *will* find it, memorise it and destroy it. Then our people will **smuggle**[2] the compound from the castle tonight, and we will move the **siphon**[3] into position after that.' Bryn Davis's assailant looked most satisfied with himself. 'We attack tomorrow, after dark,' he finished.

Cad, the ground beneath her feet crumbling like eggshells, battled the urge to scream. Rage, a true sharp hate with teeth in it, roared within her as she fought the desire to stab her emerald hairpin through the culprit's heart.

Why? thought Cad, completely **baffled**[4]. *Why would you do this, unless you have gone stark raving mad?*

As Cad peered into the eyes of the army's commander, the person ordering the death of their own family, she found no answer. At that moment, Cad realised the eyes of the person she had once known were no longer alive, but dead. Changed, they had become the eyes of a stranger.

The once stunning green **beacons**[5] of love now shone with the **empathy**[6] of a **hangman**[7]. In that **desolate**[8] moment, Cad knew her family would never **reunite**[9]. She knew her dreams of a **reconciliation**[10] had blown away like dust in the wind. One look at those eyes and Cad's dreams had vanished, and her heart **splintered**[11] like a shattered lance. In that instant, like rain clouds parting to reveal a **shimmering**[12] sun, Cad knew exactly what she must now do.

As Cad eyed the emerald hawk earrings **glinting**[13] in her mother's ears, and as Siân Cadwaladr listened to her man, Cad vowed that no matter what, no matter when, she would

---

1 **arresting** *(adj)* attracting attention. *(s)* bewitching, engaging. *(ant)* repellent.

2 **smuggle** *(v)* move something secretly. *(s)* sneak, slip.

3 **siphon** *(n)* any of a variety of devices that involve the flow of liquids through tubes.

4 **baffled** *(adj)* totally confused. *(s)* bewildered, perplexed, confounded. *(ant)* enlightened.

5 **beacon** *(n)* a source of inspiration or light. *(s)* giver, provider.

6 **empathy** *(n)* the understanding of the feelings of another person. *(s)* compassion. *(ant)* disregard.

7 **hangman** *(n)* an executioner who hangs condemned people.

8 **desolate** *(adj)* very unhappy, melancholy, gloomy or lonely. *(s)* forlorn, dismal. *(ant)* joyful.

9 **reunite** *(v)* come or get back together. *(s)* reconcile, reunify. *(ant)* split, separate, estrange.

10 **reconciliation** *(n)* the repairing of friendly relations. *(s)* reuniting, reunion. *(ant)* estrangement.

11 **splinter** *(v)* break or cause to break into pieces. *(s)* shatter, split.

12 **shimmer** *(v)* shine. *(s)* twinkle, glisten, sparkle, glint. *(ant)* dull.

13 **glint** *(v)* give out a small gleam or flash of light. *(s)* glimmer, shine, shimmer, sparkle. *(ant)* dull.

help Llywelyn keep the bracelet from the hands of this mad woman forever.

Time to act, she thought.

Cad scanned the scene, and thankfully, in the **furore**[1] of Slippy's slithering, the guards had not quite closed the tent. Cad, Rhys and Slippy sneaked through, and out of the tent **undetected**[2].

Though neither friend realised at the time, as Cad had slipped her emerald hairpin back into her pocket, due to rage, despair and heartbreak, her hand had **misjudged**[3] its position. As she'd let go of the magical pin, it had **skimmed**[4] her pocket, falling onto the floor, where it would become visible. Little did Cad then know that many centuries would pass before she saw that emerald hairpin again.

---

1 **furore** *(n)* a disturbance caused by excitement or anger. *(s)* commotion, rumpus. *(ant)* tranquillity.

2 **undetected** *(adj)* not found or perceived. *(s)* unseen, unnoticed. *(ant)* detected, seen.

3 **misjudge** *(v)* form a wrong opinion of. *(s)* miscalculate, mistake. *(ant)* understand.

4 **skim** *(v)* move quickly through the air or on a surface. *(s)* glide, slide, sail.

CHAPTER TWENTY-THREE

The Archer

Cad, her tears now dried, had counted the steps from the tent back to the moat, noted how many, then **calculated**[1] the distance to the keep. This information was **crucial**[2] to her plan's success. The staircases of the keep's twin towers led to the top of the castle's walls and the crenels where the archers crouched, waiting for the army to advance. It mattered not; their arrows were **ineffectual**[3], because before one archer could draw back a bow, they would all be reduced to ashes.

Now in her room, Cad needed to work fast: there was little time. 'Dylan, you're by far the best archer amongst us. Do you think you could shoot a flaming arrow at a distant moving target and hit it?'

'What?' muttered Dylan, half asleep. 'I'm not *that* good at the butts.' He stretched, yawning. 'What's all this about?' He shook his head, oblivious to what Cad and Rhys had witnessed beyond Catrin's walls. There had been no time to explain yet.

To save Catrin, Cad must act now. How long it would take for her ring to refill with power was now a complete unknown, but she hoped that would be before nightfall. For her plan to succeed, they must strike at dusk. They must attack before Siân's henchmen and spies smuggled out the

1 **calculate** *(v)* determine mathematically or by reasoning. *(s)* establish, tally. *(ant)* guess.

2 **crucial** *(adj)* of absolute (complete) importance. *(s)* critical, vital, key. *(ant)* trivial.

3 **ineffectual** *(adj)* not producing a desired effect. *(s)* ineffective. *(ant)* effective.

barrels and pots needed to test their Greek-fire-breathing beast. To **ambush**[1] Siân tomorrow would be too late.

In this predicament, Cad would share nothing with the knights: no Owain Glyn, no Sir Robert, for she trusted no one. With nothing to lose, Cad would execute her plan. She knew not if her father lived, but if she did nothing, she would no longer be here to find out by tomorrow night. It was do, or die.

'Dylan, shake the sleep from your head and solve this cipher's puzzle. I need the **proportions**[2] of each ingredient. Those amounts are vital, and I need them *now*!'

Dylan's eyes widened as Cad continued whipping out orders.

'Rhys, you *must* sleep lest you fail to **function**[3]. And you, Dylan, then wake Rhys in two hours. Rhys, if he has not cracked the cipher by then, you must take over with that fresh head of yours.'

Cad was almost panting.

'What about you?' asked Rhys. 'You must get some sleep too. You've not fully recovered from your stupor.'

'I spent two days in that torpor, and if I don't succeed today, chances are I'll die tomorrow; I can sleep forever then,' said Cad **flippantly**[4], but feeling the opposite. Inside, her heart had shrivelled to the size of a plum.

'If *you* can skip sleep, then so can I,' replied Rhys. 'I'm an expert **night owl**[5], hence my chess **expertise**[6].'

Cad studied him, her heart swelling at the boy's **stoicism**[7]. She and he were cut from the same cloth.

'Well, there is no way *I* can fire a **longbow**[8] and hit a moving target with a flaming arrow,' Cad conceded. 'And neither can you.' In turn, she pointed at Rhys and Dylan. 'There's only one

---

1 **ambush** *(v)* make a surprise attack from a hidden position. *(s)* assault.

2 **proportion** *(n)* a part that makes up a whole. *(s)* amount, quantity. *(ant)* whole.

3 **function** *(v)* work in a specific way. *(s)* operate, perform. *(ant)* malfunction.

4 **flippantly** *(adv)* in an unserious way. *(s)* frivolously, jokingly, cheekily. *(ant)* seriously.

5 **night owl** *(n)* someone who is often wakeful or active at night.

6 **expertise** *(n)* expert knowledge or skill. *(s)* ability, prowess. *(ant)* inability.

7 **stoicism** *(n)* the quiet tolerance of hardship or discomfort. *(s)* fortitude, endurance. *(ant)* agitation.

8 **longbow** *(n)* a large bow for shooting arrows.

boy I know who is capable of that. He shines at the archery **butts**[1] and can split an apple at two hundred and fifty yards. But he might need some **persuading**[2]. Come, Rhys, if you're not going to sleep, you may as well help me with this one. Your **cajoling**[3] **charms**[4] **trump**[5] mine.'

Rhys jumped to attention, Slippy and a dagger at his belt. Cad hid her dagger in her tunic, where she could grab it if need be.

'What's all this about?' Dylan clutched the cipher.

'Dylan, I promise to tell all just as soon as I can, but right now, I need the exact quantities of that recipe's components.' Cad gestured towards the cipher in his hands. 'It's a matter of life and death. We'll return shortly, so please study it, solve it and then we act.'

Dylan nodded, disquiet in his eyes, as he pulled the bedding up to his neck, hiding the cipher he now read beneath it.

'Focus hard on this task. It's crucial,' said Cad.

Dylan's head popped up from beneath his blankets and nodded.

'Saviour's nails! I almost forgot the important part,' said Cad. 'When the physician calls by to see you shortly, you have a ghastly bout of worms and need a huge dose of vermifuge. But you don't take it; you keep it for me. Do you understand?' Cad inspected Dylan's face for **confirmation**[6] of what she'd asked.

'Yes.' Dylan nodded, but looked baffled.

'Come with us, Fishy. We might well need your powers of persuasion too,' said Cad, as she left with Rhys to seek out one of Catrin Castle's most **illustrious**[7] archers, the squire, Bryn Davis.

---

1 **butt** *(n)* an archery shooting target or range.

2 **persuade** *(v)* convince someone to do something by arguing or reasoning. *(s)* coax, cajole. *(ant)* dissuade.

3 **cajole** *(v)* persuade to do something by sustained coaxing. *(s)* entice, tempt. *(ant)* compel, force.

4 **charm** *(n)* the power of attracting or pleasing others. *(s)* appeal, charisma. *(ant)* unattractiveness.

5 **trump** *(v)* surpass (better). *(s)* beat, outdo, outshine. *(ant)* lose to.

6 **confirmation** *(n)* proof. *(s)* evidence, verification. *(ant)* denial.

7 **Illustrious** *(adj)* well known and respected for past achievements. *(s)* acclaimed. *(ant)* unknown.

CHAPTER TWENTY-FOUR

Blackmail

When Cad and Rhys marched up to Bryn, demanding an immediate private **audience**[1], the squire's expression hardened. A few moments passed before he paused from his duties. Then for a beat, he looked like he might laugh in their faces. It was only when the pages flashed their concealed daggers, and Fishy bared her huge **canines**[2] at Bryn, that he snapped orders at the boys who were preparing arrows beside him, and followed Cad and Rhys to a secluded **alcove**[3], Fishy softly padding along behind them.

Without preamble, Cad said, 'We know you cheated. In the joust, we know you cheated.'

Bryn stayed silent, but Cad saw his jaw **flex**[4].

'And we have proof of it,' **chimed in**[5] Rhys.

Bryn swallowed.

'How's your head these days?' asked Cad, with a **jut**[6] of her chin. 'After you *injured* it so badly a few weeks back.'

Not one to break easily, Bryn stayed silent.

---

1 **audience** *(n)* a meeting with a person or people. *(s)* interview, reception.

2 **canine** *(n)* a pointed tooth found towards the front of the mouth, often enlarged in carnivores (meat eaters).

3 **alcove** *(n)* a recess (hollow or indentation) in a wall. *(s)* niche, nook, bay. *(ant)* protrusion.

4 **flex** *(v)* move or extend through muscle contraction. *(s)* activate. *(ant)* relax.

5 **chime in** (phrase) join in a conversation. *(s)* interrupt, comment, contribute, add.

6 **jut** *(n)* a point that sticks out. *(s)* protrusion. *(ant)* retraction.

'I'm *sure* you'd remember such a dreadful beating?' Cad's tone **oozed**[1] with sarcasm as she cast a knowing glance at Rhys.

On the way over to find their archer, in view of what they were about to ask him to do, she'd told Rhys about Bryn's near-**fatal**[2] battering by the man who now fought alongside her mother.

'Well?' said Cad with impatience.

Bryn didn't answer her, but his eyes now flickered with unease.

Rhys turned to Bryn and, with nerves of steel, stared him out.

To Cad's astonishment, Bryn broke first.

It must be all that chess, she thought, admiring Rhys's **gall**[3].

'Proof! What *proof*?' spat Bryn, arrogance twisting his face.

Without taking his eyes from Bryn's, Rhys unfurled his fist. Two metal **bolts**[4] lay in his palm.

Bryn's eyes flitted to Cad, to the bolts, and back again.

'Bryn, you're looking a little **whey-faced**[5],' said Cad, with fire in her eyes.

Bryn flinched, as if to snatch the bolts from Rhys's palm, but Fishy flew at him so fast, the squire reeled, his footing faltering. Before Bryn blinked, Rhys had **stashed**[6] the evidence in his tunic: Cad had lent him one of hers, one with many covert pockets. Bryn Davis would need to **unpick**[7] each **seam**[8] to find those bolts.

'We have more than just those two,' said Cad. 'Rhys here removed all of them.'

Bryn stood his ground, but Cad saw him floundering.

'Bryn, it would seem you're a craven **coward**[9].' Cad's hand touched her dagger, Fishy guarding her. 'Had your armour not been bolted to your saddle when we jousted, a mere page such as I, on a pony, would have unseated you from your grand destrier.'

---

1 **ooze** *(v)* give a strong impression of. *(s)* exude, display, drip, exhibit, demonstrate.

2 **fatal** *(adj)* causing death. *(s)* lethal, deadly. *(ant)* harmless.

3 **gall** *(n)* bold and cheeky behaviour. *(s)* impudence, nerve. *(ant)* timidity.

4 **bolt** *(n)* a long pin with a head that screws into a nut, used to fasten things together.

5 **whey-faced** *(adj)* having a face the colour of whey (a pale yellowish liquid). *(s)* pallid. *(ant)* flushed.

6 **stash** *(v)* keep in a hidden place. *(s)* hide, conceal, stow, secrete. *(ant)* reveal, unpack.

7 **unpick** *(v)* undo the sewing of something, often stitch by stitch.

8 **seam** *(n)* a line formed where two pieces of fabric are sewn together. *(s)* join, closure.

9 **coward** *(n)* a person lacking bravery. *(s)* weakling, milksop, chicken. *(ant)* hero, heroine.

'And you ignored Cad's request for a **mercy pass**[1],' Rhys interjected, **contempt**[2] in his voice.

'What do you want?' Bryn eventually hissed through tight lips.

Cad pondered his question. How much of her plan should she reveal to him? Was Bryn Davis her mother's spy? Cad longed to discover the contrary.

'Your archery skills,' she finally said, gauging his reaction. Bryn looked genuinely surprised.

'Go on,' he said, lifting his chin.

Bryn was no fool, for Cad was sure he knew her to be a girl, and he would try to **goad**[3] her into capitulating first, but she wouldn't fall for his red herrings.

'If you want to live another day,' Cad paused, making sure she'd delivered that part slowly, 'then you must do as we ask with no questions.'

There it was; she'd said it. Cad studied Bryn's face. What was he thinking? Was he planning to run to tell Siân? Was he the one who would smuggle out the deadly Greek fire to fuel the dragon's fiery breath? Cad wished she had the time to use her ring. To follow him. To spy on him. But there was not time. If she didn't strike Siân tonight, they would all be ashes by the morrow. Bryn Davis posed a tremendous risk, but she had no choice. He was the only squire capable of firing a burning arrow at a moving target, and hitting it.

Bryn now stood stock-still, his hands on his hips, his face blank. He seemed to appraise Rhys, who glowered back, not flinching an inch. He squinted at Cad, then down at Fishy, who pulled her lips back over bared **fangs**[4].

Cad's heart bounced off her chest. She wore her straightest game-playing face, giving nothing away. Neither she nor Bryn had revealed to anyone, apart from Rhys, that she'd saved his hide that day. She suffered not one **iota**[5] of guilt over **blackmailing**[6] the squire thus. But would he walk away?

'What do you mean by "live another day"?' Bryn eventually asked, his interest **piqued**[7].

---

1 **mercy pass** *(n)* a sign given to indicate that an opponent wishes to end that particular jousting pass.

2 **contempt** *(n)* lack of respect. *(s)* disdain, scorn, dislike. *(ant)* admiration.

3 **goad** *(v)* annoy or provoke into a reaction. *(s)* badger, prod, push. *(ant)* calm.

4 **fang** *(n)* a long sharp tooth at the front of the mouth, especially a canine tooth in dogs.

5 **iota** *(n)* a tiny amount. *(s)* bit, jot, mite. *(ant)* lot.

6 **blackmail** *(v)* manipulate someone through threats. *(s)* extort, intimidate.

7 **pique** *(v)* arouse the interest or curiosity of someone. *(s)* rouse, stimulate. *(ant)* bore.

Got you, thought Cad, relieved.

Taking nothing **for granted**[1], Cad scoured Bryn's face for signs of deceit, her eyes **boring**[2] into his, but she saw only clouds of uncertainty dull their **vivid**[3] greenness. He was unaware of the Greek fire; she was sure. Since the day she'd saved his skin, whenever the opportunity arose, she'd checked his bruised face for clues of why someone had beaten him so. She recognised when Bryn's eyes revealed doubt, for she'd seen them up close. They showed that same uncertainty now: he knew not of Greek fire and she would take the risk.

Cad nodded at Rhys, who retrieved a pouch from his belt. This pouch didn't hold Slippy, but on oddly shaped **clay**[4] pot. A whiff of brimstone wafted by, and Bryn scowled at Rhys as though Rhys had released the deadliest of farts.

'It's not me, clod pate,' **retaliated**[5] Rhys, scowling back.

Cad, her eyes alight with **mirth**[6], and swallowing the most unwelcome of giggles, was astounded at Rhys's **audacious**[7] outburst.

Well, I never! Rhys price calling Bryn Davis a clod pate!

Bryn, face like **granite**[8], remained silent.

'It's brimstone,' said Cad, eyeing the clay pot.

Bryn screwed up his eyes, about to speak.

'Remember, no questions, please,' said Cad, trying to **appeal**[9] to the squire's better side, and if not that, his desire to live. 'We have little time. Can you fire a flaming arrow at a moving object up to two hundred and fifty yards away and hit the target?' asked Cad.

Bryn nodded, opening his mouth when Rhys said, 'No questions.'

Bryn nodded again.

'Good. Then tonight, you come to our quarters just before dusk. Beforehand, conceal your

---

1 **take for granted** *(v)* assume to be happening or given. *(s)* suppose, expect. *(ant)* disbelieve, doubt.

2 **bore** *(v)* drill a hole into (often used figuratively as it is here). *(s)* stare, penetrate.

3 **vivid** *(adj)* (of a colour) intensely deep or bright. *(s)* vibrant, radiant. *(ant)* dull, muted.

4 **clay** *(n)* a stiff and sticky soil that can be moulded when wet and baked into pots and such like. *(s)* earth.

5 **retaliate** *(v)* react to or fight back. *(s)* respond, retort, counter. *(ant)* excuse.

6 **mirth** *(n)* amusement. *(s)* cheer, merriment, glee. *(ant)* misery.

7 **audacious** *(adj)* daring and bold or showing a lack of respect. *(s)* brave, insolent. *(ant)* reticent, respectful.

8 **granite** *(n)* a hard rock often used as a building stone.

9 **appeal** *(v)* make a heartfelt request. *(s)* plead. *(ant)* discourage.

longbow up in the crenels overlooking the tilt yard, and be prepared to shoot flaming arrows before dark.'

'These will be your targets,' said Rhys, handing the small, stinking clay pot to Bryn.

'That won't be easy,' said Bryn, his eyes flitting between Cad and Rhys.

'No one said it would be easy,' said Cad, 'but you'll be saving Catrin Castle and all her **residents**[1].'

Bryn gulped, his eyes wide, his **pallor**[2] paler than before. Cad felt sure he knew nothing of Siân's plans.

'Is my target the giant trebuchet?'

Rhys looked at Cad, a moment passing between them.

'Yes,' Cad eventually said. 'The trebuchet is one of them.'

Bryn studied the young page before him.

Cad was sure she saw admiration in those searching green eyes, or did Bryn simply yearn to reveal her secret? Cad looked away. There was more to do than fathom Bryn Davis. For today, she must rely on him and, perhaps foolishly, assume he wasn't Siân's spy.

'Dusk,' Cad repeated to Bryn, before turning to Rhys and saying, 'Come, for we are in dire need of a physician.'

---

1 **resident** *(n)* a person who lives somewhere. *(s)* inhabitant, dweller, citizen.

2 **pallor** *(n)* a pale and unhealthy appearance. *(s)* sallowness, pastiness. *(ant)* rosiness.

CHAPTER TWENTY-FIVE

Sabotage and Chess

'We may be rid of Peggy and Goodwife Hughes, but if Owain Glyn finds me skulking around the castle, he'll lock me up.'

Cad and Rhys scuttled back to their quarters, armed with stinking worming potion.

'But the ring – will it refill before nightfall?'

'I don't know. As Dewi seems to have the bracelet some distance from us, it's impossible to gauge. We can't risk the wait; the **stakes**[1] are too high. I must try to avoid Owain.'

'Or distract him,' said Rhys, stifling a yawn, which Cad spotted. 'I'm fine. I'm fine,' he said too quickly, trying to hide it. 'Like you, I can sleep tomorrow.'

Cad appreciated, and feared, the **gravity**[2] of his words: if they failed tonight, there would be no tomorrow.

'Do you trust Davis?' Rhys sounded **sceptical**[3] of her decision to involve him.

She shot him a piercing look. 'I don't know, but in a few hours, we'll find out.'

Rhys didn't mention Bryn again. 'If your ring doesn't refuel in time, I could distract the knights while you go to the dungeons,' he said, with a shrug of his shoulders.

'What do you have in mind?' Cad frowned; it was her turn to sound sceptical now.

'Their love of chess.'

---

1 **stakes** *(n)* the risks. *(s)* consequences, threats.

2 **gravity** *(n)* seriousness. *(s)* importance, significance. *(ant)* triviality.

3 **sceptical** *(adj)* not easily convinced, having doubts. *(s)* dubious, uncertain. *(ant)* certain.

'Chess! We're under siege. My father is possibly dead. Are you mad? How can chess possibly help?'

'But that's the point,' replied Rhys, his voice kind. 'No one knows the attack is imminent.

It's broad daylight, and an **impromptu**[1] chess match, one of **tremendous**[2] **guile**[3] between two skilful players, would act as a fitting decoy.'

Cad's expression changed.

'The people would enjoy some secret gambling, and once the coin comes out, so will the dice. The **betting**[4] and the hard beer will both flow, and you'll be free to roam unnoticed.'

'My word!' Cad nodded in amazement. Rhys was right. She **assessed**[5] the bailey, which bustled with busy folks. They all appeared tense, **hunched**[6] and desperate for respite from boiling water **vessels**[7], assembling arrows, fixing armour, **salting**[8] foods, fearing for their lives.

'Which opponent do you have in mind?' asked Cad, as they approached the door to their quarters, a **gaggle**[9] of geese scattering at their feet.

'Why, our very own Dylan,' replied Rhys, as they entered their room.

Dylan must have heard his name because he shot out of bed.

'I think I understand the compound's quantities,' he **gushed**[10], beaming. 'What in God's name is this potion, for it will stink to high heaven?'

Cad and Rhys exchanged side-eyed looks, Cad signalling to Rhys with the slightest of head shakes.

'We're not sure,' she said quickly, 'but it burns.'

Cad felt dreadful keeping the truth from Dylan, but it was the best choice at this point. Why terrify her friend when all she needed from him was a decent chess game? The fewer people

---

1 **impromptu** *(adj)* done without prior planning. *(s)* spontaneous. *(ant)* planned.

2 **tremendous** *(adj)* extremely great in size or excellence. *(s)* immense, amazing. *(ant)* slight, small.

3 **guile** *(n)* clever or imaginative intelligence. *(s)* cunning, shrewdness. *(ant)* candour.

4 **betting** *(n)* the action of gambling on a game or such like for money. *(s)* speculating, chancing.

5 **assess** *(v)* evaluate or judge. *(s)* consider, gauge. *(ant)* misjudge.

6 **hunch** *(v)* lift the shoulders and bend the top of the body forward. *(s)* bow, stoop. *(ant)* straighten.

7 **vessel** *(n)* a container. *(s)* vat, barrel, cask, drum.

8 **salt** *(v)* preserve food using salt. *(s)* conserve.

9 **gaggle** *(n)* a flock of geese.

10 **gush** *(v)* speak quickly and enthusiastically. *(s)* enthuse, effuse, babble. *(ant)* drawl.

privy to the plan, the better; right now, that was her, Rhys and Bryn Davis.

'I suspect Goodwife Hughes and Peggy were making this potion. For whom, we don't know.'

Cad cast an eye towards Rhys as they placed their stinking vermifuge down on the table beside the dose that the physician had left for Dylan.

'By the way, I don't have worms,' cried Dylan, his face a picture of indignation. I had to persuade the physician that I was sure I do!

'Nor do we,' replied Cad. 'I'm sorry the physician had to inspect your rear.'

Cad winked, pretending that she and Rhys had suffered the same **fate**[1]. 'Needs must. In the place where we kept Fishy, there are barrels full of what Peggy and Mrs Hughes were making. I intend to **sabotage**[2] them.'

'With what?' asked Dylan, his face incredulous.

'With this,' Cad's nose wrinkled as the disgusting smell filled the room.

'I intend to pollute the barrels with brimstone, for that is what vermifuge is: brimstone. Too much of one component, and I hope the liquid will fail to **ignite**[3].'

Dylan gaped, looking amazed as she turned her attention to the cipher he'd handed to her.

'They won't detect **foul play**[4], for the smell is already foul.' Cad smiled at her play on words but didn't mention the clay pots that she wouldn't spoil. 'You've done a mighty fine job with this cipher; you are indeed sharp of mind,' said Cad with a grateful grin.

Dylan beamed back at his friend.

'So much so,' Rhys added, 'that you and I should play a well-deserved game of chess.' Rhys winked at Dylan, who would understand he meant a bout of chess that involved the exchange of coin.

'Come, Dylan,' Rhys called, collecting his prized chess set. 'Let us play outdoors in the bailey, for it is a beautiful day to gather bets from the guards. I will **stake**[5] the **wager**[6].' He wiggled his hips and jiggled the coins in the purse at his belt.

---

1 **fate** *(n)* an unavoidable outcome. *(s)* destiny, lot.

2 **sabotage** *(v)* deliberately damage or prevent something. *(s)* spoil, ruin. *(ant)* aid.

3 **ignite** *(v)* catch fire. *(s)* burn, light. *(ant)* extinguish.

4 **foul play** *(n)* criminal behaviour. *(s)* villainy, crime, wrongdoing.

5 **stake** *(v)* gamble (risk) money on the outcome of something. *(s)* pledge, wager.

6 **wager** *(n)* an act of betting money on the outcome of a game or unpredictable event. *(s)* stake, bet.

'Boys,' said Cad, as they left, 'keep an eye out for May. When you see her arrive in the bailey, bring your game to a fitting end and fire up the crowd. Then start another game and get them throwing dice and betting on arm-wrestling. By then, the guards will be thirsty for strong beer. I need all eyes off me and on the coin they hope to win.'

'Understood,' said Rhys, with a **mock**[1] **salute**[2], as he ushered Dylan through the door, giving him no chance to speak or protest.

When the boys had gone, Cad took both ciphers and placed them on the table. One parchment held the trebuchet's plans, the other, the **supposedly**[3] long-lost recipe for Greek fire.

Then, Cad rinsed her face, ate some bread and cheese and, although exhausted, sat at the table and memorised every last **digit**[4], symbol, mark and meaning of the Greek-fire cipher. When satisfied she'd lodged all meanings in her mind, she hid the trebuchet's plan away but held the other above the metal plate whence she'd taken her cheese. Grasping its edge, she picked up a candle and held its flame to the vellum's curled corners. It took but a moment to light. Cad's eyes followed the flames as they licked and danced, turning the parchment black, its hot remains fluttering down onto the plate beneath them.

Mesmerised[5], she watched the cipher burn, willing fate to **decree**[6] that no other parchments held the deadly instructions for Greek fire, the secret Byzantine weapon that **Emperor**[7] Romanos, its first user, had vowed would never reach foreign hands for fear of its devastating effects if turned on its creators.

Aware of the horrors wielded by this wildly **destructive**[8] weapon, Cad didn't want it to fall into another's hands, especially those of her mother and uncle. With Greek fire and the power of the Gwalch Gem bracelet in their control, the world would be an **abominable**[9] place. Whether her father lived or died, she would not let that happen.

---

1 **mock** *(adj)* not real. *(s)* imitation, simulated. *(ant)* real.

2 **salute** *(n)* a raising of the hand to the head in formal recognition of someone. *(s)* acknowledgement. *(ant)* shun.

3 **supposedly** *(adv)* believed. *(s)* apparently, allegedly. *(ant)* unlikely.

4 **digit** *(n)* a number represented by a single symbol used alone or in combinations.

5 **mesmerise** *(v)* hold the complete attention of. *(s)* captivate, enthral. *(ant)* bore.

6 **decree** *(v)* to order by decree (usually having the force of law). *(s)* command, dictate.

7 **emperor** *(n)* a ruler of an empire. *(s)* sovereign, monarch.

8 **destructive** *(adj)* causing huge damage. *(s)* ruinous. *(ant)* constructive, beneficial.

9 **abominable** *(adj)* extremely bad. *(s)* dreadful, appalling. *(ant)* admirable, good.

With **uncharacteristic**[1] patience, Cad waited until the parchment was **nought**[2] but black ash. Then she extinguished the candle, walked over to her bed, beckoned Fishy onto it, and rested against her pillows. She would allow herself a quick nap.

'Fishy,' she said, staring at her dog, 'don't let me sleep too long.'

Fishy's tongue **lapped**[3] lovingly at Cad's face in response, as Cad hoped her body's rhythms would wake her in good time to execute her plan.

---

1 **uncharacteristic** *(adj)* in a way that is not usual. *(s)* unexpected, novel. *(ant)* characteristic.

2 **nought** (pronoun) nothing. *(s)* naught.

3 **lap** *(v)* lick repeatedly and especially noisily. *(s)* wash, slap, slosh.

CHAPTER TWENTY-SIX

Secret Sacks

Cad woke feeling like death itself. May squawked as Fishy licked Cad's face. Both had ensured she would not sleep too long. It was daytime, and to her pets, sleeping in the light meant either sickness or 'wake up soon'. Cad had trained them well.

Still dressed in the tunic she'd worn since visiting Owain Glyn, she sniffed. It wasn't pleasant but what did she care? Catrin was under siege. There would be **ample**[1] time to wash tomorrow, if tomorrow ever came.

With a gaping yawn, Cad rose, walked over to the table, and picked up the plate that held the cipher's burned ashes. To ensure they weren't discovered, she mixed their blackened remains with the reeds on the floor.

Thankful for small mercies[2], she eyed the vial by her bed. The ever-**dependable**[3] Rhys had left her a tad more potion to dull the pain in her ribs. She hoped it wouldn't **blunt**[4] her wits too much. However, she remained confident, as the dose she'd taken earlier had seemed **adequate**[5].

Although wrought with anxiety, Cad quashed the shaky sensation, **securing**[6] the bandages

---

1 **ample** *(adj)* enough or more than enough. *(s)* abundant, plenty. *(ant)* insufficient, meagre.

2 **thankful for small mercies** (phrase) grateful that one's situation is not as bad as it might be.

3 **dependable** *(adj)* reliable and trustworthy. *(s)* unfailing, steadfast, loyal. *(ant)* unreliable.

4 **blunt** *(v)* weaken the power of. *(s)* dull, deaden. *(ant)* sharpen, intensify.

5 **adequate** *(adj)* enough or good enough. *(s)* satisfactory, sufficient. *(ant)* inadequate.

6 **secure** *(v)* fix, attach or fasten firmly. *(s)* tighten. *(ant)* open.

nursing her ribs and strapping the dagger to her belt, which she then obscured with her tunic. How long before they discovered these daggers missing, she neither knew nor cared. She would deal with that **snag**[1] if it arose. Right now, she would pay her pony a swift visit and do her **utmost**[2] to sneak past the crowd gathered at the chessboard in the bailey.

Peeping through the door, she saw that the boys had **exercised**[3] the **wisdom**[4] to play in a quiet corner near the chapel's entrance. Because of this, Cad could reach the stables and then double back to the keep unseen. She could not say the same for the gate which led beneath the gardens and moat and out into the occupied tilt yard. But that mattered not, for if she left the castle again, she must use her ring, lest an arrow greet her the minute she did so.

Had Cad been stronger of mind and body, and not poisoned, she might have risked masquerading as a spy and duping the soldiers on the other side of Catrin's walls. But as beleaguered as she was, she must risk her ring instead, and have **faith**[5] that its powers might last long enough to see out her plan.

Cad opened her door and **wedged**[6] a stone in the bottom of its jamb, leaving it just wide enough for Fishy's nose to push open. Then she beckoned May into the yard and signalled for her to hide and wait. May feared falconers, and was the master of hiding in plain sight, fleeing Cad's room whenever folks approached. Hence, Cad's shuttered windows were **seldom**[7] locked. May came and went as she pleased. But today, Cad needed May to hear her calls. For without May's help, tonight's plan would be scuppered.

Time was now critical. Aware of this, Cad **sidled**[8] out of her room, sticking close to the walls. She bristled as she passed the **barricaded**[9] well where she'd almost drowned but a few days back; the castle's residents were still oblivious to its traitorous poisoning. Owain Glyn had avoided

---

1 **snag** *(n)* an unexpected problem. *(s)* issue, hitch, obstacle. *(ant)* boon, benefit.

2 **utmost** *(n)* the greatest extent. *(s)* best. *(ant)* worst.

3 **exercise** *(v)* apply. *(s)* employ, utilise, use.

4 **wisdom** *(n)* the quality of having experience or good judgement. *(s)* intelligence, insight. *(ant)* foolishness.

5 **faith** *(n)* trust and belief. *(s)* confidence, hope. *(ant)* mistrust.

6 **wedge** *(v)* force or place into a tight space. *(s)* jam, shove, stuff.

7 **seldom** *(adv)* not often. *(s)* hardly ever, rarely, scarcely. *(ant)* often.

8 **sidle** *(v)* walk in a furtive (secretive) manner. *(s)* slink, edge. *(ant)* stride.

9 **barricade** *(v)* defend or block with a barricade (barrier). *(s)* blockade. *(ant)* open.

panic, keeping that fact concealed, and Cad deemed him right to do so. But it mattered not: if her plan failed, there would be few occupants left at Catrin in need of water.

*

'Flash,' cried Cad, having navigated the bailey and into the stables unseen. 'Flashy,' she gushed, patting her pony's neck and inhaling her **heavenly**[1] smell. Cad glanced down and noticed Flash's water pail was but a third full. Cad swallowed hard, that sight reminding her how horribly grave the situation was.

'Cad,' sang a cheery voice from behind her, 'what are you doing here?'

Cad twirled to see Ellis Williams's grinning face.

'I thought you were **confined**[2] to your room?'

'I am,' whispered Cad. 'You've not seen me.' She winked at Ellis with a knowing grin.

'Of course not,' he laughed, plonking down a bucket with a slosh.

Cad looked at it, her face serious.

'Her water needs a top-up,' said Ellis, **motioning**[3] at Cad to move.

Cad watched as Ellis poured the liquid life into her pony's bucket.

'Not betting on the chess match?' Cad asked, searching for the opportune time to approach Ellis.

'I've no interest in it. I don't even wager on the jousts. How are you?' Ellis pointed to Cad's ribs.

'Much improved,' she lied, thanking the potion for dulling her pain. 'Ellis,' she said, her voice tiptoeing forward.

'Yes,' he chirped, filling Flash's **manger**[4] with golden hay.

'Do you trust me?'

Ellis halted his labours and met her gaze, his brow furrowed at her incongruous question.

'Well, yes. Of course,' he answered, clearly confused.

Cad supposed he'd never needed to think of this before.

'The thing is, I see you with my pony. I see you with the other horses. You have a good heart.'

---

1 **heavenly** *(adj)* very pleasing. *(s)* glorious, wonderful. *(ant)* dreadful.

2 **confine** *(v)* keep within certain limits. *(s)* enclose, imprison. *(ant)* release.

3 **motion** *(v)* direct with a movement of the hand or head. *(s)* gesture, signal, beckon.

4 **manger** *(n)* a trough from which animals feed. *(s)* feeder, crib, fodder rack.

Ellis peered at her, his eyes narrowing.

'So, I trust *you.*'

Ellis turned to face her fully but said nothing. Cad swiftly scanned the stables, stepping outside of Flash's stall, and back in before continuing.

'I need a favour, but you cannot ask me why. Please, trust me **implicitly**[1].'

The boy's eyes widened, but he gave a brief nod.

'I need you to meet me outside the keep, and bring Flash with you.'

Ellis frowned.

'You can pretend you're taking her to the **smithy**[2] to have a loose shoe nailed.'

Ellis still didn't speak, but Cad continued.

'Bring her **rugged**[3], for I need her to carry some sacks which we must quickly conceal beneath the rug.'

Ellis looked at Flash and the giant destrier, Midnight, who pawed at the straw in his stall.

'How will I know when to bring Flash?' was all that the good egg, Ellis Williams, asked.

'I'll send May in here as a signal for you to leave.'

'May! Who's May?'

'My **goshawk**[4].'

Ellis's mouth dropped open.

'May will swoop in and land on Flash's rear, but she'll stay only a short while, so keep an eye open for her. Flash will likely **neigh**[5]. May's done this many times **afore**[6].'

'You have a goshawk?' Ellis marvelled.

'Yes. A blind one,' said Cad, smiling. 'I'll tell you more tomorrow,' she added, trying to believe there would be a morrow.

'As soon as you see May, bring Flash into the bailey, to the foot of the keep. I'll hide there until

---

1 **implicitly** *(adv)* in an implicit (absolute) way. *(s)* completely. *(ant)* restrictedly.

2 **smithy** *(n)* a blacksmith's (a person who works with metals) workshop. *(s)* forge.

3 **rugged** *(adj)* (of a horse) having a rug placed over the horse to keep it warm or dry.

4 **goshawk** *(n)* a large white-grey hawk with cream coloured underwings. *(s)* raptor.

5 **neigh** *(v)* make a whinnying sound like that of a horse. *(s)* bray, nicker, whicker.

6 **afore** *(prep)* before.

I see you. May's presence will signal the boys to bring their match to a fitting **finale**[1]. The game will **divert**[2] folks' attention from us.'

Ellis nodded, listening as though his life depended on it. Which, of course, unbeknownst to him, it did.

'Once we load Flash with the sacks, you take them back to the stables and hide them where they'll be safe, **accessible**[3] only to me.'

'I'll cover them with a rug at the back of the **tack**[4] room,' said Ellis. 'That's near the rear door, should you need a swift exit.'

'Wise boy,' replied Cad, remembering he'd been there when the sinister monk had **unnerved**[5] the horses. Though at the time, Ellis had not spotted the hooded figure, thinking a fox had been the culprit.

'I'll return at dusk to retrieve the sacks. I don't know yet if I'll need her, but have Flashy tacked up for me, ready to ride. And use Bryn Davis's tack. You'll need new bolts for the saddle.'

'Bolts?' Ellis's jaw dropped.

'Long story. But yes. Bolts to secure me to his saddle. You'll see the holes if you look closely enough. Don't ask,' she finished, seeing his mouth ready to speak. 'I'll explain another time.'

'But Cad, you can't ride with broken ribs. It will be agony, and you might fall again.'

'Let me decide that,' Cad said, knowing she still had a tad of remaining potion **at her disposal**[6].

Ellis raised his arms, his face screwed up. 'But you can't leave the castle because of the siege. Why do you need Flash?'

'No questions, please,' said Cad, a **beseeching**[7] **note**[8] to her voice. 'Flash *must* wear Bryn's saddle. It will be too big, so tighten her **girth**[9] well.'

---

1 **finale** *(n)* the (dramatic) last part of something. *(s)* end, climax, conclusion. *(ant)* beginning.

2 **divert** *(v)* draw the attention of someone away from something. *(s)* distract, redirect. *(ant)* focus.

3 **accessible** *(adj)* able to be reached. *(s)* handy, available. *(ant)* inaccessible.

4 **tack** *(n)* the equipment used for horse riding.

5 **unnerved** *(adj)* made to lose confidence or courage. *(s)* alarmed, worried. *(ant)* encouraged.

6 **at one's disposal** (phrase) available to use as one wishes.

7 **beseech** *(v)* ask someone urgently or fervently. *(s)* implore, beg, plead. *(ant)* offer.

8 **note** *(n)* a sound or tone that expresses feelings or attitude. *(s)* intonation, inflection.

9 **girth** *(n)* a strap attached to a saddle and fastened around a horse's fore belly to hold the saddle in place.

Ellis sighed, and stroked Flash on her velvet **muzzle**[1].

'Are you sure you're happy to help me?' asked Cad, genuinely concerned at having to involve such an innocent and kind page as Ellis.

'If it involves Flash, I'm in,' he said with a **courageous**[2] smile, which Cad saw clean through.

'Thank you,' she said, touching his shoulder. 'I'll never forget your kindness. And I promise, I'll explain more when I can.'

Before she made to leave, she gave her beloved Flash, and the **brooding**[3] Midnight, a last pat. Ellis waited, then picked up the empty pail.

'Oh, and by the way,' Cad turned back to face Ellis, 'the sacks will stink of farts. Blame it on Flash's backside if folks ask.'

Ellis shook his head in silence, but grinned at Cad, who smiled back.

It was time to collect the all-important vermifuge from her room. After that, she would head to the keep and into the dungeons, where she would start the big boulder rolling down the hill.

---

1 **muzzle** *(n)* the nose and mouth of an animal. *(s)* snout.

2 **courageous** *(adj)* undeterred by danger or pain. *(s)* brave, plucky. *(ant)* cowardly, timid.

3 **brood** *(v)* sulk (be bad tempered). *(s)* mope, pine. *(ant)* be content.

CHAPTER TWENTY-SEVEN

Sabotage

To Cad's dismay, sabotaging the barrels of Greek fire with worming medicine proved to be more difficult than anticipated, and she'd feared that dusk would arrive before she finished. Yet this had not been a task to rush, and there had been many barrels to pollute.

Using her dagger, she'd **carved**[1] out a tiny hole in the top of each barrel, then placed in a thin reed. With her mouth full of the **vile**[2]-tasting vermifuge, she'd blown it through the reed and into the barrels until her cheeks ached, willing it to do the trick. If her **overall**[3] plan succeeded, the traitors would **abandon**[4] these barrels, for their waiting **recipient**[5], Siân, would no longer be able to reach them. But just in case it failed, Cad had **sullied**[6] each barrel and burned the Greek fire recipe **to boot**[7]. No one would get their hands on that now.

Cad grinned. After **ingesting**[8] this amount of vermifuge, even if Cad survived a Greek fire

---

1 **carve** *(v)* cut a hard material, often to make an object or design. *(s)* sculpt, form.

2 **vile** *(adj)* very unpleasant. *(s)* nasty, foul, horrid. *(ant)* pleasant.

3 **overall** *(adj)* taking all into account. *(s)* master.

4 **abandon** *(v)* leave alone or behind. *(s)* discard, forsake, ditch, dump. *(ant)* keep.

5 **recipient** *(n)* a person or thing that receives something. *(s)* receiver. *(ant)* giver, donor.

6 **sully** *(v)* spoil or pollute. *(s)* contaminate, taint, mar. *(ant)* purify.

7 **to boot** (phrase) in addition to. *(s)* also, as well.

8 **ingest** *(v)* swallow or absorb into the body. *(s)* consume, eat.

attack, she would spend tomorrow with her rear fixed to a **latrine**[1], and not a worm in sight for miles.

Now back up in the keep, and exhausted by her work with the barrels, Cad skulked in a stinky corner where lazy guards often **urinated**[2]. Because it stank, no one bothered her. Folks ignored the **scruffy**[3], somewhat smelly page, cap over his eyes, hauling sacks of goodness knows what up from the lower floors. Whilst a siege ensued, the **abnormal**[4] became **commonplace**[5]. Besides, many were busy betting on the chess match, the dice and the arm-wrestling stirred up by the boys. With Llywelyn away, the cats would play, and Owain Glyn and Sir Robert were, fortuitously, nowhere to be seen.

Cad had filled two sacks with the clay pots that she had previously tripped over in Fishy's room. With broken ribs, hauling the pots up through the long passageways on her own was slow and painful going. Now forced to work alone, she trusted only her three friends, all of whom were occupied elsewhere. She was already **out on a limb**[6] relying on Bryn Davis, but that would be just this once. Anyway, they might all be ashes by tomorrow. With time now pressing, Cad longed for Bryn to show up, and without Siân **in his midst**[7]. Her stomach swirled at that thought.

Outside the keep, Cad shooed away some waddling ducks, and side-stepping their droppings, gave the shrillest of whistles before moving back inside. Two **burly**[8] guards clattered down the internal stairs, apparently eager to join the now **raucous**[9] games. Fortunately, they didn't care a jot for Cad's presence. She relaxed a mite, exhaling with relief then breathing hard. Time seemed to stand still as her gaze darted in every direction, **pre-empting**[10] threat as she waited for May to arrive.

Come on, May!

---

1 **latrine** *(n)* a toilet, especially a communal (shared by many) one.

2 **urinate** *(v)* pass waste water from the bladder. *(s)* wee, pee.

3 **scruffy** *(adj)* untidy or dirty. *(s)* bedraggled, messy, dishevelled. *(ant)* tidy, neat.

4 **abnormal** *(adj)* anything that is not the normal way or situation. *(s)* unusual, uncommon. *(ant)* normal.

5 **commonplace** *(adj)* usual. *(s)* normal, ordinary, routine. *(ant)* unusual, abnormal.

6 **out on a limb** (phrase) at risk. *(s)* vulnerable. *(ant)* strong, secure.

7 **in his midst** (phrase) near him. *(s)* with him, around him, in his group.

8 **burly** *(adj)* large and strong. *(s)* sturdy, strapping, brawny. *(ant)* puny, weedy, weak.

9 **raucous** *(adj)* making a harsh, loud noise. *(s)* boisterous, unruly. *(ant)* orderly, placid.

10 **pre-empt** *(v)* take action to prevent something happening. *(s)* anticipate.

After what seemed ages, cheers and **jeers**[1] grew from the games as guards won and lost their **illicit**[2] bets. Back to the wall, Cad still waited. To steady her thoughts, she counted in her head, when to her utter relief, May **glided**[3] from the sky and into the keep, landing on Cad's shoulder with aplomb. Cad fed the goshawk pork fat, stroked her head, and said, 'Flash. Go now. Find Flash.'

And with that, May sailed away on her short flight across the bailey and into the stables.

Cad stilled, but her body vibrated with tension as she waited for Ellis to lead Flash to the keep. All the while, she mentally urged the **pandemonium**[4] from the games to divert any unwanted attention.

The waiting almost killed Cad, her chest so tight it hurt. What little time slipped by felt like aeons. Cad surveyed the bailey, then the full sacks, and the bailey again.

'Come on, Ellis,' she muttered, fidgeting, knowing May would have landed on Flash's **rump**[5] and taken off again by now. It was a trick she'd taught May for fun, showing off to Dylan and Rhys. Little had Cad known then how crucial that trick would turn out to be.

By the chapel, the noise from the gambling quietened, and Cad hoped the boys' guile would persuade the guards to continue betting.

'Come on, Ellis,' she urged, dancing from foot to foot. She grabbed the sacks in anticipation of his arrival, knowing that if someone stopped her, she'd have much explaining to do.

Now frantic with apprehension, Cad peeped into the bailey again, but Ellis and Flash were nowhere to be seen. To carry both sacks across the bailey would cripple her ribs, but there was no way she'd get away with making two journeys. Nor did she have time to do so if she was to meet Bryn in her quarters before dusk. But it seemed Ellis wasn't coming with Flash, so she must at least try.

With little choice, Cad waited until the coast cleared, then hauled the sacks onto the stairs leading to the upper floors. When disturbed, the sacks stank like nasty farts, and would draw attention from the ladies above if Cad didn't get into the open at once.

---

1 **jeer** *(n)* a rude remark. *(s)* boo, hiss, jibe. *(ant)* cheer, compliment.

2 **illicit** *(adj)* not allowed or illegal. *(s)* forbidden, banned. *(ant)* allowed, permitted.

3 **glide** *(v)* move smoothly and continuously. *(s)* sail, float, drift. *(ant)* hurtle, careen.

4 **pandemonium** *(n)* noisy disorder and confusion. *(s)* chaos, uproar, tumult. *(ant)* calm, order.

5 **rump** *(n)* the hind part or backside of a mammal. *(s)* rear, bottom, behind, buttocks.

Cad squatted, desperately trying to protect the pots. She twisted her body as her ribs screamed in pain, and managed to grab one sack. Then she yanked it up over her shoulder and did the same for the second.

'Save us all!' she cursed, breathing through the pain, which even the potion couldn't now quell. Somewhat wobbly, Cad balanced the sacks over each shoulder, gripping them just below her **collarbones**[1]. On the count of three, she hauled herself to her feet. As she stood, one sack **dislodged**[2] its position with a clatter. Sickened, Cad waited for the sound of smashing pots, but none came. It seemed luck had granted a **reprieve**[3]. She planted both feet hard, regaining her balance to ensure the sacks were as stable as possible. Then with tentative steps, she exited into the bailey.

Once outside, Cad made sure her cap hid her eyes. Head down, she **doddered**[4] out and towards the stables where, to her huge relief, she heard the clip-clop of Flash's shoes. So relieved, Cad looked up to see a flush-faced Ellis leading Flash by a **halter**[5], his eyes wide, his face sweaty. One look at him, and Cad saw something was amiss. She quickened her pace, putting as much distance as she could between herself and the guards spectating the games. The moment she reached Ellis, their eyes met, but Cad quickly shook her head to silence him.

Without speaking, Ellis lifted Flash's rug, hung the sacks from either side, **tethered**[6] them with a **rein**[7], and **slung**[8] the rug back over before anyone looked their way. Ellis turned Flash to lead her to the stables, but before he did, he whispered, 'Hugh Hughes was sniffing around the **stalls**[9] just now. I couldn't leave sooner for him asking questions.'

On hearing that name, Cad thought of Goodwife Hughes and what might have become of her. Where were she and Peggy hiding while nursing their wounds? But this being the wrong

1 **collarbone** *(n)* one of the two bones joining the breastbone to the shoulder blades.

2 **dislodge** *(v)* force or knock out of position. *(s)* displace, move, shift.

3 **reprieve** *(n)* a cancellation or postponement (delay) of something unpleasant. *(s)* let-off *(ant)* continuation.

4 **dodder** *(v)* move in an unsteady way. *(s)* hobble, shuffle, totter. *(s)* stride.

5 **halter** *(n)* a rope or strap fitted around the head of an animal used for leading or tethering it. *(s)* head collar.

6 **tether** *(v)* tie something up to restrict movement, fix securely. *(s)* fasten, bind. *(ant)* untie, release.

7 **rein** *(n)* a strap attached to a horse's bit or head-collar, often used in pairs to guide a horse by its rider or leader.

8 **sling** *(v)* (informal) throw (past tense: slung). *(s)* fling, chuck, toss.

9 **stall** *(n)* a holding compartment for an animal, enclosed on three sides. *(s)* cubicle.

time for **speculation**[1], she shook the questions from her head. Then signalling Ellis to go, Cad lifted her chin, pointing it towards the stables.

On her way back to her room, Cad blinked at the sun's glare, which hung low in the sky. She thanked the heavens it was a dry night. It would soon be dusk. At least the boys were succeeding because merry cheers rose from the corner as guards **swigged**[2] beer and rubbed their hands together, **gleeful**[3] at the thought of the coin they would win.

Wet-faced women still stirred drums of boiling water, their filthy children playing at their feet. The castle's **standards**[4] had slipped in these siege days. Folks ate when and where they could. Mealtimes in the great hall were **haphazard**[5] and rushed. Cad wondered why she'd seen neither Sir Robert nor Owain Glyn recently. Were they secretly plotting with Dewi and Siân? Cad hoped with all her heart they were not. As Cad strode through the bailey towards her room, as if to torment her, Llywelyn's face sprang into her mind, but it was too unbearable and she pushed him away. She would consider her father's whereabouts tomorrow, if she were still here, that was. Right now, heading back, her step surprisingly light considering her predicament, she thought of Bryn and hoped he would appear before dusk,

Cad admitted that her hands were tied, and that she could do little else now. The plan depended on her, Bryn Davis and May, only two of whom Cad could trust for sure.

---

1 **speculation** *(n)* the forming of a view without firm evidence. *(s)* guesswork, conjecture. *(ant)* reality.

2 **swig** *(v)* drink in big gulps. *(s)* guzzle. *(ant)* sip.

3 **gleeful** *(adj)* very pleased. *(s)* delighted, joyful. *(ant)* miserable, glum.

4 **standard** *(n)* the level of quality or attainment of someone or something. *(s)* excellence.

5 **haphazard** *(adj)* lacking organisation. *(s)* random, chaotic. *(ant)* methodical.

CHAPTER TWENTY-EIGHT

On Tenterhooks

Cad **loathed**[1] the **confines**[2] of her room, and now flopped on her bed, ran through a checklist in her head. **Loyal**[3] Fishy lay beside Cad, head resting between her front paws. All was in place; she could do nothing more now but wait for Bryn to arrive and try to block out the sounds of **merriment**[4] rising from the other side of the bailey, where her friends played chess, dice and arm-wrestling as a decoy.

Rhys's idea had worked a treat. The guards and siege-weary castle folks seemed thrilled to have some respite from the terrifying thoughts of attack. Little did they know someone had poisoned their water supply, and a giant machine was poised to hurl boulders the size of the moon at them. Then after that, even Catrin's moat would burn like hell's **furnace**[5] as the army invaded with a fire-breathing monster to **incinerate**[6] all who lived there. Cad shuddered, pulling Fishy closer to her. May perched on the foot of Cad's bed, her head cocked, twisting at the slightest of sounds.

---

1 **loathe** *(v)* feel intense dislike or disgust for. *(s)* hate, despise, detest. *(ant)* adore, love.

2 **confines** (plural noun) the borders of a place with regard to restricted freedom. *(s)* limits, boundaries.

3 **loyal** *(adj)* remaining consistent and true. *(s)* trusty, reliable, dependable, faithful. *(ant)* disloyal.

4 **merriment** *(n)* fun, gaiety and high spirits. *(s)* cheer, joy. *(ant)* misery.

5 **furnace** *(n)* an extremely hot place. *(s)* fire.

6 **incinerate** *(v)* destroy by burning. *(s)* burn.

Cad sniffed. She still wore her stinky tunic. There'd been no time for **vanity**[1]; she had much bigger fish to fry. Her dagger was still at her belt, her emerald ring on her right thumb, where it would remain **idle**[2] until switched to the left. She sipped at some water, and prayed the remnants of vermifuge she'd inadvertently swallowed while sabotaging the barrels, would stay in her **bowels**[3] a while longer. Cad thought of Rhys as she downed the very last of the pain-killing potion from the vial. Gagging at its vile taste, she stood, and with the one clay pot she'd brought from the dungeons, began to practise the **manoeuvres**[4] with May.

May learned fast, and the clay pot she must carry was lighter than a **coney**[5], so it should be easy for her. May needed to feel for the grip required for the perfect **purchase**[6] of the clay containers. It didn't take long, as Cad had **presumed**[7]. After a few test runs, May alighted back whence she came, at the foot of Cad's bed, head twitching to the sounds in the bailey beyond.

Up and down like a **jack-in-the-box**[8], Cad checked the bailey from behind the open shutters of her window. No sign of Bryn, and dusk was closing in. Her chest tightened with unexpected sorrow, and an overwhelming wave of remorse and **melancholy**[9] crushed her. How rash she'd been to involve Bryn Davis. How reckless to involve the squire she was certain had cheated in a joust to reveal her true gender. The squire she had shot with her sling, and spent time for in the tower. The squire who loathed her.

Cad's head fell into her hands. Pain, regret and fear crippled her. What had she done? How foolish she'd been to think Bryn would help her.

In her despair, she almost missed the batting of wings and air swooshing past her cheek, but both snapped her from misery. May had flown out through the open window. Someone was approaching. Cad's heart flipped. Who was it? She almost dared not look beyond the wooden slats, lest it be Rhys, Dylan or even Owain Glyn approaching. Her heart thudded as her gaze slid

---

1 **vanity** *(n)* too much pride in one's own achievement or appearance. *(s)* narcissism, conceit. *(ant)* modesty.

2 **idle** *(adj)* currently not working. *(s)* dormant, inactive, unoccupied. *(ant)* working.

3 **bowel** *(n)* the guts below the stomach. *(s)* insides, innards.

4 **manoeuvre** *(n)* one or several movements requiring care and skill. *(s)* action, procedure, exercise.

5 **coney** *(n)* a rabbit. *(s)* bunny.

6 **purchase** *(n)* a firm contact or grip. *(s)* hold, toehold. *(ant)* release.

7 **presume** *(v)* assume something but without certainty. *(s)* suppose. *(ant)* confirm.

8 **jack-in-the-box** *(n)* a toy in a box which jumps up via a spring when the lid is opened.

9 **melancholy** *(n)* sadness. *(s)* sorrow, woe, desolation, gloom. *(ant)* happiness.

towards the bailey. Was it him? With horrid doubt, she peeked through the shutter's gaps.

Taken aback by her reaction, Cad gasped as she caught a glimpse of Bryn striding towards her door, carrying a lit lantern in one hand and a sack in the other, his **brazen**[1] demeanour, wide shoulders and **bold**[2] stride revealing nothing of her plan, although he knew not exactly *all* that it **entailed**[3]. Not yet.

All of a dither[4], Cad snatched open the door before he knocked, and beckoned him inside. Set to blurt out, 'You came,' she thought better of it.

A low growl **gurgled**[5] from Fishy's throat, who had shot to Cad's side the moment Bryn entered.

Bryn glared at Cad, his eyes saying, *Call off your dog.*

'Off, Fishy,' said Cad, gesturing to her dog that for now, Bryn was friend not foe.

Bryn sniffed, his nose wrinkling in disgust. 'Your dog farted, or was it you?' He took a step away from Fishy.

Cad ignored his comments. 'Have you got the arrows?'

'In the sack.' Bryn nodded and looked towards it.

Well done my girl, May.

Cad had sent May to deliver a note to Bryn a short time before, containing Cad's **explicit**[6] instructions. Because Bryn had known Cad's **requirements**[7] for as short a time as possible, he would have little time to pass intelligence to the enemy if he were a traitor.

Maybe you'll come good after all, she **reasoned**[8], **scrutinising**[9] his eyes for signs of fear but finding none. He was either brave or a skilled liar. *He's probably both,* she thought, struggling to see his positive side. After all, they'd needed to blackmail him in exchange for his **cooperation**[10].

---

1 **brazen** *(adj)* pushy and shameless. *(s)* bold, brash, blatant. *(ant)* shy, timid.

2 **bold** *(adj)* lacking fear. *(s)* courageous, brave, daring. *(ant)* timid, scared.

3 **entail** *(v)* to involve. *(s)* require, demand.

4 **all of a dither** (idiom) being in a state of confusion, distress or nervous agitation.

5 **gurgle** *(v)* make a bubbling sound. *(s)* burble, babble.

6 **explicit** *(adj)* clear and detailed. *(s)* plain, direct. *(ant)* vague.

7 **requirement** *(n)* something that is wanted or needed. *(s)* wish, demand.

8 **reason** *(v)* form logical judgements. *(s)* think, figure, conclude.

9 **scrutinise** *(v)* look, inspect or examine closely and thoroughly. *(s)* study, search. *(ant)* glance.

10 **cooperation** *(n)* help. *(s)* assistance, participation. *(ant)* refusal.

She didn't ask after the well-stocked, burning lantern she'd requested, for he held that in his hand.

'Come further inside. Move from the window.'

Bryn, his eyes blank, did as she asked.

Once away from the window, Cad stooped to pick up the pongy pot, gingerly unscrewing its lid. Bryn's attention followed her moves. Cad handled the pot like a baby, lest it break and the precious Greek fire be lost to the reeds scattered on her floor. Silent, Bryn didn't move, but his nose wrinkled in further disgust. He studied Cad as she wrapped the arrowheads he'd brought in strips of torn tunic, and sewed the **fabric**[1] onto each one with **deft**[2] stitches. She hoped Bryn wouldn't question her sewing skills.

I must act boyish, she reminded herself.

Cad pulled the thread extra tight to ensure the cloth bindings stayed on the arrowheads before dipping each one into the pot of Greek fire, soaking them with the stinking liquid.

'What is that?' Bryn eventually asked, yielding to his curiosity.

'It burns,' was all Cad said.

Bryn muttered something and screwed up his face.

Even though he was deeply involved, Cad debated which details to share with this squire, who was about to fire the burning arrows required to execute her plan. What exactly did he need to know? She'd thought of little else this afternoon. Though now he was here with her, willing to help, albeit blackmailed to do so, she yearned to halve her burden. Cad longed to unload its heavy weight onto someone else's shoulders – after all, they were all hiding beneath the same cloak now – but something stopped her. Rashness was often her downfall, and to share all with Bryn now would be foolhardy.

I mustn't, she thought, before letting out a whistle for her goshawk.

Shortly after, May glided back into the room. Bryn's brows shot skywards, yet he said nothing, clearly masking his **impressed**[3] expression. May settled, clutching Cad's shoulder, her head

---

1 **fabric** *(n)* cloth. *(s)* material, hangings, drapery.

2 **deft** *(adj)* neatly skilful and quick. *(s)* adept, able, capable, adroit. *(ant)* clumsy, lumbering.

3 **impressed** *(adj)* showing or feeling approval or respect. *(s)* influenced, fascinated. *(ant)* unimpressed.

twitching at Bryn's unusual presence. Cad fed her **morsels**[1] of meat, **placating**[2] her and letting her know Bryn was an **ally**[3] – for now.

'Where did you get that goshawk?' Bryn finally asked, looking like he hated himself for doing so.

'She was blinded and left to die by the falconers. I rescued her.'

Bryn blinked a few times, but said nothing. Instead, his attention **tracked**[4] down towards Fishy, who bared her **splendid**[5] canines at him.

'*You* didn't throw Fishy into the moat, did you?' snapped Cad, suddenly horrified at that thought and wondering why Fishy was baring her teeth so much. But before the words finished leaving her mouth, Bryn was shaking his head, and she believed him. His eyes spoke the truth.

'I love dogs. They're nicer than people. Loyal.'

Cad saw sorrow flit across Bryn's eyes. Taken aback, she cleared her throat and said, 'Bryn, I know we have our **issues**[6], and it's most odd for you to be here at my behest, but trust me, if only this once. It's important. If we fail tonight, there might be no Catrin Castle tomorrow.'

Bryn didn't flinch. Not a trace of emotion crossed his face. Cad's heart sank: Was he poised to say no? Was he that heartless, or did he not believe her?

In horrid limbo, Cad felt she was drowning in those green eyes of his, her fate held firmly in his hands.

Bryn looked away, then squatted to face Fishy. Fishy locked eyes with his; her ears flat as if weighing him up. Cad wondered what on earth Bryn was doing, when Fishy lunged forward and gave his nose an almighty wet lick.

Bryn ruffled Fishy's fur, then stood, his glare boring into Cad.

Cad struggled to hold his gaze, but did.

'I'm all ears,' he finally said, his face an unreadable page.

---

1 **morsel** *(n)* a small piece or amount. *(s)* mouthful, bite, nibble, bit. *(ant)* chunk.

2 **placate** *(v)* make less angry or hostile. *(s)* pacify, soothe, calm. *(ant)* enrage.

3 **ally** *(n)* a person that helps another in a task. *(s)* aide, associate, supporter. *(ant)* opponent.

4 **track** *(v)* follow the movements or trail of something or someone. *(s)* trace.

5 **splendid** *(adj)* impressive. *(s)* magnificent. *(ant)* unimpressive.

6 **issue** *(n)* difficulty. *(s)* problem, disagreement. *(ant)* agreement, accord.

CHAPTER TWENTY-NINE

Midnight Mayhem

Cap pulled low, Cad climbed up to the battlements that overlooked the tilt yard and the occupying army. She panted, just about keeping up with Bryn, as weary-looking archers nodded at him, **unperturbed**[1] by his presence. Bryn would have worked for most of them, replenishing their arrows many a time before. If they noticed the stench of Greek fire, none mentioned it, probably blaming their comrades' farts instead. Due to the siege, the crenels were **sparsely**[2] **manned**[3]. Arrows could not **effectively**[4] reach the occupying army from here and, as it was dusk, many of the archers would be eating while they could.

Cad's window of opportunity fell between the greyness of the dying dusk and the inky blackness that followed it.

'Bryn, whatever you do, keep that lantern lit. Without it, you *cannot* light the arrows.'

He nodded. 'I made sure to fill it, as your note requested.'

In her head, Cad plotted her strategy and hoped that Bryn's assailant had successfully tested the fire-breathing machine as he'd promised Siân he would. Success hinged on this: the Greek-fire siphon being moved into position **parallel**[5] to Catrin's moat. Cad also prayed Siân's secret

---

1 **unperturbed** *(adj)* not anxious or concerned. *(s)* untroubled, unworried. *(ant)* perturbed.

2 **sparsely** *(adv)* low in numbers. *(s)* thinly, barely. *(ant)* heavily.

3 **man** *(v)* defend or staff. *(s)* crew.

4 **effectively** *(adv)* in a way that gets the desired result. *(s)* successfully. *(ant)* ineffectively.

5 **parallel** *(adj)* side by side, having equal distance between. *(s)* aligned, lateral. *(ant)* perpendicular.

stocks[1] of Greek fire were all but sabotaged by her with the vermifuge in Catrin's dungeons. If the man and Siân were concealing more Greek fire in their camp, and the Byzantine history she'd studied was true, then it would ignite and burn their tents to ash in seconds. Even though the army was her enemy, that thought turned Cad's stomach. Her village had burned to the ground.

'It's in **self-defence**[2],' Cad muttered, knowing many lives would be lost, and perhaps that of her adoptive mother, Siân.

Bryn shot her a confused look, seeing her hands tremble as she removed the arrows from the sack.

'You have five flaming arrows. The others are just plain heads. I didn't have enough of the burning substance to make more.'

Bryn stared at her, an odd expression on his face. Cad wondered what he was thinking, but continued regardless.

'You'll see May; she'll carry the clay pots you saw in my room. When she swoops low and drops one, you fire a burning arrow. Do not hit my goshawk,' added Cad, her voice dagger sharp.

'What do you take me for?' hissed Bryn. 'But it's darkening, so I'll be blind shortly. Then I *will* kill your hawk. Even I'm not that good a shot.'

'We move soon. Very soon. Watch carefully for May. She's silent and swift. If you miss her, we miss our chance. You're starting the fires.'

'Where are *you* going?' asked Bryn, astounded to see Cad turn to leave.

'To plant the pots.' Her heart slammed her chest so hard it hurt.

Bryn frowned. 'You mean to say you're leaving Catrin to sneak amongst that army?' He almost laughed. 'And you think your little pots of stinky stuff will set that entire camp on fire?'

'I'm stealthy when need be.' Cad touched the ring on her thumb. 'Especially on my pony, as you well know.' She glared at him, twisting the knife over the joust and his cheating.

'You're a **lunatic**[3],' he **scoffed**[4]. 'You'll be dead in seconds. I'll say my **farewells**[5] to you now, *Master Cad*.'

---

1 **stock** *(n)* a supply. *(s)* store, reserve, stockpile.

2 **self-defence** *(n)* the defence (protection) of one's self.

3 **lunatic** *(n)* a person showing a confused state of mind. *(s)* maniac, madperson.

4 **scoff** *(v)* speak in a mocking or derisive way. *(s)* ridicule, deride, sneer. *(ant)* praise, respect.

5 **farewell** *(n)* a parting wish for well-being. *(s)* goodbye, send-off. *(ant)* hello, greeting.

And with that **snide**[1] tone in his voice, Bryn Davis retrieved his longbow, readied his arrows, lantern by his side, and gazed out between the crenels in wait of May, the blind goshawk. He didn't look at Cad again.

Cad wanted to kick him, but Bryn's words rang in her ears as she made to leave. He was right, of course. The enemy would **slaughter**[2] Cad in seconds if they saw her, if she didn't have her ring, which she **sincerely**[3] hoped had refilled to adequate power.

With darkness creeping closer, Cad left the **fortification**[4], descending the stone steps two at a time, almost flying headlong more than once. To her relief, the chess game had become an **epic**[5] session with tables now boasting cards and dice. Strong beer flowed like a **fountain**[6].

Amid[7] cheers, laughter, and raucous merriment, the once-peaceful corner by the chapel was alive and loud. Her father would be irked if he were here, but this was the scenario she'd planned. And she tried not to think of Llywelyn.

As she scooted into the bailey, Cad caught Rhys's eye and nodded towards the passage that ran beneath the gardens and moat into the tilt yard. Then she **skirted**[8] by the gamers and straight to her room. She grabbed the last piece of kit she'd borrowed from the armament store, then sprinted to the stables as fast as her ribs would allow.

'Ellis,' gasped Cad as she approached Flash's stall, holding her ribs and panting. 'Help me into this armour.'

Cad wheezed as she **brandished**[9] the metal plates, her chest tight from the run.

Agog, the boy sprang into action, helping Cad into Bryn Davis's **oversized**[10] upper-body armour.

'Cad—'

---

1 **snide** *(adj)* slyly mocking. *(s)* scornful, spiteful. *(ant)* complimentary.

2 **slaughter** *(v)* kill. *(s)* butcher, destroy, murder, slay.

3 **sincerely** *(adv)* in a sincere (true and heartfelt) or genuine way. *(s)* really, truly. *(ant)* insincerely.

4 **fortification** *(n)* a defensive or reinforced wall or place. *(s)* defences.

5 **epic** *(adj)* grand in character or scale. *(s)* monumental, extraordinary. *(ant)* understated.

6 **fountain** *(n)* an ornamental creation in a pool, pond or lake that pumps jets of water into the air.

7 **amid** *(prep)* surrounded by, in the middle of. *(s)* among, amidst, between, during. *(ant)* outside.

8 **skirt** *(v)* go round or pass closely by. *(s)* circle, dodge. *(ant)* face.

9 **brandish** *(v)* wave as a threat or in excitement. *(s)* shake, wield, display. *(ant)* conceal.

10 **oversized** *(adj)* something that is bigger than the usual size. *(s)* too big. *(ant)* undersized.

'No questions,' she snapped, batting away his words. 'Is Flash saddled?'

Ellis nodded.

'Then grab a **mounting block**[1] and help me up.'

Ellis grabbed the nearest block. Cad followed him into Flash's stall. Midnight, adjacent, **bucked**[2] and **whinnied**[3] his **disapproval**[4].

'Don't worry, Midnight, you're coming too,' said Cad.

'What?' cried Ellis, but Cad cut him off with a glare. Ellis didn't question her again.

With a giant heave, and wincing, Cad hauled herself into Bryn's oversized saddle.

'Ellis, do up her girth, over-tight. I can't risk the saddle slipping.'

'Cad, you're scaring me. This saddle is way too big for Flash.'

'Do it,' snapped Cad, hating her **harshness**[5], but night was falling fast. She would apologise tomorrow … 'Now, bolt my armour to the saddle.'

Ellis's eyes almost doubled in size.

'Now!' she barked, then added, 'Please.'

Ellis quickly screwed the bolts into place, his hands shaking so much he struggled to tighten them. Cad watched, her heart pounding, her hands trembling too. She wore no **gauntlets**[6]: she would require **dexterity**[7] for this job.

'Now get the sacks from the tack room and bring two **panniers**[8].'

'Flash.' Cad gently stroked her pony's arched neck, 'You must trust me. I need that brave girl from the joust.'

Cad patted Flash firmly, and the pony let out a low whinny.

Ellis returned, and with no instruction from Cad, deftly attached the panniers and began filling them with the clay pots that held the Greek fire.

'Ellis, you're a quick learner. Thank you for this.'

---

1 **mounting block** *(n)* a raised step upon which someone stands to help them mount a horse.

2 **buck** *(v)* (of a horse) put the head down between the front legs and kick high with the rear.

3 **whinny** *(v)* make a neighing sound like that of a horse. *(s)* nicker, whicker, bray.

4 **disapproval** *(n)* the negative opinion of. *(s)* dislike, objection. *(ant)* approval.

5 **harshness** *(n)* the quality of being harsh (cruel or severe). *(s)* meanness, spite. *(ant)* softness.

6 **gauntlet** *(n)* an armoured glove made from hardened leather or metal.

7 **dexterity** *(n)* skill in performing tasks, especially with the hands. *(s)* adroitness. *(s)* clumsiness.

8 **pannier** *(n)* a bag or basket carried by an animal, vehicle or person.

Cad's mind sprinted, replaying the plan she'd already played out a thousand times.

Calm, Cad, calm, she chanted in her head.

Ellis finished his work and looked at Cad, giving her a silent nod.

'Now listen hard, Ellis Williams. There are two further things I require of you. Do you understand?'

He nodded.

'The first is, you take that bold beast, Midnight, and you loose him into the bailey. Then you pursue him as though he's escaped. Listen out for Flash's hooves as we canter by, then catch him and return him to his stall. But you might not see me, you'll just hear me. Don't ask.'

Cad shook her head before Ellis could say another word.

Ellis sucked in a deep breath.

'You've got all that?' asked Cad.

He nodded, glancing at Flash and Midnight.

Then she leaned across from Flash and grasped Ellis's shoulder, **fixating**[1] on his searching eyes. He froze beneath her grip.

'Now for the more important part. When you've done that, you get Rhys, Dylan and Fishy and you all hide in that damned oubliette.'

Cad trusted Rhys would strap Slippy to his belt.

'Why are you saying this? Why?' Ellis was spluttering now.

'No questions. No time. You *must* trust me. Rhys will lead you down to the hellhole. He knows the way. And do not leave the oubliette until I come for you. Do you understand me?'

Ellis's body turned **limp**[2] beneath Cad's grip, his face the colour of milk. There was no time for **niceties**[3].

'You all go straight to the oubliette. You stay there. You take no one else but Rhys, Dylan and Fishy, and you *do not move*. If I don't come for you within a day, then I won't be returning at all. In that event, you must leave the oubliette, but beware as you do.'

Cad didn't dare tell him why, and the poor boy didn't ask.

---

1 **fixate** *(v)* direct the eyes fixedly. *(s)* focus.

2 **limp** *(adj)* lacking internal strength or structure, not stiff or firm. *(s)* floppy. *(ant)* stiff, rigid.

3 **nicety** *(n)* nice or polite social behaviour. *(s)* civility, chit-chat, small talk. *(ant)* rudeness.

Looking stunned, Ellis nodded, his face grey as he **beheld**[1] his precious horses, but Cad shook her head, reading his mind. If her plan failed, the horses would be stuck in their stalls. There was nothing in this world Cad could do to alter that, and her heart broke as she observed the odd stablemates, Flash and Midnight.

Dashing a tear with her sleeve, she said, 'Now go.'

With a click of her tongue, Cad backed Flash from her stall as Ellis led the disgruntled Midnight from his. Midnight whinnied, his head tossed back, the whites of his eyes rolling. The gaming **revellers**[2] would flee as the wild stallion **rampaged**[3] through the bailey. **Ergo**[4], no one would notice the cantering of Flash's invisible hooves, for they would mistake them for those of the **stampeding**[5] Midnight.

Her nerves **frayed**[6], Cad readied Flash and waited as Ellis, with a slap of reins to Midnight's rear and a loud *yarhhh,* **unleashed**[7] the **livid**[8] stallion. Then, with arms flailing like a **windmill**[9], Ellis raced after Midnight, shrieking warnings to the **unsuspecting**[10] folks in the bailey.

It was now time for Cad to face the unknown **whim**[11] of fate.

---

1 **behold** *(v)* observe something (past tense: beheld). *(s)* see, watch.

2 **reveller** *(n)* a person who is enjoying themselves in a noisy way. *(s)* partygoer. *(ant)* party-pooper.

3 **rampage** *(v)* rush wildly. *(s)* storm, charge, tear, riot. *(ant)* saunter.

4 **ergo** *(adv)* for that reason. *(s)* therefore, hence, consequently, as a result, thus.

5 **stampede** *(v)* (usually of an animal) run wildly. *(s)* bolt, charge, tear. *(ant)* saunter.

6 **frayed** *(adj)* showing the effects of trauma or tension. *(s)* frazzled, worn.

7 **unleash** *(v)* release from a rein or leash. *(s)* free, unbridle, loose. *(ant)* leash.

8 **livid** *(adj)* extremely angry. *(s)* furious, fuming, seething. *(ant)* calm, content.

9 **windmill** *(n)* a building with large sails that converts wind power into energy.

10 **unsuspecting** *(adj)* feeling no suspicion. *(s)* unaware, ignorant, oblivious. *(ant)* aware.

11 **whim** *(n)* a desire or change of mind. *(s)* fancy, whimsy. *(ant)* certainty, belief.

CHAPTER THIRTY

Face to Face

Flash danced on the spot, clearly disturbed by Midnight's **expulsion**[1] from the stables, and no doubt sensing the tension emanating from her master's body mounted upon her back.

'Easy, girl,' cooed Cad, soothing Flash as she placed her emerald ring onto her left thumb, hoping it had gained enough power to work for her and the large animal beneath her. It had worked when cuffed to Rhys. Now bolted to Flash's saddle, Cad prayed it had charged sufficiently. Her stomach rolled as she pressed her right thumb into the ring's centre.

Please work! Please!

But Cad didn't need to worry. Flash **reared**[2], spooked by the **flare**[3] of dazzling green light shooting from the ring. Cad had predicted this reaction, and now leaned into the pony's neck to **pacify**[4] her. Pats and coos quickly stilled Flash, who trusted her master to guide her.

Cad glanced down at her hands and then her pony's hooves before moving: she couldn't see either, so she shortened the reins and **spurred**[5] on her mount, clicking Flash into a canter and out of the stable doors.

---

1 **expulsion** *(n)* the action of forcing something or someone to leave. *(s)* removal. *(ant)* admission.

2 **rear** *(v)* (of an animal) rise up onto the hind (back) legs.

3 **flare** *(n)* a sudden burst of bright light or flame. *(s)* flash, dazzle, glare.

4 **pacify** *(v)* calm the agitation, anger or excitement of. *(s)* soothe, appease. *(ant)* provoke.

5 **spur** *(v)* encourage. *(s)* urge, hurry, motivate, drive. *(ant)* discourage.

In the bailey, which was now chaotic, Midnight had already cleared Cad's path. **Drunken**[1] guards **bellowed**[2] at Ellis to catch the **insane**[3] stallion. Dogs, ducks and chickens scrambled to safety. Terrified parents scooped up their children, while cats **clambered**[4] up onto shoulders to avoid being trampled by the **barrelling**[5] horse.

As Cad cantered Flash across the bailey, she glanced at the games corner where Rhys and Dylan were frantically clearing away chess pieces and **discarded**[6] dice. Poor Ellis, looking mortified, tried to **entice**[7] a cornered Midnight with a rosy apple.

Cad guided Flash as close to Ellis as she could, and with **stoic**[8] determination kept her mount on track. Flash's invisible hooves pounded the bailey as they passed Ellis on their way to the gate that would take Cad out of Catrin, under the moat, and into the army-occupied tilt yard. She hoped Rhys had opened the gate as she'd requested, and that she and Flash would fit through it.

Without slowing, Cad **careered**[9] past the keep's entrance and saw Ellis reach out to grab Midnight's halter. A few more yards and Cad would be at the gate. If Rhys hadn't opened if for her, she would be stuck inside the castle, her plan in **tatters**[10].

Sweat trickled down her face as she approached the thick wooden gate. With **immense**[11] relief, Cad slowed to find it was wide open. She leaned forward, almost lying on her pony's **mane**[12] to avoid bashing her head, and cantered through the passageway. All the while, she hoped that the enemy soldiers hadn't noticed the hidden route into Catrin, because if they had, their invasion would be far easier than they'd anticipated.

The dark passage and its low ceiling and narrow sides proved **treacherous**[13]. More than once,

---

1 **drunken** *(adj)* intoxicated because of drinking too much alcohol. *(s)* drunk, inebriated. *(ant)* sober.

2 **bellow** *(v)* shout loudly and deeply. *(s)* holler, roar, cry, yell. *(ant)* whisper.

3 **insane** *(adj)* foolish, mad and irrational. *(s)* crazy. *(ant)* sensible.

4 **clamber** *(v)* move or climb in an awkward manner. *(s)* scramble, scrabble, scale.

5 **barrel** *(v)* move in a fast and uncontrolled way. *(s)* careen, career. *(ant)* amble, saunter.

6 **discarded** *(adj)* thrown aside, as no longer useful or desirable. *(s)* abandoned, dumped. *(ant)* retained.

7 **entice** *(v)* tempt or attract. *(s)* lure, cajole, persuade. *(ant)* dissuade, deter.

8 **stoic** *(adj)* the tolerating of difficulty without complaint. *(s)* hardy, tough. *(ant)* weak.

9 **career** *(v)* move in a quick, uncontrolled manner. *(s)* race, gallop. *(ant)* dawdle.

10 **tatters** *(n)* shreds of some sort (ruin). *(s)* bits, pieces.

11 **immense** *(adj)* large in scale or degree. *(s)* great, enormous, huge. *(ant)* tiny, small.

12 **mane** *(n)* the long hair on the back of an animal's neck such as a horse or male lion.

13 **treacherous** *(adj)* presenting hidden or unforeseen dangers. *(s)* hazardous, perilous. *(ant)* safe.

Cad's knees collided with the wall. If she lifted her head, she would take a huge knock to it, especially while bolted to the saddle. Flash kept her nose low as Cad slowed her to a trot, then stopped before the exit gate. She'd asked Rhys to leave it **ajar**[1] so she could nudge it open and gauge the **terrain**[2] before entering the camp.

'Flash, it's now or never.'

Cad patted her pony's neck, her arm feeling as if it belonged to someone else. She sucked in several deep breaths before exhaling slowly and whispering, 'Walk on.'

With the toe of her boot, Cad pushed open the gate just enough to pass through it, choosing the softest ground to follow, lest Flash's hooves **clanged**[3] on rocks. Luckily for Cad, the tilt yard was soft, therefore soundless underfoot. Near-darkness rendered the **vast**[4] camp a myriad of shadowed outlines. The enemy was winding down for the evening, as she guessed it would. Lanterns glowed inside tents, casting soldiers' shadows as they readied for sleep, or the night **patrol**[5], whichever came first.

Now faced with her **adversary**[6], Cad drew Flash to a halt, standing parallel to the moat. With one hand on the reins, the other fished inside the pannier for an invisible clay pot. She removed one, twisted off the top, and emptied its contents into the moat. Then, as if handling **priceless**[7] treasure, but struggling to steady her hands, she repeated this with four more pots, abandoning the now visible empty containers on the ground. To leave them here like this, in full view, was a **colossal**[8] risk, but she had little choice: she was bolted in place and her panniers must be light when she finished, for Flash might need to gallop like the wind at the end.

By the time she'd finished pouring Greek fire into the moat, sweat trickled between her shoulder blades, soaking her back. For the next stage of the **assault**[9], Cad turned

---

1 **ajar** *(adj)* slightly open. *(s)* cracked, unfastened. *(ant)* closed, shut.

2 **terrain** *(n)* a stretch of ground or its features. *(s)* area, land, environment.

3 **clang** *(v)* cause or make a loud clang (ring). *(s)* clank, resound, reverberate.

4 **vast** *(adj)* large or immense. *(s)* enormous, colossal, gigantic. *(ant)* small, insignificant.

5 **patrol** *(n)* an operation to keep watch over a specific area or place. *(s)* guard, vigil.

6 **adversary** *(n)* an opponent or enemy (rival). *(s)* foe, combatant. *(ant)* ally.

7 **priceless** *(adj)* so precious that a value cannot be put on it. *(s)* rare, high-priced. *(ant)* worthless.

8 **colossal** *(adj)* exceptionally large or great. *(s)* massive, enormous, huge. *(ant)* tiny.

9 **assault** *(n)* a military attack. *(s)* offensive, strike, onslaught.

Flash towards the camp's main body and signalled for her to walk on. Cad felt her pony's reluctance, smelled her sweat, willing her to stay quiet. Even a single whinny from Flash might prove disastrous. If the enemy heard Cad, she could flee: she was invisible, but she needed first to plant the Greek-fire pots in **precisely**[1] the right places.

With the utmost caution, Cad steered Flash to the trebuchet's massive silhouette, which filled the darkening sky. It loomed above Catrin like a **mammoth**[2] skeleton of wood and rope. But this destructive machine was far from dead. As Cad neared it, she reached into her pocket and pulled out a handful of invisible cheese, scattering it on the ground. That would occupy any dogs for a while, she hoped.

Now on high alert, Cad weaved her way through the tents, her breaths **shallow**[3] and rapid, her hands wet with sweat. Then she circled the back of the trebuchet as silently as Flash's hooves would allow. Lanterns lit the **weathered**[4] guards **stationed**[5] at its base. All looked hungry for food, beer and their beds. This would be tricky. Cad couldn't **dismount**[6]; Ellis had secured her using bolts through the saddle. It was far from ideal, but Cad had feared if she were separated from Flash, one or the other might reappear. It was a strange thought at this time, but Cad wondered if Flash was aware of her own invisibility – she doubted it.

As she took in the situation, a sudden **bolt**[7] of dread **jolted**[8] Cad: she realised how swiftly darkness was falling. If she didn't hasten now, Bryn wouldn't see May, and even in this light, hitting the moving targets would prove tricky.

I have little time left, she thought, approaching the trebuchet's base at an unguarded corner. She took out a clay pot and placed it on one of the wide wooden **struts**[9] which made up its vast frame. Then, at roughly equal distances, she placed another four alongside it. Nine clay pots remained: five for May and four for the fire-breathing monster. That would be when, and if, she

---

1 **precisely** *(adv)* in a precise (exact) way. *(s)* absolutely, just. *(ant)* vaguely.

2 **mammoth** *(adj)* extremely large. *(s)* huge, colossal. *(ant)* tiny.

3 **shallow** *(adj)* not deep.

4 **weathered** *(adj)* aged or worn by long exposure to the weather. *(s)* wizened.

5 **station** *(v)* put in a place to watch or guard something or someone. *(s)* post, position, locate.

6 **dismount** *(v)* get off something that one rides. *(s)* descend, alight. *(ant)* mount.

7 **bolt** *(n)* a shock. *(s)* surge, flash, dart.

8 **jolt** *(v)* push or move roughly. *(s)* jerk, lurch, rattle.

9 **strut** *(n)* a bar that performs part of a supporting framework for something.

found it, for Cad was sure it **lurked**[1] nearby, **equipped**[2] to spray **hellfire**[3] over Catrin Castle.

'You disgusting pig!'

Cad's heart almost stopped as her head whirled to see who'd insulted her.

'You stink like a **cesspit**[4],' bellowed a guard.

Cad flinched so hard, had she not been bolted to Flash, she would have tumbled in terror. Then as her heart calmed, she remembered she and Flash were invisible.

'It ain't me,' the guard's **colleague**[5] said, an **indignant**[6] look on his face.

The **grousing**[7] guard wafted his nose, and pointing at his mate's backside, fled the stench. Oblivious to Cad and her actions, he couldn't see the invisible clay pots **oozing**[8] particles of the devil's own brimstone, and had blamed his comrade instead. Cad hoped the stench from the moat had not yet raised suspicions, for she despaired it soon would.

As darkness raced forth, Cad had to locate the dragon fast. Her eyes scoured the camp; her heart pounded in her ears. Sweat soaked her undergarments, the armour baking her even in the cool of dusk. Flash twitched, urged on by Cad into a brisk walk: a trot would be too noisy.

As dusk **succumbed**[9] to darkness, rings of lanterns flickered to life in the camp.

Where is it? Where is the siphon?

Time was running out.

---

1 **lurk** *(v)* be or remain hidden, hang about. *(s)* loiter, skulk. *(ant)* appear, materialise.

2 **equip** *(v)* supply with the necessary items for a specific purpose. *(s)* issue, provide. *(ant)* deprive.

3 **hellfire** *(n)* the fires regarded by some as existing in hell.

4 **cesspit** *(n)* a pit containing waste liquid or sewage for disposal.

5 **colleague** *(n)* a person with whom one works. *(s)* associate, workmate, co-worker.

6 **indignant** *(adj)* angry or annoyed at what is perceived as unfair. *(s)* offended, irate. *(ant)* content.

7 **grouse** *(v)* to complain about trivial things. *(s)* moan, whine, grumble, whinge. *(ant)* compliment.

8 **ooze** *(v)* gently flow or seep. *(s)* bleed, creep, issue. *(ant)* gush, pour.

9 **succumb** *(v)* give in or give way to. *(s)* yield, submit, surrender, capitulate. *(ant)* withstand.

CHAPTER THIRTY-ONE

Fireworks

Aware that time was slipping by, Cad weaved Flash amongst the tents, grateful for what little light remained. Terrified it would soon be too dark, she feared the fire-breathing dragon was still in the tent at the camp's rear. Perhaps its test run had failed? Maybe Siân's deputy, Bryn's assailant, hadn't positioned the siphon by Catrin's moat as he'd said he would? Had their Greek-fire mixture proved useless, its proportions **askew**[1]?

If Cad didn't find the dragon soon, the trebuchet would be her sole target, for the arrows she'd asked Bryn to fire would not reach to the back of the tents if that's where the dragon remained. Cad had **salvaged**[2] twenty clay pots of Greek fire from the room beneath Catrin, and she'd used one to make five flaming arrows for Bryn. That left nineteen pots for her to dot around the army's camp as **incendiary**[3] devices.

Now dogged by fear of failure, Cad searched amongst the tents in vain, her heart hanging with every step Flash took. Her search proved futile. She couldn't find the dragon near the moat, yet she needed to call May before it was too dark. She must change her plan; perhaps they'd not moved the dragon after all. Cad headed for the camp's rear, where earlier with Rhys, she'd seen Siân with the Greek-fire siphon.

As she made her way through the camp, she placed single clay pots on top of random tents

---

1 **askew** *(adj)* wrong. *(s)* awry, incorrect. *(ant)* correct.

2 **salvage** *(v)* rescue. *(s)* save, recover. *(ant)* abandon, lose.

3 **incendiary** *(adj)* designed to cause fires. *(s)* inflammable, combustible.

until she reached the tent where she'd seen her mother and Bryn's assailant that morning. Then, as quietly as she could, she steered Flash to the back and placed a pot there. If the dragon was still inside, there at least remained an outside chance this Greek-fire **grenade**[1] might explode if the camp burned, taking the monstrous siphon with it.

For a single beat, her adoptive mother's image, and her being inside the tent, assailed Cad's thoughts, but she banished it at once. No matter the sacrifice, she must save Catrin Castle. Torn, she turned Flash and cantered back towards the moat, skirting the camp's **perimeter**[2] so no one would hear her. Once she arrived, Cad drew her pony to a halt, then she whistled for May.

For what felt like a lifetime, Cad waited, scouring the dusky sky for her goshawk. May had never before failed her. The waiting tortured Cad. What would normally be **divine**[3] cooking smells rose from the camp, but tonight they sickened her. She swallowed her **nausea**[4]. At least the soldiers would be distracted by their stomachs and the strong beer which flowed at nights.

Suddenly, wings flapped past Cad's face, circling her head. She stifled a shocked cry as her heart rate **rocketed**[5].

Damned bats!

Nocturnal[6], they **emerged**[7] at dusk, and soon the sky would host a **flock**[8].

Unlike the bats, May was blind, using her ears and **innate**[9] abilities to fly, so no matter how dark, or despite Cad's invisibility, she should find Cad and Flash with ease. But where was she? Nightfall was but a breath away, and Bryn needed light to shoot his arrows.

Cad's eyes swept the battlements, but the crenels hid their occupants and she saw nothing. She hoped Bryn's lantern still burned because it struck Cad that if May failed to show, her plan was doomed.

Come on, May, Cad thought as a crippling unease cloaked her body.

---

1 **grenade** *(n)* a small (often) hand-thrown bomb or stun device.

2 **perimeter** *(n)* the boundary of an area. *(s)* border, periphery, edge. *(ant)* centre.

3 **divine** *(adj)* very pleasing. *(s)* glorious, wonderful. *(ant)* dreadful.

4 **nausea** *(n)* a feeling of sickness. *(s)* queasiness, biliousness. *(ant)* wellness.

5 **rocket** *(v)* (of an amount) increase quickly. *(s)* soar, escalate. *(ant)* plummet.

6 **nocturnal** *(adj)* occurring, done or active at night.

7 **emerge** *(v)* become visible. *(s)* arrive, surface. *(ant)* disappear.

8 **flock** *(n)* a group or gathering of.

9 **innate** *(adj)* naturally occurring. *(s)* inborn, instinctive. *(ant)* learned.

She will show. She will show.

Cad glanced everywhere, then focused on the sky. Dare she risk a louder whistle and raise suspicions? Cad slipped two fingers of each hand into her mouth, inhaled deeply, and blew out, creating the loudest, shrillest whistle she could muster. She was outside the castle walls after all. Perhaps May had not heard her, even with her acute senses.

Desperate, and full of trepidation, Cad studied the sky for signs, when, as if from nowhere, claws gripped her invisible shoulder. Relief hit Cad like a thunderclap. Her hands shook as she stuffed invisible pork into May's beak whilst grabbing a clay pot from the pannier. Then she lifted May with her free hand, offering the pot to her **talons**[1]. As quick as a wink, May grasped the pot. Cad gave the command May had learned earlier, and May soared above the camp. When almost out of Cad's sight, May stopped rising and batted her wings in a **hover**[2].

After a few more steady beats, May released the pot of Greek fire.

Heart pounding, breaths on hold, Cad scrutinised the battlements, waiting to see flames fly forth and strike the pot mid-flight. The burning arrow would **detonate**[3] the Greek-fire grenade, just like those Chinese fireworks she'd seen painted in pictures.

Eyes **peeled**[4], Cad watched, but no arrow came, and the pot crashed to earth, landing in the camp. Cad expected the guards to swarm where it fell – and soon.

Weak with despair, Cad pictured her father, her friends, and the residents trapped inside Catrin. Then she whistled May back. Within moments, the hawk clawed her shoulder. Cad, hands shaking, trying not to drop the treats, pushed pork into May's beak, gave her another Greek-fire grenade, and commanded her to fly.

May soared, hovering before the battlements, then she freed the grenade.

Cad, eyes fixed on May, swiped at a circling bat and held her breath. **Numb**[5] with foreboding and **helplessness**[6], Cad saw the grenade leave the hawk's claws. Then her eyes turned to the battlements.

---

1 **talon** *(n)* a sharp claw, particularly one belonging to a bird of prey. *(s)* nail, fingernail.

2 **hover** *(n)* a process of staying in the air in one place.

3 **detonate** *(v)* explode or cause something to explode. *(s)* ignite.

4 **eyes peeled** (idiom) remaining vigilant or carefully watching (someone or something).

5 **numb** *(adj)* being unable to think or feel. *(s)* paralysed, stupefied. *(ant)* feeling.

6 **helplessness** *(n)* the inability to do anything at all. *(s)* powerlessness. *(ant)* ability.

Come on, Bryn.

Something shot out from between the crenels; a flame, like a shooting star. It flew through the darkness, climbing, climbing, climbing. Then just like those Chinese fireworks, an **eruption**[1] blasted forth, followed by a shower of shimmering stars, which rained down on Siân Cadwaladr's camp.

'Yes!' cried Cad. Then she whistled again.

With a soft swish, May landed and Cad repeated the **drill**[2]. Another fiery arrow shot from between the crenels. Cad gasped as the spectacular explosion showered a wider area of the camp with Greek-fire flames.

Then reality hit her like a **tidal wave**[3]. **Aghast**[4], Cad froze for a moment as tents burned. Soldiers scattered, their clothes ablaze. Mayhem ensued, as horrid thoughts of her burning village surfaced. Cad despised the **horrific**[5] scene playing out before her, but she called May again, and Bryn Davis shot down the fourth deadly grenade, spraying its red-hot contents over Siân's unsuspecting army.

The **inferno**[6] roared, consuming all in its path. The stench sickened Cad: a mixture of Greek fire and horror filled her nostrils. She sought some kind of solace, telling herself Catrin, and all her people, would have suffered this same **atrocious**[7] fate, and at the hands of *her* own mother. Tears blurred Cad's vision as she handed the last of the clay containers to her **obedient**[8] **servant**[9], May.

Practised now, Bryn's blazing arrow split the final clay pot, releasing its deadly contents directly over the monster trebuchet that loomed above Catrin Castle. Fire began licking its legs, lighting the dry wood with ease. Commanders barked frantic orders. Soldiers ran to and from the moat, full pails in each hand, their efforts futile. Little did the oblivious troops know that

---

1 **eruption** *(n)* an act of something being forced out of something or somewhere. *(s)* blast, explosion.

2 **drill** *(n)* the correct procedure. *(s)* practice, routine.

3 **tidal wave** *(n)* an extremely large wave. *(s)* storm surge, tsunami.

4 **aghast** *(adj)* shocked or horrified. *(s)* astounded, stunned, appalled. *(ant)* unaffected.

5 **horrific** *(adj)* causing horror. *(s)* ghastly, atrocious, grisly. *(ant)* pleasant.

6 **inferno** *(n)* a large and out of control fire. *(s)* blaze.

7 **atrocious** *(adj)* extremely unpleasant. *(s)* dreadful, appalling, vile. *(ant)* wonderful.

8 **obedient** *(adj)* one who is willing to do as is asked or expected. *(s)* compliant, dutiful. *(ant)* disobedient.

9 **servant** *(n)* a loyal and helpful supporter. *(s)* follower, devotee.

the water from the moat would further fuel the devil's fire, for Cad had sullied it with Greek fire.

When the final pot had exploded directly above the moat, the **hapless**[1] fire crew, faces aghast, mouths wide, watched it ignite. As the water burned like the depths of hell itself, Siân Cadwaladr's army began to leave their camp, fleeing like rats from a burning **barn**[2].

Unable to find joy at her success, Cad peered up at the battlements, her eyes searching the crenels for signs of Bryn. The crenellations were filling with castle folk **craning**[3] to see the army that had held them **hostage**[4], apparently, now destroy itself with fire.

The **intense**[5] heat rising from the moat forced Cad to turn away, and as she twitched her reins to steer Flash towards the gate to leave, she noticed her hands. Their reappearance meant that she and Flash would be visible in a matter of moments.

Despite the carnage unfurling before her, with soldiers **deserting**[6] in **droves**[7], Cad and Flash were not yet safe. They must flee the scene fast, though it now seemed all over for Siân Cadwaladr: her army appeared doomed.

---

1 **hapless** *(adj)* unlucky. *(s)* unfortunate, doomed. *(ant)* fortunate.

2 **barn** *(n)* a big farm building for storing animal feed, grain or livestock (animals). *(s)* outbuilding.

3 **crane** *(v)* stretch one's body or neck to see something. *(s)* extend. *(ant)* retract, shrink.

4 **hostage** *(n)* someone unwillingly held to be exchanged for something else. *(s)* captive, detainee. *(ant)* captor.

5 **intense** *(adj)* of great strength. *(s)* severe, fierce, extreme. *(s)* mild.

6 **desert** *(v)* leave in a way that is disloyal. *(s)* flee, abandon. *(ant)* stand by, remain.

7 **drove** *(n)* a large number of people or things. *(s)* horde, crowd, throng. *(ant)* one, individual.

CHAPTER THIRTY-TWO

Mother

Cad steered Flash from the flaming moat and towards the gate that would take her from the **havoc**[1] of the tilt yard and back into Catrin's bailey. What awaited her there, she didn't know, but she must think fast.

As she made to move, an unexpected sadness struck her. It wasn't just the horrific scene she'd caused; it was her father. At the thought of Llywelyn still missing, sorrow clung like a wet cloak, yet she must reach the gate. She spurred Flash onwards.

Cad was almost there, when an almighty whooshing sound followed by an ear-splitting boom spooked Flash, who sprang sideways and lost her footing, almost collapsing onto her side. With swift reflexes, Cad leaned in to the stumbling **mare**[2] and managed to pull her to an **ungainly**[3] halt. Had Flash rolled, Cad would have been crushed beneath her, for she was still bolted in place.

'Come on, girl. We can do this,' Cad muttered to Flash.

With the gate in sight, but all her strength sapped, Cad tightened the reins and relaxed her knees off her pony's ribs, trying to steady the terrified beast. Cad was now fully visible, yet riding an invisible pony. Had any soldiers remained nearby, they would have died of fright, not fire. The sinister sight unnerved even Cad.

---

1 **havoc** *(n)* destruction. *(s)* damage, devastation, catastrophe. *(ant)* peace.

2 **mare** *(n)* a female horse.

3 **ungainly** *(adj)* clumsy. *(s)* awkward, lumbering. *(ant)* elegant, graceful.

'Easy, girl,' she whispered, clicking Flash on, when another enormous blast from the camp's rear, louder than the first, caused Flash to rear in **abject**[1] terror. A fireball **mushrooming**[2] from the tent where she'd seen the dragon this morning **ravaged**[3] the camp, **obliterating**[4] all in its wake.

Cad fought to steady Flash, who reared again. No matter what, Cad must keep Flash on her feet. Flash danced, jigging on the spot, throwing her head as another flare of orange, followed by a boom, ascended from the camp. Cad's stomach dropped in horror. Not at the deafening explosion, but at what it had lit up before her.

As if conjured from thin air, a colossal destrier, its sweat-soaked chest glowing grey-white in the moonlight, stood as if carved from **marble**[5]. The warhorse towered before her and Flash. Cad's heart screamed as if it might burst from despair. She recognised the horse immediately, and a hurt, so **profound**[6], unlike any she'd experienced before, tore at her **core**[7].

Time faltered. The night sky, now lit with the red and orange **hues**[8] of the burning Greek fire, glowed as if the sun shone from a secret place. The behemoth trebuchet and its surrounding canvas tents would fuel this inferno for hours, illuminating Catrin Castle like a ship's beacon from a shore. Distant sounds drifted into Cad's ears. Whether they were cries of joy from Catrin behind her, or screams of terror from the camp before her, she couldn't say. All arrived via a long and darkening tunnel.

Fighting a faint that threatened to **smite**[9] her, Cad's eyes met those of the destrier's rider, Siân Cadwaladr. But too **distraught**[10], Cad couldn't hold her mother's icy gaze. Instead, she focused

---

1 **abject** *(adj)* something bad experienced to the maximum degree. *(s)* complete, absolute, extreme. *(ant)* minimal.

2 **mushroom** *(v)* increase rapidly. *(s)* burgeon, spread, grow. *(ant)* diminish, shrink.

3 **ravage** *(v)* cause great damage to. *(s)* destroy, devastate.

4 **obliterate** *(v)* wipe out. *(s)* destroy, eradicate. *(ant)* create, establish.

5 **marble** *(n)* a form of limestone often polished and used in sculpture, architecture and kitchen worktops.

6 **profound** *(adj)* (of feelings, qualities, or emotions) intense, deep or great. *(s)* extreme. *(ant)* superficial, shallow.

7 **core** *(n)* the part that is central. *(s)* heart, inside, interior. *(ant)* edge, outside.

8 **hue** *(n)* a colour, tone or shade. *(s)* aspect, tinge, tint.

9 **smite** *(v)* conquer or defeat. *(s)* beat, quash, crush. *(ant)* lose to.

10 **distraught** *(adj)* extremely worried and upset. *(s)* distressed, desperate. *(ant)* calm, serene.

on the emerald earrings glittering from beneath the hood that partly **shrouded**[1] the stunning, yet **stony**[2] face.

'Evidently your ring works without the Gwalch Gem bracelet being nearby to power it.'

Cad said nothing as her mother's long, **slender**[3] hands removed the monk's cowl to reveal her blonde hair.

Cad gasped at what she saw, then chided herself for showing emotion.

Her mother's face wore no remorse, her features cold and hard.

Cad hadn't been surprised to see her mother beneath the monk's hood, for Cad had recognised the **magnificent**[4] steed at once, and guessed it would be Siân. Nor did the monk's outfit **faze**[5] Cad, because she now accepted she'd recognised those slim fingers when they'd trapped her and John in the oubliette. Perhaps, back then, she'd been **loath**[6] to admit they belonged to their mother.

But what shocked and saddened Cad most as she stared at the smug face, was that Cad's emerald hairpin was now holding Siân's hair in place. Cad hadn't used the hairpin today, and with everything else **afoot**[7], hadn't noticed it missing. The stunning gift, given to Cad by her father, now **adorned**[8] her mother's hair.

I will not cry. I will show you nothing more of my feelings – not ever.

Cad averted her eyes from the pin, not wanting to give her **callous**[9] mother the **satisfaction**[10] of seeing her grief. It was the last gift her father had given to her, and now he might have **perished**[11]. One look at her mother's **deadpan**[12] face told Cad that she would never own that hairpin again.

---

1 **shroud** *(v)* envelop or cover to prevent from being seen. *(s)* conceal, mask, hide. *(ant)* reveal.

2 **stony** *(adj)* (of the face) showing no sympathy. *(s)* unfriendly, cold. *(ant)* friendly.

3 **slender** *(adj)* slim and graceful. *(s)* delicate. *(ant)* chubby, plump, fat.

4 **magnificent** *(adj)* spectacular, impressive and awesome. *(s)* superb, superlative. *(ant)* unimpressive.

5 **faze** *(v)* (informal) cause upset. *(s)* disturb, disconcert. *(ant)* calm.

6 **loath** *(adj)* unwilling or reluctant (not wanting to do something). *(s)* opposed, hesitant, averse. *(ant)* eager.

7 **afoot** *(adj)* in preparation or progress. *(s)* happening, underway.

8 **adorn** *(v)* make more attractive or beautiful. *(s)* decorate, embellish. *(ant)* strip.

9 **callous** *(adj)* cruel and heartless. *(s)* hard, unfeeling, uncaring. *(ant)* compassionate.

10 **satisfaction** *(n)* enjoyment. *(s)* pleasure, delight. *(ant)* dissatisfaction.

11 **perish** *(v)* lose one's life. *(s)* die. *(ant)* thrive, live.

12 **deadpan** *(adj)* without expression. *(s)* stony, blank. *(ant)* animated.

Her mother clearly intended to keep it as some sort of **trophy**[1].

Siân cocked her head. Was she waiting for Cad to speak? Expecting a reaction, perhaps? Well, she could wait, for Cad was done with Siân now.

Using just her knees, Cad squeezed Flash into a walk and towards Catrin's secret gate.

'Did you think it would be *that* easy?'

The **menace**[2] dripping from Siân's voice **jarred**[3] Cad, but she didn't look back, and continued to walk Flash away.

For an instant, Cad contemplated the dagger sheathed at her waist, but even she, with her overwhelming fury rising, could not do that to Siân. The depth of Cad's despondency **triumphed**[4], stopping her from reaching for the weapon. Grief fuelled her sorrow, not violence.

'Callwen bach, lucky for you that I found your beloved hairpin this evening. Had I come across it earlier, when you evidently dropped it in my tent, Catrin would now be ablaze instead of my camp.'

That comment caused Cad to pull Flash to a halt, but she didn't face her mother.

'Callwen, I locked the gate. You cannot return to Catrin.' Siân's voice was almost a **cackle**[5]. 'Perhaps you should seek your *father's* help instead.'

At that, Cad's heart turned to stone. Her hand went for the dagger and yanked it from its sheath. On a **sixpence**[6], Cad turned Flash, primed to charge at the destrier. It was too late. Her mother had already spurred the grey-white stallion into a flying gallop and was disappearing from view. The monk's habit flapped behind her in the wind, as Greek fire whipped through her devastated camp. Flash would never catch the destrier – never. To chase Siân would be futile. A mixture of loathing and despair gripped Cad as she turned her pony back towards what she now knew was the locked gate.

Then to add to her anguish, just as Cad had suspected they might, a final few troops loyal to Siân and under her command, crept from the burning camp and began to approach her. Some

---

1 **trophy** *(n)* a souvenir of an achievement. *(s)* reminder, prize, memento.

2 **menace** *(n)* threat or intimidation. *(s)* ominousness, warning. *(ant)* protectiveness.

3 **jar** *(v)* shock or disturb. *(s)* shake, jolt, rattle. *(ant)* appease, please.

4 **triumph** *(v)* be successful. *(s)* succeed, win, prevail. *(ant)* lose, fail.

5 **cackle** *(n)* a harsh and loud laugh. *(s)* crow, snigger.

6 **turn on a sixpence** (phrase) turn quickly and easily (with agility).

came on horseback, some on foot, but they were coming, and they came for Cad. Should she flee? Some rode destriers and would chase her, others carried long **pikes**[1].

Cornered, Cad glanced about, quickly reckoning which escape route would prove most **favourable**[2]. Flash jogged beneath her, sensing an imminent gallop, but Cad saw no best way, for the enemy closed in on all **flanks**[3].

I must gallop at them, then change ***tack***[4], she thought, bracing herself for speed, when, from behind, a whooshing sound, like birds swooping, filled the air. Her head turned towards the noise, and her mouth dropped open. From the highest battlements of Catrin Castle, falling like rain, came a curtain of arrows heading straight for Siân's soldiers.

'Bryn Davis,' cried Cad, spurring Flash onwards, hoping and praying that somehow she could open the gate. Although she no longer had her magical hairpin, she must try to get into Catrin before more of Siân's **cronies**[5] crawled from hell's inferno. The raging fires and blazing moat illuminated Flash and her like a brightly lit target.

Lady Luck, it seemed, sought to abandon Cad. On reaching the gate, reality hit: it was closed as Siân said it would be, and being tethered to the saddle meant Cad couldn't dismount Flash to try to open it.

Cad fiddled, trying to loosen the saddle's bolts, but Ellis had so well tightened them that her attempts proved futile. Should she try to ride Flash into the gate and **ram**[6] it down? But Cad knew that no matter how obedient and brave Flash was, she would refuse to canter into a solid door. Flash was a horse, and Cad couldn't reason with her over this.

Stumped as to her next move, at the edge of her vision, Cad caught the silhouette of a running man. Although not overly tall, his outline was stocky and his hair dark, and he was gaining ground on her fast. She squinted, and to her horror, she saw her mother's henchman, the same man who'd beaten Bryn almost to a **pulp**[7]. He was running towards her, followed by two other men.

---

1 **pike** *(n)* a long thin, wooden weapon with a pointed metal head on the end. *(s)* spear.

2 **favourable** *(adj)* to the benefit of. *(s)* advantageous, beneficial. *(ant)* unfavourable.

3 **flank** *(n)* the left or right side of someone or something.

4 **tack** *(n)* a direction or course of action.

5 **crony** *(n)* a companion, close friend or associate. *(s)* comrade, colleague.

6 **ram** *(v)* crash into something violently. *(s)* batter, hit, strike.

7 **pulp** *(n)* a soft, wet shapeless mass of something.

Again, Cad quickly tried to fathom an escape route, but all were severely hindered by fire. Her options now shrank to one gap through the blaze; she must flee. But as Cad was about to spur Flash on to freedom, a loud thud, clanging of metal, and wood splintering, grabbed her attention.

Her head swivelled towards the locked gate, which, with a bang, burst open, **clouting**[1] the wall as it did. Through it marched Bryn Davis, longbow in his hands. He stopped, planted both feet out wide, and as speedy as a **greyhound**[2] on a coney, he whipped an arrow from his **quiver**[3] and fired. It shot past Cad's head and hit her mother's man square in his right shoulder.

On seeing this, one of the man's accompanying soldiers turned and fled, as the other took Bryn's second arrow in his backside. The skewered man yelled and leaped, dancing a jig as he tugged at the arrow **protruding**[4] from his **buttock**[5].

'Yarhhh, Flash!' yelled Cad, grasping her moment. Flash sprang into a canter, thundering straight for the gate into the passageway.

'Bryn, come on!' screamed Cad as she sped by the squire who was shooting at her pursuers. But he didn't budge. Instead, he spread his feet further, pulled back his bow as if it might snap in two, then loosed his last arrow.

Cad didn't see its **destination**[6], for she was now beyond the passage, back in Catrin's bailey and heading straight to the stables to unbolt her armour from Bryn's saddle.

Had Cad remained on the battle field, she would have seen Bryn's final arrow lodge firmly in the henchman's left shoulder, and she would have wondered why Bryn had not killed the man who'd beaten him half to death; the very same man who'd planned, with her mother, Siân, to burn Catrin Castle to the ground.

Then she would have seen Bryn turn and run like the wind down the passage and arrive safely in the bailey. And finally, with the help of some fellow squires, Cad would have seen Bryn and his friends barricade the inner gate closed with whatever they could find to do so.

---

1 **clout** *(v)* strike with the hand or something hard. *(s)* blow, knock, smack.

2 **greyhound** *(n)* a tall slender, speedy dog used since ancient times for hunting but now bred for racing.

3 **quiver** *(n)* a portable case used for holding an archer's arrows.

4 **protrude** *(v)* extend above or beyond a surface (stick out). *(s)* poke out, jut, project. *(ant)* withdraw.

5 **buttocks** *(n)* the bottom. *(s)* backside, behind, rump, rear, bum.

6 **destination** *(n)* the place where someone or something is going to. *(s)* objective, target. *(ant)* starting point.

CHAPTER THIRTY-THREE

Half Truths

The night of the great fires, Catrin Castle did not sleep. The inhabitants gasped with a mix of horror and joy, as an almighty explosion roared from the rear of the camp, expelling a flaming fireball that annihilated all in its wake. Catrin's **jubilant**[1] residents spectated from atop the battlements as the colossal trebuchet burned through the night like a beacon of hope. None had known that a fire-breathing beast, stuffed **to the gills**[2] with Greek fire, had detonated that blast. Nor would they ever find out, for Cad would not share the recipe she'd learned from the cipher, whose ashes lay strewn among the reeds in her room.

'Callwen, please sit.'

Sir Owain Glyn gestured to the **plush**[3] sofa in his quarters.

Cad hesitated, never having seen his personal rooms before; they were fit for a king, like her father's **suite**[4]. Despite her success in smiting the siege, Cad's heart dragged, wishing her father were here. She must find him – dead or alive.

Owain poured two cups of water. Cad assessed her position, deciding just how much she should tell the Knight Hawk. She was convinced Siân had tripped up when saying Cad should

---

1 **jubilant** *(adj)* expressing or feeling great happiness. *(s)* joyful, ecstatic. *(ant)* miserable.

2 **to the gills** (informal phrase) fully. *(s)* completely, totally.

3 **plush** *(adj)* expensive and luxurious. *(s)* deluxe, lavish. *(ant)* spartan, cheap.

4 **suite** *(n)* a set of rooms. *(s)* living quarters.

seek her father. Did Siân know where her **estranged**[1] husband was? How could she know he wasn't at Catrin, and that Cad must 'find him'? Was Siân holding him prisoner? That idea sickened Cad, for she now realised her adoptive mother had lost her mind. The woman she'd faced last night, the woman who'd trapped her and Prince John in the oubliette, was not the woman Cad once knew. Siân suffered a sickness of the mind, for this was the only explanation for her **heinous**[2] crimes. Since giving birth to Prince John, Siân had never been the same. With overwhelming sorrow, Cad now saw that.

'Please,' Owain repeated, wrenching Cad from her thoughts and gesturing for her to sit.

Reluctant, she perched on the edge of the velvet sofa, her clothes stinking of sweat, fire and fear. She'd not changed since seeing him some days past. Her eyes darted about the room.

'We are alone,' said Owain, his voice gentle.

'The walls have ears,' replied Cad, 'and legs,' she added, **alluding**[3] to the tunnels she now knew existed.

Owain's **jagged**[4] eyebrows met in confusion at her comments, but he didn't pursue them.

'Callwen, we have much to discuss. You must trust me.'

His upturned palms and open face pleaded with Cad to share her experience. Stubborn and resolute, Cad would reveal only necessities, and save the rest for her father. First, she would seek some answers of her own, and then she would give Owain Glyn his.

'Has anyone seen Goodwife Hughes these past days?'

Owain showed **authentic**[5] surprise, seemingly taken aback by such a **banal**[6] question. 'Well, I believe her to be **bedridden**[7] by the sickness. Do you wish for her care again, once she is able? I can arrange this when she is well.'

Cad weighed him up. Owain Glyn wouldn't have reacted thus had Goodwife Hughes been making Greek fire for *him* in the dungeons. Nor was he aware that the goodwife had probably

---

1 **estranged** *(adj)* no longer friendly or close to someone. *(s)* parted, separated. *(ant)* united.

2 **heinous** *(adj)* wicked. *(s)* evil, monstrous. *(ant)* admirable.

3 **allude** *(v)* call attention to indirectly, suggest. *(s)* hint at, imply. *(ant)* announce.

4 **jagged** *(adj)* rough or sharp. *(s)* spiky, ragged. *(ant)* smooth.

5 **authentic** *(adj)* genuine, original or traditional. *(s)* real. *(ant)* false, fake.

6 **banal** *(adj)* boring or obvious from lack of originality. *(s)* predictable. *(ant)* original.

7 **bedridden** *(s)* confined (stuck) in bed because of sickness or old age. *(s)* housebound.

fled Catrin via underground tunnels known to a mere few. Cad doubted they'd ever see Mrs Hughes at Catrin again. For whom had the goodwife and Peggy toiled thus, she wondered? Cad had **ruminated**[1] on that question ever since seeing them in the **basement**[2].

Having given it some consideration, Cad didn't bother to ask of Peggy, now convinced neither worked for Owain Glyn, her father's closest friend and ally.

Steeling[3] herself to tell her story, Cad sat on the sofa.

'There is much to tell, Sir Owain.'

She reached for her water cup. Her thirst raged, and she finished it in one gulp.

Where do I begin? she thought, placing her cup on the low table before her.

In a straight-backed chair, Owain waited as Cad settled into the plush velvet. Exhausted and desperate for sleep, Cad braced herself, then told Owain Glyn her story, **omitting**[4] all the parts she didn't want him to hear.

---

1 **ruminate** *(v)* think about deeply. *(s)* consider, contemplate, ponder.

2 **basement** *(n)* the floor of a building that is below ground level. *(s)* cellar. *(ant)* attic.

3 **steel** *(v)* mentally prepare for something difficult. *(s)* strengthen, fortify, brace. *(ant)* weaken.

4 **omit** *(v)* leave something out. *(s)* exclude, skip. *(ant)* include, add.

CHAPTER THIRTY-FOUR

Keeping Secrets

After **recounting**[1] only the chosen parts of her story, Cad left Owain's suite and heaved her **dog-tired**[2] body down towards the bailey and her room. Once in the open, a hideous smell filled her nostrils, foul, **acrid**[3], and one that would haunt her for the rest of her days. Smoke as thick as fog sullied the air; ashes fell from the sky like unseasonable snow. Vats no longer boiled in the bailey. Catrin's gates would open later, her outside freshwater springs accessible once more. Children cheered, waving makeshift flags. Dogs barked, and even the ducks and geese clucked in oblivious excitement.

Regardless of the **jubilation**[4], Cad's heart lay heavy in her chest as she made for her quarters. She must sleep soon lest she fall sick. Her ribs ached, and her head swam in a sea of fatigue, still muddled with remnants of poison and heartache at the loss of her mother. For Cad now accepted, Siân was lost to her family, forever. The ice she'd seen in her mother's eyes had sealed that fate for Cad. The mother she'd once known had gone to a faraway place.

Tears **welled**[5], and Cad swallowed hard as she pictured the magical hairpin that had held Siân's hair in place. The emerald hawk earrings glittering at Siân's ears, and the monk's habit she'd

---

1 **recount** *(v)* tell someone about something. *(s)* narrate, describe, convey.

2 **dog-tired** *(adj)* being extremely tired. *(s)* exhausted, fatigued. *(ant)* fresh, energetic.

3 **acrid** *(adj)* unpleasantly pungent or bitter. *(s)* choking, harsh. *(ant)* pleasant, sweet.

4 **jubilation** *(n)* a feeling of great happiness. *(s)* joy. *(ant)* misery.

5 **well** *(v)* to rise or pool. *(s)* accumulate. *(ant)* drain.

openly **flaunted**[1] to Cad. In doing so, Siân had fully intended Cad to know that she had been the one to trap her and Prince John, her own child, in the oubliette. Without shame or remorse, Siân had **gloated**[2], then fled. Was Dewi involved, for she'd not seen him? Were the two allies, or enemies now? And which of them controlled the Gwalch Gem bracelet if so?

Cad's mind **flagged**[3], **weariness**[4] fogging her judgement.

I must think on this tomorrow, she thought, too shattered to follow anything more, and knowing sleep would come when her head touched her pillow. More than anything else, she yearned to curl up with Fishy for days. To sleep, and forget the Greek fire and those soldiers, all human, who'd fallen at her hands. Sorrow smothered her.

In this mire of tangled emotions, tears like pearls slid silently from her eyes, soaking her cheeks. Oblivious to her wet face, Cad hobbled past the kitchens where celebration cakes and breads baked. But Cad's **appetite**[5] had died along with Siân's army, for even the heavenly smell of sweet pastry failed to rouse her hollow stomach.

As she neared her room, Cad's thoughts strayed back to Owain Glyn. He'd listened intently as she'd described the incendiary liquid. He'd listened closely when she'd revealed that secret tunnels **riddled**[6] Catrin's basement. A **labyrinth**[7] probably designed by Sir Robert Evans, for she'd found the maps in his rooms. He'd listened when she'd shared Bryn Davis's brave actions. How he'd helped her when he need not have. How he'd risked his life to open the locked gate into the tilt yard.

But Owain Glyn had not listened when she'd shared her mother's part in this **evil**[8], for she'd not been able to tell him. Cad had tried to utter the words that still clogged her throat. The words that speared her heart with agony each time they blighted her mind. Perhaps she would tell Owain Glyn one day. But before that day arrived, she must know her father's fate.

---

1 **flaunt** *(v)* display ostentatiously (openly) to cause envy, admiration or defiance. *(s)* parade, exhibit. *(ant)* hide.

2 **gloat** *(v)* dwell on one's own success with smug pleasure. *(s)* revel, smirk. *(ant)* commiserate.

3 **flag** *(v)* become tired. *(s)* slow, weaken, falter. *(ant)* revive.

4 **weariness** *(n)* extreme tiredness. *(s)* exhaustion, fatigue. *(ant)* liveliness.

5 **appetite** *(n)* one's natural desire to eat in order to sustain the body.

6 **riddle** *(v)* fill with something (often undesirably so). *(s)* penetrate.

7 **labyrinth** *(n)* a complicated network of passages. *(s)* maze, warren.

8 **evil** *(n)* bad. *(s)* wickedness, wrongdoing. *(ant)* good.

At the **prospect**[1] of seeing Rhys, Dylan, Fishy, May and even Slippy the toothless adder, Cad's burden eased a tad. And although she didn't sense it, the corners of her mouth lifted a little.

As she headed to her friends, Cad halted and glanced yonder, beyond the sealed well shack. Should she visit Flash and Ellis now? She peered down the bailey towards the stables. Flash was fine, for Owain Glyn had told her so. No, Flash would wait, happy to be reunited with Midnight after her atrocious ordeal in the burning tilt yard.

Close to exhaustive collapse, Cad let prudence prevail and made straight for her room, preparing to tell Rhys and Dylan that she would reveal all once she awoke, whenever that might be. As Cad reached her door, she cast a glimpse back at the bailey, eyeing the smoke that drifted from the still **smouldering**[2] trebuchet which lay beyond Catrin's walls. Cad's job was done.

About to enter her quarters, and allowing herself a great yawn, Cad moved to open the door when something caught her eye. Since Bryn Davis had helped to save her skin with his shower of arrows, she'd not seen him in the castle. But she saw him now, and shook her head. Was she seeing things? **Hallucinating**[3]? Were Physician Jordan's demons back again?

Not trusting what she saw, she blinked hard, her mouth dropping open. Bryn hadn't seen her, for he was bent forward, feeding a dog as a black cat swirled between his **shins**[4]. Cad recognised both animals at once. There was no mistaking that tri-coloured terrier, or that soot-black cat. Furthermore, it was the first time she'd *ever* seen them in the castle like this. Hitherto, they seemed to have miraculously appeared when she'd needed them. Now she wasn't so sure …

Rooted[5] to the spot, she frowned as Bryn smiled at the animals. He then stood and turned towards the keep, the terrier she'd dubbed Skip, and the cat she'd named Sooty, happily following at Bryn's heels.

Had she not been so devoid of energy, she may well have sprinted after Bryn to ask who owned them. But she already knew the answer to that question. For the way they'd **interacted**[6] with Bryn only moments ago, they were clearly his companions – his pets.

---

1 **prospect** *(n)* the likelihood of a future event or possibility occurring. *(s)* expectation.

2 **smoulder** *(v)* burn slowly and with no flame. *(s)* smoke, glow. *(ant)* blaze.

3 **hallucinate** *(v)* see or experience something that isn't real. *(s)* imagine.

4 **shin** *(n)* the bony front of the leg below the knee.

5 **root** *(v)* cause to remain immobile through amazement or fear. *(s)* rivet, stick.

6 **interact** *(v)* communicate or be involved with directly. *(s)* mix, associate. *(ant)* separate.

As all three **sauntered**[1] into the keep, she remembered when she'd accused Bryn of throwing Fishy into the moat. He'd been appalled, **professing**[2] he preferred dogs to people, and she'd believed him.

Cad thought of the joust, when it seemed Bryn had wanted to reveal her gender. Could she have misjudged him? Had he perhaps been trying to help her after all, afraid he'd maimed her? But why challenge Cad to a duel, knowing he might hurt her? And him mounted on Lightning and she riding little Flashy. It made no sense.

Bone-tired[3], Cad's head spun. Too weary to find the answers, she conceded that her questions must wait. But as hard as she tried to turn away, she couldn't. Bryn had **ambled**[4] into the keep, Skip and Sooty trotting at his heels.

As Cad watched the **enigmatic**[5] squire leave, she couldn't help but wonder if the boy who'd been **instrumental**[6] in helping her save Catrin Castle, might just be **harbouring**[7] even greater secrets than she.

To be continued.

1 **saunter** *(v)* walk in a slow and relaxed manner. *(s)* stroll, amble. *(ant)* hurry, hasten.

2 **profess** *(v)* claim that one has a feeling or quality. *(s)* declare, state.

3 **bone-tired** *(adj)* being extremely tired. *(s)* exhausted, fatigued. *(ant)* fresh, energetic.

4 **amble** *(v)* move or walk slowly. *(s)* saunter, stroll. *(ant)* stride.

5 **enigmatic** *(adj)* mysterious and hard to make out. *(s)* puzzling. *(ant)* straightforward.

6 **instrumental** *(adj)* involved in and importantly so. *(s)* active, significant. *(ant)* uninvolved.

7 **harbour** *(v)* hold a thought or feeling in the mind, especially secretly. *(s)* nurture, foster, entertain.

LEARN WITH THE CADWALADR SERIES

The Cadwaladr Chronicles: Book 3 – Siege forms part of *The Cadwaladr* integrated education series.

When you have finished *The Cadwaladr Chronicles* series, it's time to move on to the following trilogy, *The Cadwaladr Quests.*

The Cadwaladr Quests series comprises a trilogy of novels, supporting workbooks and vocabulary revision notebooks.

Find all *The Cadwaladr Quests* books online via your local Amazon store.

The Cadwaladr Quests: Book 1 – Tangled Time

Other supporting books:

The Cadwaladr Quests: Book 1 – Tangled Time – Workbook

The Cadwaladr Quests: Book 1 – Tangled Time – Vocabulary Revision Notebook

11+ Vocabulary, Comprehension and Verbal Skills – Workbook 1

*

The Cadwaladr Quests: Book 2 – Race For The Gold

Other supporting books:

The Cadwaladr Quests: Book 2 – Race For The Gold – Workbook

The Cadwaladr Quests: Book 2 – Race For The Gold – Vocabulary Revision Notebook

*

The Cadwaladr Quests: Book 3 (the finale) – Cat's Eye

PARENTS, GET FIVE FREE COMPREHENSION EXERCISES

Parents, to receive your free comprehensions (with answers) based on *The Cadwaladr Chronicles: Book 3 – Siege,* please leave a review for *Siege* on Amazon and email a screenshot to:

freebies@slager.co.uk.

I will add you to my mailing list[1] and send you the comprehensions by email.

1 You can unsubscribe from the mailing list at any time. Further details will be emailed to you as soon as you are added.

REVIEWS, PLEASE!

If you've enjoyed *The Cadwaladr Chronicles: Book 3 – Siege*,
please leave a review on Amazon.
Thank you!

ERRATA AND INFORMATION

To report any **errata**[1], please email: **errata@slager.co.uk.**
If you would like information about new books in *The Cadwaladr Chronicles* series, please visit:

SLAGER.CO.UK

You can stay up to date with S. L. Ager, author of *The Cadwaladr Chronicles* series, on social media:

facebook.com/SLAgerAuthor
instagram.com/SLAgerAuthor
linkedin.com/in/SLAgerAuthor
pinterest.com/SLAgerAuthor
twitter.com/SLAgerAuthor
tiktok.com/@s.l.agerauthor

1 **erratum** *(n)* an error in writing or publishing (plural: errata).

Printed in Great Britain
by Amazon

28167460R00119